EX AUDITU

An International Journal for the Theological Interpretation of Scripture

VOL. 27   **2011**

Ex Auditu is published annually by Pickwick Publications, an imprint of Wipf and Stock Publishers, 199 West 8th Avenue, Suite 3, Eugene, Oregon 97401, USA

SUBSCRIPTIONS

Individuals:
U.S.A. and all other countries (in U.S. funds): $20.00
Students: $12.00

Institutions:
U.S.A. and all other countries (in U.S. funds): $30.00

This periodical is indexed in the ATLA Religion Database, published by the American Theological Library Association, 300 S. Wacker Dr., Suite 2100, Chicago, IL 60606, Email: atla@atla.com, www: http://www.atla.com/; *Internationale Zeitschriftenshau für Bibelwissenschaft; Religious and Theological Abstracts; and Old Testament Abstracts.*

Please address all subscription correspondence
and change of address information to Wipf and Stock Publishers.

©2012 by Wipf and Stock Publishers
ISSN: 0883-0053
ISBN: 978-1-62032-212-3

EX AUDITU

An International Journal for the Theological Interpretation of Scripture

Klyne R. Snodgrass, Editor
Stephen J. Chester, Associate Editor
D. Christopher Spinks, Associate Editor

North Park Theological Seminary
3225 West Foster Avenue
Chicago, Illinois 60625-4987
USA

Tel: (773) 244-6243
Fax: (773) 244-6244
email: ksnodgrass@northpark.edu
Web site: http://wipfandstock.com/journals/ex_auditu

EDITORIAL BOARD

Terence E. Fretheim, Luther Seminary, St. Paul, MN
Richard B. Hays, The Divinity School, Duke University, Durham, NC
Jon R. Stock, Wipf & Stock Publishers, Eugene, OR
Miroslav Volf, Yale Divinity School, New Haven, CT
John Wipf, Wipf & Stock Publishers, Eugene, OR

THE EDITORIAL BOARD MEMBERS AND CONSULTANTS represent various disciplines and denominations. Theological interpretation of Scripture is a task to be taken seriously by scholars who are committed to the Christian faith and tradition. However, as one editorial consultant stated: "Let people gradually get used to the idea that a sane hermeneutics is both oriented in advance toward agreement/consent and is simultaneously exigent, discriminating, critical."

EDITORIAL CONSULTANTS

Richard Bauckham
University of St. Andrews, Emeritus
St. Andrews, Scotland

M. Daniel Carroll R.
Denver Seminary
Denver, Colorado

Jan Du Rand
Emeritus, University of Johannesburg and Extraordinary Professor, North West University

Willie Jennings
The Divinity School
Duke University
Durham, N. Carolina

Robert Johnston
Fuller Theological Seminary
Pasadena, California

R. Walter L. Moberly
University of Durham
Durham, England

Kathleen M. O'Connor
Columbia Theological Seminary
Decatur, Georgia

Iain Provan
Regent College
Vancouver, B.C.

Anthony Thiselton
University of Nottingham
Nottingham, England

Augustine Thompson
University of Virginia
Charlottesville, Virginia

Marianne Meye Thompson
Fuller Theological Seminary
Pasadena, California

Kevin J. Vanhoozer
Wheaton College
Wheaton, Illinois

Geoffrey Wainwright
The Divinity School
Duke University
Durham, N. Carolina

Sondra Wheeler
Wesley Theological Seminary
Washington, D.C.

William H. Willimon
Bishop of the North Alabama Conference
The United Methodist Church
Birmingham, Alabama

N. T. Wright
St Mary's College, University of St Andrews, Scotland

CONTENTS

Announcement of the 2012 Symposium	v
Abbreviations	vi
Introduction *Klyne Snodgrass*	viii
A Christian View of Wealth and Possessions: An Old Testament Perspective *Hugh G. M. Williamson*	1
Response to Williamson *James K. Bruckner*	20
Poverty and Paul's Gospel *Bruce W. Longenecker*	26
Response to Longenecker *Aaron Kuecker*	45
A Patristic View of Wealth and Possessions *Helen Rhee*	51
Response to Rhee *Bradley Nassif*	78
Blessings, Curses, and the Cross *Kelly Johnson*	82
Money and Possessions: A Biblical Perspective *Jonathan J. Bonk*	100
Response to Bonk *Liz Mosbo VerHage*	128

Contents

Decorum and Deeds in 1 Timothy 2:9–10 in Light of *Ephesiaca* by Xenophon of Ephesus Gary G. Hoag	134
Response to Hoag Lyn Nixon	161
Wealth, Lordless Powers, and the Rule of Christ Mark Husbands	169
Response to Husbands William Myatt	192
Money and Possessions Will Willimon	196
Annotated Bibliography on Money and Possessions	203
Presenters and Respondents	217
Ex Auditu – Volumes Available	219

ANNOUNCEMENT OF THE 2012 SYMPOSIUM

North Park Theological Seminary in Chicago, Illinois, is pleased to announce that the twenty-eighth Symposium on the Theological Interpretation of Scripture will take place September 27–29, 2012. The symposium will start at 7:00 p.m. on September 27 in Nyvall Hall and will extend through a Saturday afternoon worship service on September 29. The theme in 2012 will be Family. The following persons have agreed to make presentations:

    Stephen Barton, University of Durham, New Testament
    Jana Marguerite Bennett, University of Dayton, Theological Ethics
    Lynn Cohick, Wheaton College, New Testament
    Jim Dekker, North Park University, Youth Ministry
    Dennis Olson, Princeton Theological Seminary, Old Testament
    Luke Powery, Princeton Theological Seminary, preaching
    Caryn Reeder, Westmont College, Old Testament
    Julie Rubio, St. Louis University, Ethics
    Mary Veeneman, North Park University, Theology

Persons interested in attending the sessions should write before September 1 to:

    Ms. Guylla Brown
    North Park Theological Seminary
    3225 W. Foster Avenue
    Chicago, Illinois 60625

Meals may be taken at North Park and assistance can be provided in finding nearby lodging.

ABBREVIATIONS

All abbreviations are as specified in Patrick H. Alexander et al., eds., *The SBL Handbook of Style* (Peabody, Mass.: Hendrickson, 1999). Items not included here, such as abbreviations of some patristic sources, will be found there.

ANRW	*Aufstieg und Niedergang der römischen Welt*
BADG	Bauer, W., W. F. Arndt, and F. W. Gingrich, and F. W. Danker, *Greek-English Lexicon of the New Testament and Other Early Christian Literature*. 2nd ed.
BDAG	Bauer, W., F. W. Danker, W. F. Arndt, and F. W. Gingrich, *Greek-English Lexicon of the New Testament and Other Early Christian Literature*. 3rd ed.
BibInt	*Biblical Interpretation*
CSEL	Corpus scriptorum ecclesiasticorum latinorum
ESV	English Standard Version
ET	English Translation
FGrH	*Die Fragmente der Griechischen Historiker*
GNO	*Gregorii Nysseni Opera*
HTR	*Harvard Theological Review*
ICC	International Critical Commentary
IvE	*Die Inschriften von Ephesos*
Int	*Interpretation*
JECS	*Journal of Early Christian Studies*
JSNT	*Journal for the Study of the New Testament*
JSOT	*Journal for the Study of the Old Testament*
JSOTSup	Journal for the Study of the Old Testament: Supplement Series
JTS	*Journal of Theological Studies*
LHB/OTS	Library of Hebrew Bible/Old Testament Studies
LXX	Septuagint
LW	*Luther's Works*, ed. Jaroslav Pelikan
MT	Masoretic Text
NAB	New American Bible
NAC	New American Commentary

Abbreviations

NICOT	New International Commentary on the Old Testament
NIV	New International Version
NovT	*Novum Testamentum*
NPNF	Nicene and Post-Nicene Fathers
NRSV	New Revised Standard Version
NTS	*New Testament Studies*
OTL	Old Testament Library
PG	Patrologiae cursus completus: Series graeca
R & T	*Religion and Theology*
RSV	Revised Standard Version
SP	Sacra pagina
StPatr	*Studia Patristica*
TDNT	*Theological Dictionary of the New Testament*
TDOT	*Theological Dictionary of the Old Testament*
TLNT	*Theological Lexicon of the New Testament*
TLG	*Thesaurus linguae graecae*
TS	*Theological Studies*
VC	*Vigiliae christianae*
WBC	Word Biblical Commentary
WUNT	Wissenschaftliche Untersuchungen zum Neuen Testament
ZNW	*Zeitschrift für die neutestamentliche Wissenschaft und die Kunde der älteren Kirche*

INTRODUCTION

The most difficult theological issue with which most of us have to deal—especially those of us who live in the Western world—is the issue of money and possessions. Jesus' sayings about money and possessions are more difficult, more confrontive, and more disconcerting than those on any other topic. The treatment of money and possessions in the rest of Scripture may not be so uniformly abrasive, but it still confronts and demands a reorientation of the way we view our possessions and what we think is important. Surely if there is any place where Christians, to say nothing of the rest of Western society, need to change their assumptions about life, this is it. Materialism is so much a part of our thinking that we do not notice it is idolatry. We are deluded by the need for protection of self and property, a feeling which comes so naturally that we cannot be objective, and we turn our eyes away from the systemic issues that prevent other people from moving out of poverty. Money can be a wonderful tool for exhibiting love and serving God's kingdom, but it is a terrible master. Scripture calls us to place money and possessions under the Lordship of Christ, but what that entails is not easily answered. The enclosed essays offer guidelines for thought. Welcome to the task.

There is a glaring omission in the essays in this volume. There is no paper from an economist. Originally one was scheduled, but due to unforeseen circumstances, the person who had committed to offering such a paper was prevented from doing so.

At the symposium twice as much time is given to discussion of the papers as to their delivery, and the journal cannot reproduce the character of those discussions, which are always stimulating and enriching. We are grateful to all who participated.

Appreciation is expressed once again to all the presenters and respondents who made a significant investment in the life of North Park. The friendship of these people is a gift we value. The authors of papers were given a chance to edit their contributions after the symposium, but the responses are essentially as they were presented. As is obvious, the views expressed are those of the authors and not necessarily those of the journal or of North Park. We also thank all those in attendance for their interest and contribution to the discussions. Special gratitude is expressed to Joel Johnson and Paul Burger, students at North Park, for their work on the bibliography and especially to Guylla Brown from North Park's staff, without whom the symposium would be impossible. Anyone who has been to the symposium knows that is true.

The Editor

A CHRISTIAN VIEW OF WEALTH AND POSSESSIONS: AN OLD TESTAMENT PERSPECTIVE

H. G. M. Williamson

Two problems confront us in trying to outline an OT perspective on a Christian view of wealth and possessions. The first is familiar enough and concerns all efforts to integrate the OT into a Christian view of any moral or ethical topic: to what extent is the OT position confirmed, modified, or completely changed by the teaching of the NT on the same subject? That is obviously a question that I cannot answer in full in the context of the present article. The value of a published symposium such as the present one, however, is that it may by its very format help us to approach an answer as we consider this topic from a variety of angles. While from a personal perspective I write as a Christian, I propose here to concentrate on the OT teaching within its own context and then to rely on the articles by colleagues in adjacent fields and the responses to guide us further in our joint hermeneutical quest.

The second problem is of more pressing concern. The OT was written over a period of many hundreds of years—some would even claim a whole millennium. During those centuries the many writers lived under diverse political and social circumstances and in different countries. Sometimes they were inhabitants of free, independent kingdoms—Israel and Judah—where it was possible to order their affairs in conformity with their own religious understanding. Other parts, however, were written in exile, where freedom of maneuver was more inhibited. Others, yet again, were written in the post-exilic community of Judah, a minor province in the mighty Persian and Hellenistic empires, where obviously much of what we regard as biblical law could not be enforced. And finally, still other parts seem to be the product of the diaspora communities—Jews, as we may now legitimately call them, who chose (more or less) to live outside the boundaries of the promised land.

It does not require any great insight to realize that in these varied and time-separated circumstances there are likely to be differences of emphasis relating to our topic so that the problem which arises is the question concerning what method or approach most securely leads to a description of the OT perspective which somehow transcends the vagaries of historical diversity. If we indulge in text-picking, we can find ways to justify more or less any position we choose. For instance, on the one hand I have frequently heard, as I am sure we all have, passionate sermons based on the early prophetic literature that would suggest as a consequence that we should all become material-free mendicants. On the other hand I have been seriously challenged when speaking on a related subject[1] to endorse what is sometimes called the "prosperity gospel" or the "health and wealth gospel," that is to say (according to the Wikipedia definition) "a Christian religious belief whose proponents claim the Bible teaches that financial blessing is the will of God for Christians." I was told that because Abraham was faithful to God he was blessed with many flocks and herds, so that clearly if anybody was not wealthy it had to be because they were unfaithful in some way. Somehow that seemed easier to believe in California, where the conversation took place, than when more recently I visited a remote area of northwest Tanzania where our home church has close links with the rapidly growing and dedicated churches but where poverty is endemic. Of course, it is unlikely that many would endorse either of these extreme positions, but they highlight the danger to which we are all prone, namely that one can usually find an OT text that seems to justify one's own favored position.

Part of the answer to this difficulty is to accept that these seemingly discordant voices are in fact giving us some important information by virtue of that very fact. No single rule or doctrine on this topic should be elevated to an inflexible truth because Scripture itself testifies to the fact that there are always exceptions, and these in turn demonstrate that it is a mistake to argue back from an individual's circumstances to a deduction about their position in the divine economy. This has important pastoral consequences that I fear are sometimes observed more in the breach than in reality, so let this first point that I have just made be written as a banner over all that will now follow.

In order to get at the heart of what I believe are the main principles of the OT view of wealth and possessions we need to come to terms as far as the available evidence allows with an appreciation of the very different nature of society then from now. Our western (supposedly liberal) democratic systems tend to place ultimate value on the opinions and position of each individual. The ideal of the system may not yet have been universally reached, but the predominant idea is that we are what

---

1. The talk in question was very similar to a Tyndale House Open Day lecture which was subsequently published and which now has been made available online: "The Old Testament and the Material World," *Evangelical Quarterly* 57 (1985) 5–22 (http://biblicalstudiesorguk.blogspot.com/2010/06/hgm-williamson-on-old-testament-and.html).

we make of ourselves. The authority of those who are in positions of political or economic leadership derives from the will of the majority beneath them. That is why we have elections for political office and meetings of shareholders in major companies. Inherited wealth or position is increasingly frowned upon, and we are encouraged to admire those who succeed against all the odds in improving themselves in their chosen sphere of life. All this has come about (and continues to develop, of course) by reaction against a previously feudal system where much more depended upon the accident of birth and where in pre-democratic times authority to rule was as much inherited as was the wealth and status that went with it.

Even allowing that this is an exaggerated caricature, it helps us to see that much against which the movement towards democracy has striven is in fact typical of the nature of society in OT times. Of course, as we shall see shortly, there are other factors to be taken into account that may help to compensate for that seemingly stark contrast, but nevertheless I find it hard to escape the conclusion that for the most part the OT takes a top-down or hierarchical view of society rather than a bottom-up, democratic view. Allow me to expand a little by way of explanation and illustration.

An obvious starting point is the presentation of God as creator. This truth is conveyed by several discrete, though not incompatible, images. In Gen 2, for instance, he appears as a craftsman or artisan (cf. 2:7, 21–22) who proceeds to some extent by trial and error. In the psalms, by contrast, the striking relevant image is of God as king who orders and keeps under control the unruly forces of natural and political chaos in order to establish a secure environment for humanity (see especially the so-called enthronement psalms, Pss 47, 93, 95–99). And that concept of God as king, though not explicitly stated, seems to be the dominant image of the more considered presentation in Gen 1, not least in vv. 26–31, to which we shall need to return.

When it comes to the material world, therefore, the underlying conviction is that it is all, without exception, the Lord's inalienable possession and that he gives it to whom he will. This truth applies at several levels. It is at his disposition that the nations enjoy their territory (e.g., Deut 32:8; cf. 2:5, 9, 19; Jer 27:1–7; Amos 9:7), and Israel in particular needs to acknowledge this (e.g., Gen 12:1–3; Deut 32:9). Furthermore this insight is at the basis of Israel's perception of land ownership within Israel (e.g., Lev 25:23), because as ultimately "his" property God has "given" it to his people for them to distribute, and in doing so he has instigated legal and social customs, such as that of the *gōʾēl*, or "kinsman-redeemer," to ensure that it remains secure at the basic levels of family and clan.

The same notions underlie the political establishment within the nations of Israel and Judah and their successor in postexilic Judah. Although inevitably there is considerable diversity here because of the changing circumstances under which the territory was inhabited, it is apparent that (for better or worse, one is inclined to remark) the kings were given by God to Israel in history[2] and that would remain the case for future improved models (e.g., Isa 9:6–7). Equally, in postexilic times all the leaders of the Judean community of whom we read (Zerubbabel, Ezra, Nehemiah) came from Babylon in response to divine calling or appointment rather than being chosen by local procedures. What is true of the top line of leadership is reflected also in the lower levels of judges, elders, heads of fathers' houses and the like.

At first sight this looks like a close forerunner of later European feudalism in which the cynical view might be taken that all was organized by privilege, reinforced by might, in such a way as to ensure that wealth, or failing wealth then at least possessions, was generated from below in order to sustain those higher up the pyramid. The flow was from bottom to top, therefore, and certainly there are passages in the OT that reflect the reality of this mournful scenario (e.g., 1 Sam 8:10–18).

At this point, however, the portrayal needs to be supplemented by another series of observations that maintain the structure, so to speak, but ideally, at least, invert the direction of wealth management. First, as regards God's own role, he turns out to be very much less demanding as a divine landlord than the deities of neighboring lands. In other countries we read of temples, their land, and their personnel as central to the national or regional economy and as demanding high forms of "taxation" to maintain the cult, which from a material point of view could be said often to have favored its priestly practitioners. In Israel, by contrast, at least as presented in the texts in idealized fashion, we find that the temple was not a major landowner and that the tribe of Levi, the primary cultic functionaries, was equally without tribal inheritance and lived dispersed throughout the other tribes and dependent on their charitable care. This seems to have characterized both the preexilic times, if Deuteronomy may be considered broadly to reflect that era, and the

---

2. I am well aware, of course, of the differences of opinion about this that seem to be expressed in, for instance, 1 Sam 8–12 and parts of the book of Hosea. Equally, the kings of the northern kingdom of Israel are universally condemned in the historical books because of the writers' southern, Judean standpoint. But by whatever means a monarchy came to be established there can equally be no doubt that it came to be seen as very much a beneficial gift of God both in history (e.g., 2 Sam 7) and in the development of hopes for the future in some of the prophets.

postexilic period when, according to Neh 13:10–12 and similar passages, the Levites were still very much dependent upon others for their general welfare. On such occasions as we read of exaggerated temple festivities, such as at the temple dedication, the requirements were donated by the crown rather than being considered a specific additional burden on the people (1 Kgs 8:62–66).

As God's supreme representative, the king in his turn was not ideally appointed for his own benefit but in order to serve the needs of the nation at large. Although there is often said to be a clear distinction between the more elevated view of kingship in the psalms and the more critical view in the historical books and some of the prophets, the fact remains that in each body of literature this ideal is maintained. It is clear from the theology stressed throughout the books of Kings, for instance, that the nation's fortunes are dependent upon the king's faithfulness and obedience to a limited range of divine demands and that his reign is assessed accordingly. Similarly in Chronicles there is a somewhat stereotypical presentation of "good" kings being rewarded with a large family, success in public building works, and victory in battle. This may seem overly simplistic in some respects, but it makes the point quite powerfully that royal privilege is not for personal pleasure but is rather a responsibility towards one's subjects. Likewise in the psalms, although the privileges of royalty are certainly highlighted (e.g., Pss 2 and 45), it remains also the conviction that the king should be the one to uphold God's justice and righteousness in a manner that will guarantee the rights of the poor and even ensure agricultural prosperity for the people (Ps 72). The prophetic ideal is not dissimilar (e.g., Isa 9:6–7; 11:1–5; 32:1; Mic 5:2–5).

Of course the fall of the monarchy inevitably led to a significant modification of this schema, but the response Israel made reflects profoundly on the underlying values that the system sought to encapsulate. Disregarding for the moment the inevitable forward postponement of royalist hopes that developed into the messianism with which we are familiar from later times, we should note two creative interpretive shifts.

First, in Isa 55:3 the promises once made to David are transferred to "you" (a plural form in the Hebrew text). In other words, those being addressed, whom we assume from elsewhere in this section of Isaiah (chs. 40–55) to be the people of God, elsewhere called Jacob/Israel and Zion/Jerusalem, now take over the role among the nations that the king once had in Israel. Just as he had been a light to his people and their guarantor of justice, now that role was to be fulfilled with respect to the gentile nations by the servant Israel (Isa 41:8–10; 42:1–9; 49:1–6, and frequently).

It has sometimes been called a "democratization" of the royal hopes, and that is acceptable provided the point is kept firmly in mind that it is the role of service that is democratized, based on Israel's anticipated faithfulness, not merely a transfer of privilege from the one to the many.[3]

Second, we need to take into account the astonishing implications of the account of the creation of humankind in Gen 1:26–31. Discussion of what is meant by being made in the image and likeness of God has been prolonged, and there seem to be several elements that have a claim to being included. Most recently, for instance, Crouch has made a strong and quite novel case for the view, based on the closely parallel language between Gen 5:1–2 and 5:3, that it is an attempt to represent humanity's divine parentage, a subject with a number of parallels elsewhere in the OT.[4] One element that can scarcely be avoided from the text as it stands is humanity's role in "dominion" over the remainder of the created order. In the ancient Near East it was generally the king who was the image of God, but here it "appears that the OT has democratized this old idea. It affirms that not just a king, but every man and woman, bears God's image and is his representative on earth."[5]

Here, then, we have two cardinal texts that reflect on the shift from a monarchical system to a more democratized system that imaginatively either makes "Israel" a servant figure in relation to other nations or, more boldly still, moves humanity as a whole into a position in relation to the created order that has its closest analogy in the image of an ideal king in relation to his subjects. My reason for drawing attention to these two examples is to illustrate in a powerful manner how the OT cannot be said to represent a single historical period or set of circumstances. Nevertheless, the OT remains true to certain principles about the ordering of society that, though far removed from our own, develops principles in ways which we can grasp easily enough and which may give us an entry into some constructive thought on our principal topic.

---

3. For a fuller account of the conclusions summarized in this paragraph, see my *Variations on a Theme: King, Messiah and Servant in the Book of Isaiah* (Carlisle: Paternoster, 1998) ch. 4.

4. C. L. Crouch, "Genesis 1:26–7 as a Statement of Humanity's Divine Parentage," *Journal of Theological Studies*, new series 61 (2010) 1–15. In making her case Crouch seeks to eliminate other possibilities, though in the case of the one argued above her arguments are weak, as she tacitly admits. The language of the passage seems to me to be strong enough to sustain a "both . . . and" rather than an "either . . . or" exegesis.

5. G. J. Wenham, *Genesis 1–15* (WBC 1; Waco, TX.: Word, 1987) 31. Wenham includes a useful and full survey of opinions on this topic, concluding that "there may be elements of truth in many of them," but that the "strongest case has been made for the view that the divine image makes man God's vice-regent on earth."

All this may seem at first sight to be somewhat removed from our primary concern with wealth and possessions. I propose, however, that it may serve to underline an overarching notion in the OT which I intend now to illustrate from a range of passages from different literary genres, namely that, as with kingship, so with individuals, the OT has no objection to ownership of wealth or possessions as such. However, one, the means of acquisition is tightly guarded; any hint of gain by oppression, theft, or corruption is vigorously condemned. Two, possession is a cause for gratitude to God; it cannot be expected automatically, so that poverty (in a relative rather than an absolute sense) comes over the course of time to be equally valued as an indication of piety. Three, possessions are thus not held for one's own benefit but for the service of the God who gives in order to do his will in the care and protection of those with less or no means to represent themselves in society.

These interrelated headlines may now be illustrated from a wide range of different passages. I should stress that these are illustrative only, and I shall be able to indicate only a sample of the other passages that might be closely compared with those analyzed here.

Amos 4:1–3

A good starting point that may already be in the reader's mind is the address to the women in Samaria in Amos 4:1–3. Here the prophet castigates the women for oppressing the poor and crushing the needy, though quite how they do so is not spelled out. In my opinion we should take two clues from the context to help us understand this condemnation. First and most obviously, they demand of their husbands, "bring something to drink." Second, more indirectly, by calling them "cows of Bashan" Amos was not just being rude but was framing his invective more pointedly. Bashan is the high plateau to the east of the Sea of Galilee, which includes what we know of as the Golan Heights, and it was famed in antiquity for its great fertility due both to the quality of its soil and its more plentiful rainfall than most of the surrounding regions. Elsewhere it is singled out for the excellence of its agriculture and pasturage (Mic 7:14) and for its fine oaks (Isa 2:13; Ezek 27:6; Zech 11:2) as well as its domestic animals (Deut 32:14; Ezek 39:18; Ps 22:12). When Amos refers to the cows of Bashan, it is likely that he has in mind their well-fed nature which would be evident just by looking at them. There is thus a probable reference in this passage to the unnecessarily indulgent lifestyles of these women with regard to both food and drink.

Now it seems unlikely that they would have directly and consciously oppressed and crushed the poor. Rather, I suspect that the reference to their demands of their husbands is to indicate that their oppression was at second hand. In order to keep up with their requirements the husbands were having to take short cuts in their dealings with others.

Incidentally, the people referred to as being oppressed need not be just small independent farmers, as is often assumed. It could equally be employees of the husbands on their own farms or estates, those who produced goods of various kinds, and the merchants or middlemen who acted on the husbands' behalf. In fact, in a recent study Houston has demonstrated how frequently the references to oppression refer to town or city dwellers rather than to the agricultural communities that mostly lived in the villages, where, he claims, archaeological evidence is not indicative of extreme poverty.[6]

This conclusion is exegetically and historically important. For too long scholars have simply assumed that the crisis of oppression to which the prophets refer related almost exclusively to small farmers, and the explanation given was based on more recent, Western capitalist models of mortgages and foreclosures. Although this may have happened from time to time, it is clear that the notion of a crisis which can be wheeled out to explain texts over a range of several hundred years (i.e., from at least the eighth century BCE in the prophets to the fifth century BCE, as testified in Neh 5) stretches credulity. Recent research has begun to take far more seriously the nature of agricultural practices as employed then, as well as more recently in some other, though not wholly dissimilar, societies. The role of patronage, for instance, is quite different from anything with which most of us are closely familiar, so that it would be a mistake to try to press ancient Israel into a more modern Western mode. But that does not empty the prophetic rhetoric of its force; it merely sends us back to the texts to investigate more carefully what class of people and what sort of labor are being referred to.

Although this is not my main point here, it is difficult not to draw an analogy with the observation that many of our Western demands for cheap goods of all kinds often cause others in manufacturing or trade to oppress their workers on our behalf. We may be as ignorant of this as the women of Samaria were, but in Amos's view

---

6. W. J. Houston, "Exit the Oppressed Peasant? Rethinking the Background of Social Criticism in the Prophets," in J. Day (ed.), *Prophecy and Prophets in Ancient Israel: Proceedings of the Oxford Old Testament Seminar* (Library of Hebrew Bible/Old Testament Studies 531; New York: T. & T. Clark, 2010) 101–16.

this would not excuse us. We should take some trouble to inform ourselves about whether the goods and services we buy are oppressive, both in terms of those who provide them and those who transport them and, where possible, we should surely move to the use of fair trade items. This is a big subject which I cannot open up here in full, but the starting point must be the need to educate ourselves better as to the consequences of our consumer society. As with Amos, we should know better than we do. Any form of wealth or possessions, including such basics as food and drink, that are obtained on the basis of injustice towards either the producers or the trade and transport intermediaries is here automatically condemned even where that oppression is effected only at second or even third hand.[7]

There are many comparable passages elsewhere in the prophets, and the nature of oppressive practices applies not only to such basic issues as the treatment in material terms of the producers but also to the manipulation of the courts and other administrative procedures to one's own advantage at the expense of those who may not be adequately represented. See, for instance, Isa 1:21–26; 3:13–15; 10:1–4; 58:3–7; Ezek 22:13; Amos 6:1–7; and Mic 2–3.

Proverbs

For a second example I turn to the quite different type of literature that we find in the book of Proverbs. The advantage here is that we may expect to find in this book reflections on how ordinary people should live. Furthermore the book itself makes clear that the proverbs were gathered over a period of several centuries (cf. 1:1; 10:1; 25:1, and most scholars would maintain that some are of even later date), so that we may assume that the book reflects a distillation of Israel's most highly prized wisdom. If so, then this may help resolve a debate that has been ongoing for a number of years, namely the identity of the intended audience.[8]

---

7. At this point I wish to highlight my respondent James Bruckner's comment that "the casual life of inattentive consumption and vague disavowal of implications is a timeless concern worth further discussion." I regard this as an observation that should be developed into a cardinal principle for ethical Christian living.

8. See, for example, R. N. Whybray, *Wealth and Poverty in the Book of Proverbs* (JSOTSup 99; Sheffield: Sheffield Academic, 1990); and J. D. Pleins, *The Social Visions of the Hebrew Bible: A Theological Introduction* (Louisville: Westminster John Knox, 2001) 452–83. A valuable assessment is offered by W. J. Houston, "The Role of the Poor in Proverbs," in J. C. Exum and H. G. M. Williamson (eds.), *Reading from Right to Left: Essays on the Hebrew Bible in Honour of David J. A. Clines* (JSOTSup 373; London: Sheffield Academic, 2003) 229–40.

One scholar, for instance, has sought to maintain that the so-called sentence proverbs (basically the whole book apart from chs. 1–9) were for what we might call the agricultural middle classes. They were people of modest means who were conscious of the precariousness of life both in absolute terms and in that it was easy to fall into poverty if they did not continue to work hard. At the same time, they were encouraged to be generous to the genuinely poor (who have no direct voice in the book, nor, incidentally, do women) and to remember that as often as not significant new wealth could only be obtained by dishonest or oppressive means. Others, however, have responded that the book was written by and for the elite.

My own appraisal is that it is almost certainly mistaken to try to find a single social or geographical setting for these proverbs. While the urban and elite setting of much of Prov 1–9 seems to be agreed, in my opinion the variety of sentence proverbs which follow should be allowed to stand. Taken on their own and based upon their content, the likelihood is that they derive from a wide variety of settings. Their very variety is what makes them so valuable as an insight into the society's widely held values.

There can be no doubt even on a superficial reading that Proverbs is much exercised with the division between rich and poor, and commentators often imply that this is directly related as a form of reward to the equally common distinction between the righteous and the wicked. Some proverbs seem to justify that simple conclusion; for instance, "Misfortune pursues sinners, but prosperity rewards the righteous" (13:21), and "The righteous have enough to satisfy their appetite, but the belly of the wicked is empty" (13:25).

In this connection, therefore, we should note on the other hand that there are a number of sayings which make equally clear that in fact wealth is by no means the most important value in life or the basis for a rigid distinction between individuals. "Better is a little with righteousness than large income with injustice" (16:8) makes wealth of lesser value than justice, thus tying in closely with what we saw in the prophets. Similar ideas are seen in the sayings "In the house of the righteous there is much treasure, but trouble befalls the income of the wicked" (15:6) and "The field of the poor may yield much food, but it is swept away through injustice" (13:23).

This last proverb is also important in another connection for us, namely in making clear that when the book speaks of the poor it does not necessarily refer only to the destitute; after all, the poor person here at least has a field. It is worth remembering, therefore, that the poor in the OT may not be as poor as we are initially inclined to think on the basis of our own modern parlance, and we should take this into account when we try to formulate principles for action in the modern world on the basis of these ancient sayings.

That takes us into the realm of another set of proverbs, namely the relation between work and laziness on the one hand and wealth and poverty on the other. Let us take as an initial example Prov 10:4: "A slack hand causes poverty, but the hand of the diligent makes rich." This is a prominent and recurring theme in Proverbs and one that, as a general rule, common sense could hardly deny. The consequences for behavior are so obvious that they hardly need spelling out, but to cite just one familiar example, "Go to the ant, you lazybones; consider its ways, and be wise. Without having any chief officer or ruler, it prepares its food in summer, and gathers its sustenance in harvest. How long will you lie there, O lazybones? When will you rise from your sleep? A little sleep, a little slumber, a little folding of the hands to rest, and poverty will come upon you like a robber, and want, like an armed warrior" (Prov 6:6–11). The consequence of poverty resulting from laziness is thus explicitly a spur to action.

Of course, the writers are aware that there are exceptions to this general rule, and that is just as well, because, as I have already stressed, we see still today, as they did then, that wealth and poverty are not awarded in direct proportion to effort expended. In fact, that is not what the proverb says in the first place; it does not promise wealth in proportion to work but only that failure to work will lead to poverty. So this proverb deserves to be read in the context of the two that immediately precede it (and this we may do without getting bogged down in the debate about the extent to which the proverbs have been deliberately arranged in a specific sequence). First, "Treasures gained by wickedness do not profit, but righteousness delivers from death" (10:2). So it is possible to gain wealth by illicit means (there is no comment on how much work is involved in that!), but the reader is urged to take a longer view of the situation. Ultimately it will not endure; whereas righteousness will not necessarily make you rich, it will at least deliver from fatal consequences. Then comes the saying, "The Lord does not let the righteous go hungry, but he thwarts the craving of the wicked" (10:3). Here again we note that the reward of the righteous is modest and that extravagant promises are avoided.

Now all this is not to say that success in life can be ascribed to the mechanical application of wisdom's rules and principles. However much the proverbs as a collection show more circumspection in what they say than some of their fiercer critics have allowed, the fact of course remains that there are exceptions even to these sayings, and other biblical books, not least Job and Ecclesiastes, tackle some of these in forceful and memorable ways. But in a sense we could say that there could not be a Job without Proverbs. It is only because Job's experience is such a blatant contradiction to standard observation that there is a problem to be discussed in the first place. And part, at least, of the answer in the book of Job is to move the source of the problem into the divine realm, where human observation no longer obtains. So there is an admitted limit on how far these kinds of proverbs can take us in ultimate terms, but that does not mean that they should therefore be ignored as providing an important element, at least, to the basis on which decisions large and small should be taken in daily living.

What guidelines, then, does Proverbs offer for this further practical matter of application? We may start by observing that poverty is spoken of in two somewhat different ways in Proverbs. On the one hand, there are many proverbs which indicate that poverty may be the outcome especially of laziness, though it can also be said to be the outcome of other causes as well. Such sayings (and they are frequent) may legitimately be taken as warnings by the wealthy to others in their own circles or families against conduct that would lose them their privileged position. To that extent the somewhat cynical view may be justified that much language that initially sounds high-minded is actually self-serving, at least from a class-orientated point of view.

On the other hand, however, the converse point is not made, namely it is never said that poverty is always the immediate fault of the poor person, so that those scholars who have claimed that Proverbs is uniformly critical of the poor are mistaken. Folly, wickedness, excessive pleasure seeking, and the like may reduce a wealthy person to poverty, but by no means are all the poor in that situation for those reasons alone. Some just are members of the poorer classes. In some cases they may themselves have suffered injustice, and here I repeat a proverb already cited earlier: "The field of the poor may yield much food, but it is swept away through injustice" (13:23). Even here it should be noted first that the subject of the saying seems to have been classed as "poor" even before suffering injustice, and second the degree of poverty that allows him to be classified as "poor" may not be as great as we might at first suppose, since he at least has a field that he may cultivate. Elsewhere, there are proverbs which speak of the poor with a degree of compassion, and at no point is there any implication that the poor deserve their position because they have all been lazy or the like. Thus we should recognize that although poverty may serve as a warning to the wealthy, that is not the whole sum of the story about poverty in

Proverbs. Some people just are poor, and it is then of interest to see what would be the appropriate response to that by others.

First, we find a number of sayings which simply encourage a kind or generous attitude: "Those who despise their neighbors are sinners, but happy are those who are kind to the poor" (14:21), or "Those who are generous are blessed, for they share their bread with the poor" (22:9). This, however, is not merely self-sacrificial, because there are other sayings, quite unexpected, which may be laid alongside these to indicate that even such kindness is not ultimately costly: "Some give freely, yet grow all the richer; others withhold what is due, and only suffer want. A generous person will be enriched, and one who gives water will get water" (11:24–25); "Whoever gives to the poor will lack nothing, but one who turns a blind eye will get many a curse" (28:27).

Second, this apparent paradox may be partially explained by those sayings that put a more overtly theological slant on this by relating care for the poor with the attitude of the creator God. "Those who oppress the poor insult their Maker, but those who are kind to the needy honor him" (14:31; cf. 17:5); "The Lord tears down the house of the proud, but maintains the widow's boundaries" (15:25); "The rich and the poor have this in common: the Lord is the maker of them all" (22:2; cf. 29:13); and "Do not rob the poor because they are poor, or crush the afflicted at the gate; for the Lord pleads their cause and despoils the life of those who despoil them" (22:22–23).

These sayings too, however, may be balanced by a couple which indicate that even in this case the Lord insures that the generous do not lose out: "Whoever is kind to the poor lends to the Lord, and will be repaid in full" (19:17), and "Honor the Lord with your substance and with the first fruits of all your produce; then your barns will be filled with plenty, and your vats will be bursting with wine" (3:9–10). There is thus a balance between what happens at the purely human level, as in our first group of sayings, and in imitation of the divine, as in the second.

Putting these sayings together suggests that underlying a concern for the poor in Proverbs are three views: first, poverty is sometimes just one of those things, a part of the created order which there is no need to question in ultimate terms; second, the proper response is, where possible, to imitate the creator who made things that way but who shows impartial care for rich and poor alike; so that, third, generosity is natural and not itself impoverishing since it fits with the created order that we find in God's world.

Psalm 72

So far, then, I have sought to illustrate my main theses from the prophets and the wisdom literature. Let me now turn thirdly to one of the psalms that helpfully fits in with the line of discussion so far, namely Psalm 72.

The psalm is a prayer to God on behalf of the king. Verse one starts with a firm and clear expression of the wish that God would grant him the ability to administer justice: "Give the king your justice, O God, and your righteousness to a king's son," and this sentiment is repeated in v. 2: "May he judge your people with righteousness, and your poor with justice." We may confidently affirm, therefore, that this psalm is first and foremost a prayer that the king will exercise social justice on God's behalf and that it will reflect God's own standard of what that is.

There seem to be two main elements in the remainder of the psalm that fill out what all this involves. In the first place there can be no doubt that externally it involves this king in international victory and prestige. The prayer is that he will "have dominion from sea to sea" with his enemies bowing before him in subjection, tribute pouring into his treasuries and all foreign kings and nations being subservient to him (vv. 8–11). Perhaps unexpectedly, this is regarded as a mark of blessing by them, for the agricultural prosperity that will result from his just rule is something in which they apparently share; they are blessed in him and they pronounce him happy (vv. 15–17). While this picture of superiority may seem to conflict with modern notions of justice, it fits closely with the pattern of thinking that we have already met elsewhere. As in the first part of the book of Isaiah, society is assumed to be hierarchically arranged. If the system is to work ideally, then it is of vital importance that the Davidic king be of unchallenged superiority. This was not merely for his own gratification, however, but in order that, under God as ultimately supreme, he might be in the position of unchallenged security from which he would be able to administer social justice in an unfettered manner.

This needs to be balanced, secondly, with the heavy emphasis in the psalm upon the insistence that it is the poor who will be favored by his just rule. This was already indicated in the programmatic v. 2 cited above. While the poor are explicitly mentioned in the second half of the line (as well as repeatedly later on), it is interesting to note the use of "your people" as the lead term in v. 2, and the term "people" recurs in vv. 3 and 4 as well. While this is clearly a general term for the king's subjects, it is qualified in two important ways. First, they are primarily God's people, "your people," as v. 2 states, and secondly the term is qualified both in this verse and in v. 4

by being closely related with the poor. In v. 2 the parallel term is "your poor," and in v. 4 we read of "the poor of the people."

What we have seen set out programmatically in the first two verses is continued in what follows. In v. 4 it is hoped that the king will "defend the cause of the poor of the people and give deliverance to the needy," while further down in vv. 12–14 the theme is again predominant, speaking of his deliverance of the needy, the poor, and those with no helper, of his having pity on them and even of redeeming their life from oppression.

Conversely, there is a muted, but undeniable, acknowledgment that this will also involve the negative task of crushing the oppressor (v. 4) and of delivering from "oppression and violence" (v. 14). Since these expressions occur in the sections that are dealing with the internal regulation of the nation, these oppressors should certainly be regarded as Judean citizens rather than foreign tyrants. The psalm alternates in a quite clear and consistent manner between internal and external affairs, so that the referent in each part is not in doubt.

Overall, a clear picture emerges from this psalm of the hopes for a king who stands very much in the place of God on earth, all victorious in his power and yet devoted to the care—depicted in legal terms—of the poor, weak, and needy in society. The consequence of such an ideal rule will be the flourishing of righteousness and peace (v. 7), and interestingly it seems to be assumed that agricultural prosperity will also follow automatically (cf. v. 16). Indeed, the king himself is likened in his good effects to that most vital of all natural elements, rain and showers (v. 6).

But of course the time came when there was no longer any king in Israel or Judah. The psalms were not abandoned, however, but were found to be of sufficient continuing value to be preserved within the Psalter of later times. The only way that we can make sense of this, it seems to me, is to accept that alongside fond memories of earlier days the psalms came to be understood as giving expression to what might come again, a restoration of the monarchy in some form, but now in the ideal to which Ps 72 gave expression, rather than its previous function as a role-model, more often frustrated than observed by a currently ruling king. In the very fact of the preservation of these psalms, therefore, the people continued to affirm their hopes that God would indeed judge the world in righteousness and that he would do it through the agency of his newly appointed king. It is a messianic hope in all but name and indicates that the pattern of the role of the authorities was deemed to supersede the chronological restrictions of the monarchical period alone.

The Law

Having looked so far at a representative passage from the prophets and the psalms together with a wider selection from Proverbs, the obvious missing element is the law.[9] Here we are fortunate to have available a recent detailed and comprehensive survey in the form of David Baker's book, *Tight Fists or Open Hands: Wealth and Poverty in Old Testament Law*.[10] Its relevance to our present thesis will be clear already from the preface in which Baker observes that "living with one's eyes open in the 'Two-thirds world' does not permit a simplistic prosperity theology; on the other hand, liberation theology's 'preferential option for the poor' emphasizes certain biblical texts and downplays others. The Old Testament both affirms the good things of this world and condemns those who monopolise them for their own benefit."

In his text of over three hundred pages Baker works systematically through every OT law that is relevant to his and our topic, commendably including in each case a section that compares relevant material from elsewhere in the ancient Near East, pointing out elements of similarity as well as difference. He groups them by subject under three major headings: "property and land," "marginal people," and "justice and generosity." His concluding citation of Deut 15:7b–8a is enough, perhaps, to indicate the large extent to which his exegesis coincides with what I have only been able to begin to explore in some of the other biblical passages: "Do not be hard-hearted or tight-fisted towards your needy neighbor. You should rather open your hand, willingly lending enough to meet the need, whatever it may be."[11]

It seems pointless to go through material which Baker has studied so fully, so that for the most part I must simply refer readers to his book for the details that they may want on some particular law or subject. In line with my practice up till now,

---

9. In his response to this paper James Bruckner makes the important point that I might have included narrative within the range of material that I consider. I entirely agree and acknowledge that this is an important field for further thought; the story of Naboth's vineyard in 1 Kgs 21 comes immediately to mind. Of course, when Bruckner goes on to comment briefly on the importance of the Abraham narratives for our topic I need to acknowledge that here I should give way to an expert on that subject; see his *Implied Law in the Abraham Narratives: A Literary and Theological Analysis* (JSOTSup 335; Sheffield: Sheffield Academic, 2001).

10. David Baker, *Tight Fists or Open Hands: Wealth and Poverty in Old Testament Law* (Grand Rapids: Eerdmans, 2009). It is relevant to observe that Baker is a British academic who lived for many years in Indonesia. After a spell back in Cambridge, England, he is now at Trinity Theological College, Perth, Australia.

11. This is cited from the NRSV whereas Baker in fact supplies his own translation on p. 315.

however, I should like to take one point and dwell on it slightly more fully by way of illustration.

Among those whom Baker labels "marginal people," brief attention is paid to the familiar pairing of "orphan and widow." This is often taken in popular commentaries to be characteristic of OT concerns as if it were distinctive. In fact, it is found very commonly in other ancient Near Eastern law codes as well as in passages that aim to illustrate the workings of an ideal society. The relevant passages have been surveyed by a number of different scholars.[12] On this two points deserve particular mention.

First, the reason for singling out orphans and widows is that they represent most acutely those classes of society who have lost their natural "champion." In the very different legal systems which then prevailed, they generally had nobody who (as husband or father) could protect their social, legal, or material rights. They may or may not have been poor; they may or may not have been destitute. The point is not so much related to the amount of their possessions as to the danger by which their status in this regard might be dramatically changed by exploitation and in turn that exploitation could come as much from neglect and oversight as by deliberate abuse. The frequency with which they occur as a pair not only in the Law but also in the Prophets and the Wisdom literature, together with their use throughout the ancient Near East, indicates that they stand as a cipher or symbol of what the writers regard as normal decent behavior. It is not that "charity" should be extended only to widows and orphans but that the attitude those in more privileged situations should

---

12. In addition to Baker's own brief treatment on pp. 189-91, there are accessible surveys in, for instance, L. Epsztein, *Social Justice in the Ancient Near East and the People of the Bible* (London: SCM, 1986) 3-42; Bruce V. Malchow, *Social Justice in the Hebrew Bible: What Is New and What Is Old?* (Collegeville, MN: Liturgical, 1996) 1-5; E. Nardoni, *Rise Up, O Judge: A Study of Justice in the Biblical World* (Peabody, MA: Hendrickson, 2004) 1-41; M. Weinfeld, *Social Justice in Ancient Israel and in the Ancient Near East* (Jerusalem: Magnes, 1995). One should also refer to the classic study of F. C. Fensham, "Widow, Orphan, and the Poor in Ancient Near Eastern Legal and Wisdom Literature," *Journal of Near Eastern Studies* 21 (1962) 129-39. The case has sometimes been made that the biblical laws on care for the orphan, widow, and stranger were in fact framed by the privileged elite in order to promote their own interests; cf. M. R. Sneed, "Israelite Concern for the Alien, Orphan, and Widow: Altruism or Ideology?" *Zeitschrift für die alttestamentliche Wissenschaft* 111 (1999) 498-507, and H. V. Bennett, *Injustice Made Legal: Deuteronomic Law and the Plight of Widows, Strangers, and Orphans in Ancient Israel* (Grand Rapids: Eerdmans, 2002). While there may be some elements of truth in these arguments, the case overall is misguided; for an informed response see B. S. Jackson, "Revolution in Biblical Law: Some Reflections on the Role of Theory in Methodology," *Journal of Semitic Studies* 50 (2005) 83-115 (esp. 99-108).

show towards them is symptomatic of how the biblical writers hope they will behave generally.

Second, there is an addition in some examples of their appearance which, so far as I am aware, is indeed distinctive to Israel; it does not seem to appear in any other body of related literature. In the prophets who come from around the start of the Babylonian exile or soon after, we find that added to the orphan and widow the figure of the "resident alien" is also joined as someone who should be treated with special kindness within the realm of social justice: "Act with justice and righteousness . . . and do no wrong or violence to the alien, the orphan, and the widow" (Jer 22:3; cf. 7:6); "The alien residing within you suffers extortion; the orphan and the widow are wronged in you" (Ezek 22:7); "Render true judgments, show kindness and mercy to one another; do not oppress the widow, the orphan, the alien, or the poor" (Zech 7:9–10; cf. Mal 3:5). The word is associated a number of times in both Jeremiah and Ezekiel with the fact that those in exile were regarded as "aliens" in Babylon, so that from their experience they should know to treat others in the same situation with compassion.

The relatively intensive use of the word at this time as well as its collocation with the orphan and widow is also found prominently in the book of Deuteronomy, e.g., "You shall not deprive a resident alien or an orphan of justice; you shall not take a widow's garment in pledge" (Deut 24:17). Most frequently this occurs in contexts where positive acts of generosity or kindness are being encouraged, and this goes along with the reminder that "you" were once aliens in the land of Egypt.

It is difficult to separate these uses in the later prophets and in Deuteronomy, though whether the earlier recollection of the sojourn in Egypt is transferred to the experience in Babylon or *vice versa* is difficult to ascertain. It is true that there are a couple of parallel references also in the earlier Book of the Covenant (Exod 22:21—linked with the widow and orphan in the next verse—and 23:9), but it is difficult to disagree with the consensus opinion that these have been added under the influence of Deuteronomy. If that is not the case, all one can say is that they had no appreciable influence on Israelite literature or thought until the later period.

As I have said, this new element in the familiar group of those who were stereotypically prone to being socially abused is without any parallel elsewhere in the ancient Near East; it seems to be characteristically Israelite or Judean. It appears to have been added as a reminder that they should learn from their historical experience of "exile," either in Egypt or in Babylon, and that they should pass on the lessons of that experience to their successors. Few if any of us have not had experiences where we have needed to know the generosity of those with wealth and possessions when we have been without. Childhood dependence is common to everyone, of course, to go no further. But what those in ancient Israel had learned collectively was that as poor and outcast people they had been given ample provision by God himself. The command to them was "go and do thou likewise." It is distressing that selfishness so often intervenes to harden hearts and blunt compassion in material as much as in other realms.

Conclusion

My argument has been, then, that on the basis of a few, but I trust representative, passages, we can see a pattern developing that transcends both the chronological and the social variety that is contained within the OT. It balances appreciation of the goodness of God in providing wealth and possessions for some with a stark warning against allowing their gain to become a dominant and hence oppressive appetite. Alongside that we have seen that those with less, including the poor (who are less well-off but not entirely without in the OT world) and the destitute are not to be judged as in any sense inferior on that basis. Rather, the challenge is to view them as members of our extended community and to act accordingly.

I am aware that my comments have been based on only a modest selection of passages, so that in due course it will be necessary to test whether other material may be fairly included within the framework. Ultimately, in a manner that I have not had space to trace here but which may be related to changing social and political circumstances, we find that in some late psalms and elsewhere in the intertestamental period the word "poor" can become a label for the spiritually rich. That, however, is a topic that runs beyond my immediate brief in this presentation, even though it may help to serve as a bridge into elements of NT and early Christian reflection which help link these OT perspectives with those found elsewhere in this Symposium volume.

RESPONSE TO WILLIAMSON

James K. Bruckner

Thank you, Prof. Williamson, for your paper, and thank you for engaging such a broad range of OT genres: the prophets, the wisdom tradition, the psalter, and the legal corpus. You have at the same time moved us into a close consideration of representative texts in each of these genres: the Bashanite bovine of Amos 4, the proverbial poor, the idea of servant dominion in Ps 72, and the widely distributed example of orphans, widows, and aliens in the law and beyond. Quite helpful for framing the paper and the broader discussion of this symposium are your clearly stated conclusions, which I take to be: "*The overarching notion is that the OT has no objection to ownership of wealth or possession as such, but . . .*"

The whole paper hangs on the glue of this little disjunctive conjunction, "but." So, what are the disjunctions? No objection to ownership of wealth or possession *as such, but* the means of acquisition is tightly guarded; any hint of gain by oppression, theft, or corruption is vigorously condemned. *But,* possessions are a cause for gratitude to God; they cannot be expected automatically, and over time poverty (in a relative sense) comes to be valued as an indication of piety. (This is not much supported in the paper, and further comment would help.) *But,* possessions are thus not held for one's own benefit, but for the service of God and for the care and protection of those with less or no means to represent themselves in society.

Significance of the Methodological Issues

Williamson has worked from a solid methodology in the selection of his representative texts. He has, it seems, succeeded in giving us a framework for avoiding the indulgence of text-picking to justify our "own favored positions." With the "vagaries of historical" context and diversity taken into account, the four text groups (prophetic, proverbial, psalmic, and legal texts) do provide us with OT principles regarding wealth and possessions that transcend their specific original situation in life. They fulfill a working hermeneutic that I happen to share and that is historically grounded, canonically consistent, and theologically relevant.

I appreciated Williamson's work in the first part of the paper to come to terms with an "appreciation of the very different nature of society then from now," particularly the contrast of the OT hierarchical view of society with western democratic systems' ultimate value of individual opinion and the belief that "we are what we make of ourselves." This question of identity ("ourselves") and "what we make" may require further reflection, especially since we conceive of identity as something mostly western and mostly individually accomplished. His salient point, however, is that we struggle with the OT partly out of the western cultural *heritage of* and *struggle against* feudalism, particularly its hierarchical structures. He has demonstrated one way through the struggle: by reading the biblical text more closely for its counter-voice in the midst of its culturally embedded hierarchical setting.

The method of the first third of the paper is necessary, not simply because the OT is often brushed aside as antiquated and presently irrelevant (i.e., to discard the kernel because of the husk), but also because some within the guild of OT studies and within the general public reread OT texts as unredeemable ideology. Rather than a cultural cradle, scholars and readers assume and conclude that the OT text perpetuates the opinions of a few privileged males to the extent that our main interpretive task is expose them as ruling class ideologues.

Thankfully Williamson has illustrated, conversely, that when cultural context is understood *as such* and named *as such* the biblical text still yields insight and a surprisingly radical critique of its own hierarchical setting. I would add that these surprises may even confront us as the Word of God. First, in the case of land ownership the land was God's to give or to take away whenever Israel oppressed its poor. (We may find a surprising present-day political application here.) Second, both levitical control and central temple priestly power were curtailed by their respective dispersion and dependence rather than by independent property ownership. Third, in the case of Davidic kings the deuteronomic historian in the voice of Samuel the prophet provided a strident counter-voice (1 Sam 8) alongside the Davidic promise (2 Sam 7). The books of Kings are surprisingly relentless in their negative assessments of kingly rule while, as Williamson indicates, Chronicles measures success by the goods and services provided for the people.

In this context the democratization of servant-kingship in Isa 55 may not be so surprising, except to those who expect or assume a monolithic OT ideology. The democratization of the image of God in Gen 1 sustains this "surprising" witness against arbitrary hierarchy. Williamson does us good service in providing two sets of heuristic texts. First, *in exile Judah shifted* from a critique of monarchy toward taking responsibility for the ideals of good dominion and placing the burden for the right use of wealth and possessions *on the community* (Isa 41, 42, 49, and 55). Second, *also in exile Judah embraced* a creation narrative that placed that responsibility and burden firmly on all human beings in the democratization of the image of God, remarkable in its ancient Near Eastern context (Gen 1:26–31; 5:1–3). More could be said here, for example, about the trajectory and development of the concept of good dominion through Isa 53 into the NT.

The Virtue of a Diversity of Voices

The heart of the paper illustrates the four-fold framework with representative texts from the Prophets, Wisdom, Psalms, and Law.

The Bashanite Bovine in Amos 4

In the illustration of the prophet Amos the wealthy wives of Samaria place an off-handed demand for food and drink on their husbands. Amos indicts them as Bashanite bovine, an image of those who are already more than well-fed. Williamson astutely places this sin with wealth in a long biblical tradition by beginning his explication with the word "incidentally."

In the canon, much oppressive sin *is* incidental, even casual. Aaron says, "I threw the gold in the fire and out came this calf" (Exod 32:24), and Adam says, "She gave me fruit from the tree and I ate." Disavowal of the source of wealth, gold, or knowledge is an ancient excuse for the most devastating rebellion against God. The casual life of inattentive consumption and vague disavowal of implications is a timeless concern worth further discussion. Williamson notes the issue in concluding this application with a caution against off-handedness, which is often the result of "second or third-hand oppression": "We should take some trouble to inform ourselves about whether the goods and services we buy are oppressive." Other texts, for example from the beginning of Isaiah, could serve as a further illustration from the prophetic corpus.

Proverbial Poor

The second representative illustration is from wisdom literature. Williamson's survey of the proverbial poor demonstrates the common general link between good living and wealth yet challenges reductionist perceptions. Key texts (Prov 13:23; 15:6; and 16:8) provide the caveat that some wicked are also wealthy. The poor are poor for a variety of reasons. They may be the victims of injustice; they may be reduced to poverty for their own wickedness, excessive pleasure seeking, and laziness; or they may simply be poor. Williamson also concludes that the poor are not to be equated with the destitute (a distinction that also could be demonstrated in Amos). The righteous response to the poor is to be generous for two reasons. First, at the purely human level generosity is enriching ("What goes around comes around"; e.g., Prov 28:27), and second, serving the poor is serving God (e.g., Prov 14:31). Here Williamson supports his conclusions that gaining wealth itself is not condemned, but gaining wealth by corruption or injustice is vigorously condemned, and that possessions are given by God for the purpose of service to God and others.

Servant Dominion in Psalm 72

The third illustration is from Psalm 72. The enduring value of this Davidic enthronement psalm for an OT understanding of wealth is delivered in the details. Setting aside the hierarchical husk and messianic trajectory, Williamson mines the psalm-prayer for its implicit relationships and theology. For the one who has been given the power of wealth and possessions, the ideals lifted to God in prayer are clear and direct: administer justice to "your people," defend the causes of "your poor," deliver the destitute, pity and save the destitute, redeem their life from oppression and violence, and "may their blood be precious" to the one in power. For further texts on the servant dominion, we might look to comments on the vindicated servant of Isaiah.

My minor question comes in the comment on v. 16 that "it seems to be assumed that agricultural prosperity will also follow automatically." Could this not also be an example of *good dominion over the environment* (abundance of grain waving on the tops of mountains, the fruit of Lebanon, and people blossoming) and included in the measure of the good use of wealth and power? An embedded theology of environmental health as a measure of the good and bad use of dominion may also be present in other texts, for example, in Hos 4:1–6 and Jer 22:26–30.

Orphans, Widows, and Aliens in the Law

In the final section on biblical law the identification of widows, orphans, and resident aliens as a cipher for vulnerable people is a helpful point for our interdisciplinary discussion. This cipher is *much used* by theologians and Williamson's footnote twelve is a valuable resource for access to the dialogue in OT scholarship.

The range of texts that echo the legal formulation of widows and orphans across biblical genres concerns anyone who is vulnerable to exploitation or neglect in regard to their social, legal, or material rights. The exilic addition of resident aliens is relevant especially in that it roots the motive for ethical behavior with wealth and possessions as a *response* of gratitude and emulation of a God who "brought you out of the land of Egypt." Inculcating gratitude in those who may not remember Egypt may be a theological theme worth broader discussion. For example, what does *memory* or *lack of memory* have to do with a Christian understanding and use of wealth and possessions?

If we choose to pursue the legal corpus beyond the phrase widows, orphans, and aliens, the book of the Covenant (Exod 21–23) with its laws of protection for poor debtors and poor plaintiffs could be a fruitful direction.[1] A sticky wicket worth further examination may be the law of the seventh year release of debt and the jubilee year of land remandation.

For Further Discussion

Williamson concludes his paper with an open door for proposals of other passages that might be "fairly included with the framework" or an adjustment of the framework itself. The genre of biblical narrative might rightly be included in the framework. Certainly the moral tale of Solomon's life could be fruitful, as he was the most prosperous man in Israel's history. Although he begins in his youth with a prayer for wisdom and continues in material blessing, he ends ingloriously in the undercurrent of acquisition and exploitation.[2] Solomon's corveé labor requirements and building projects made him an oppressive pharaoh in his own land and led to a great public outcry and rebellion in the north under Jeroboam. Could this narrative also fit within the framework?

Close readings of other well-known narratives that hinge on wealth and possessions might also serve within the framework, such as stories of gain and loss and their attendant voices and relationships. For example, the paradigmatic Joseph was righteous in prison and in poverty, then righteous in power over his brothers and over Egypt. (His bones are said to have helped to part the water at the Reed Sea in rabbinic tradition; see Ps 114:1, 3–5). These are narratives that reflect good and bad character in relation to wealth and in relation to poverty, as well as the exercise of good and bad dominion.

---

1. See J. Bruckner, *Exodus* (NIBC; Peabody, MA: Hendrickson, 2008) 205, 213, and 217.

2. See Helen R. Graham, "A Solomonic Model of Peace," in *Voices from the Margin: Interpreting the Bible in the Third World* (ed. R. S. Sugirtharajah; London: SPCK, 1991) 214–26.

In addition, within this framework and its banner of the virtue of diverse voices is the question of risk, the risk of wealth and possessions. I suggest that the binary code of *greed versus generosity* is worth investigation (cf. Deut 15:7b–8a). It is treated well in David Baker's *Tight Fists or Open Hands*.[3] Cain and Able come to mind, as do the widow of Zarephath with Elijah, Ruth with Naomi, and Esther and her risk in the Persian court. Each of these narratives is an opportunity to measure the spectrum of values within wealth, the impoverished wealthy and the wealthy poor, the impoverished poor and the true wealth of some wealthy persons. Williamson just mentions the possibility of the theme of the wealth of the poor in some late psalms and intertestamental writings. Perhaps they can be elucidated more fully.

My pressing question, however, is Do we really want to set aside the Abrahamic blessing and covenant as a topic and as a representative text, or do we want to engage it more fully? Several related questions follow. Can the current erroneous health and wealth reading (that Abraham was blessed because he was faithful) remain unchallenged? Is this not a necessary text in a discussion of wealth and possession? Do not the principles of the Abrahamic covenant set the stage for the texts that follow? For better or worse, does not God's Abrahamic promise of blessing and of *being a blessing* continue as the foundation of Israel's collective memory of God's initiative with them? Do not those promises sustain them through exile and the rebuilding of a broken community?

We may be rightly cautious around the extreme misuses of "the blessing" in health and wealth gospels, since we, in the West, share, in large measure, in actual health and wealth. Nevertheless, many less than prosperous communities in the Christian church may yet benefit from a responsible reading of the Abrahamic narrative, its context of sojourn, uninvited risk and danger, and more to the point, its rooting in the purpose of the promised blessing of wealth and possessions. First, Abraham is blessed in order that he may become a blessing, and second and perhaps surprisingly, God's election of Abraham is not a result of Abraham's faith, which follows, nor a result of Abraham's goodness. Rather, election and blessing are simply God's initiative. In Gen 20 Abraham's lack of faith and his deceit led to a deathly illness in Abimelech's clan and put the promise of a child with Sarah in jeopardy. God told Abimelech that he was blameless and implies Abraham's guilt. Nonetheless, Abraham's wealth increased, and Abimelech's wealth decreased. This is purely blessing through election, not blessing through believing.

---

3. David Baker, *Tight Fists or Open Hands: Wealth and Poverty in Old Testament Law* (Grand Rapids: Eerdmans, 2009).

POVERTY AND PAUL'S GOSPEL

Bruce W. Longenecker

Typically we think of Jesus as preaching "good news to the poor" (Luke 4:18) and Paul as preaching "good news to the Gentiles" (Gal 2:7). Being primarily concerned to evangelize Gentiles, Paul (it seems) had little interest in giving theological consideration to the poverty that engulfed vast swathes of the Gentile world. In this way of looking at things, while Paul depicts himself as "an Israelite, a descendant of Abraham, from the tribe of Benjamin" (Rom 11:1; cf. Phil 3:5–6), he stands outside of the currents of mainstream Judaism, whose Scriptures and traditions were full to the brim of strategies for alleviating the miseries of the poor and of prophetic denunciations of the abuses against the poor by those economically more secure. Sensitivities to the plight of the poor seem to have informed the ministries of Jesus, the early Jesus followers in Jerusalem, James the brother of Jesus, and others associated with the nascent Jesus movement, but it is usually imagined that Paul sat lightly toward the deeply-entrenched Israelite heritage regarding care for the poor in his efforts to evangelize Gentiles. He simply had other fish to fry, or so it seems.

In fact, however, the reality is much different. The plight of the poor has a strong foothold within Paul's apostolic ministry and the theological contours of his gospel. In the paragraphs below, overviews of the following issues will be offered: Paul's collection for the poor among Jesus followers, economic structures within the Greco-Roman world, and passages from Pauline texts demonstrating the "theological DNA" that pertains to poverty.

Paul's Collection for the "Poor among the Saints in Jerusalem" (Rom 15:26)

When we think of Paul and the poor, our thoughts tend to gravitate as a case study to the funds that Paul collected on behalf of "the poor among the saints in Jerusalem" (Rom 15:26). Beyond Rom 15 we learn of Paul's efforts for this "collection" primarily from the Corinthian letters: 1 Cor 16:1–4 and especially 2 Cor 8–9.[1] Although this

---

1. Some scholars would include Gal 2:10 within the passages that speak of Paul's collection efforts. I do not for reasons that will become clear below.

collection is not exhaustive of the pertinent data relevant to reconstructing Paul's attitude toward poverty, it is nonetheless an extremely suggestive initiative on his part that helps to reveal how poverty registered on his theological radar.

Doing our best to date Paul's collection efforts suggests that Paul dedicated five or so years of his life to this project—during the years 53 through 58 CE. During that time Paul did his best to entice members of Jesus groups that he had already founded to contribute to the fund, and then took it upon himself to deliver the fund to Jesus followers based in Jerusalem.[2]

There is much that we do not know about the collection effort. We can broadly suspect that a leading motivation behind his efforts was to demonstrate something of the unity of the Jewish and Gentile Jesus followers, a unity poignantly evidenced by their mutuality in caring for each other in times of economic need. An "economic" description of his motivation is evident in 2 Cor 8:13-14, where Paul seeks to enlist Corinthian support of his collection by speaking of it as involving "a question of a fair balance between your present abundance and their need, so that their abundance may be for your need." In 2 Cor 9:12 he speaks of the collection as a means of making provision for "the needs of the saints." But there were needy people everywhere, and among them needy Jesus followers spread throughout the Mediterranean basin, so an economic motivation alone cannot explain Paul's choice of Jesus followers in Jerusalem as the beneficiaries of the collection. Something more is in view here than simply the care for some Jesus followers by other Jesus followers.

This causes us to imagine that Jesus groups in Jerusalem are to be the beneficiaries of Paul's collection precisely because the symbolic value of Gentile followers of Jesus offsetting the needs of Jewish followers of Jesus seems to have been irresistible to Paul. It was to be a tangibly compelling symbolic gesture testifying to the unity of Jew and Gentile in Christ, a unity that Paul had often fought hard to protect throughout his ministry. The closest Paul gets to revealing this motivation for his collection efforts is in Rom 15:26-27. There he presents the collection as an occasion for Gentile Jesus followers to "share their [material] resources with the poor among the saints at Jerusalem" as a form of debt owed to them, because Gentile Jesus followers "have come to share in their [i.e., Jewish] spiritual blessings," and so are to seek to be "of service to them [i.e., Jewish followers of Jesus] in material things."

If the collection served this symbolic function, it was unlikely to have been a paltry amount of money that Paul carried to Jerusalem. With many people in

---

2. For my attempt to date these matters, see my *Remember the Poor: Paul, Poverty, and the Greco-Roman World* (Grand Rapids: Eerdmans, 2010) 338-44.

Jerusalem being suspicious of Paul (see the discussion of Rom 15:30–31 below), it would have run completely contrary to Paul's hopes and intentions to have brought only a meager collection to Jerusalem as a symbol of the mutuality between Jews and Gentiles in Christ. For this reason, we can imagine that the funds Paul eventually brought to Jerusalem were sizeable. Perhaps Paul spent five years collecting funds precisely in order to avoid a scenario in which he brought a derisory amount to the Jewish followers of Jesus in Jerusalem.

But the purposes behind the collection cannot simply be restricted to the symbolic. The symbolic purpose of the collection itself relies on a more fundamental significance of the collection. It testifies to the transformation of Gentile Jesus followers to the extent that they are digging into the resources that they have in order to assist others in need.

This may sound like simple kindness to us, but it is important to recognize that, rightly or wrongly, in the Greco-Roman world Gentiles were not known to care for the poor. There was, of course, some degree of caring for the poor in the Greco-Roman world, but to the Jewish mind it was so negligible as to be virtually nonexistent. Jews excelled at caring for the poor and needy among their number, while to the Jewish mind Gentiles did not. Imagine then the amazement that might have transpired when Paul brought his collection to the Jesus followers in Jerusalem. That seems to be the way Paul hoped his collection would be received. His hopes to unleash consolidation among Jewish and Gentile Jesus followers in a single stroke, lashing together Jesus followers in unity across ethnic boundaries, were based on this testimony of the transforming power of God within predominately Gentile members of his community. By their willingness to donate some of their own resources to offset the needs of others, Gentile Jesus followers were testifying to the fact that the Spirit of the God of Israel was moving among their midst in a powerful and unprecedented way.

Accordingly, the collection was devised to help remove the offense of Paul's "law free" mission to the Gentile world, an offense that had dogged his mission for many years. When the proceeds of Gentile generosity were brought right into the heart of Jerusalem, Jewish followers of Jesus there would be brought face to face with tangible evidence of the transformation of Gentile followers of Jesus, ensuring that Paul's "law free" mission among the Gentiles would be invigorated and unencumbered by distractions from that point on.

Paul's hopes were high, but so too were the risks, as he well knew. Even as he was wrapping up his collection efforts when writing to Jesus followers in Rome, Paul seemed cognizant that many in Jerusalem had deep misgivings about him and that grave dangers might await him if he participated in the delivery of the collection, rather than simply allowing others to take the collection to Jerusalem, as he had earlier imagined.[3] So, when laying out his plans to deliver the collection to Jerusalem, Paul adds this poignant note (Rom 15:30–31):

> I appeal to you, brothers and sisters, by our Lord Jesus Christ and by the love of the Spirit, to join me in earnest prayer to God on my behalf, that I may be rescued from the unbelievers in Judea, and that my ministry to Jerusalem may be acceptable to the saints.

Paul's suspicions that trouble may be waiting for him in Jerusalem probably proved correct. The Acts of the Apostles depicts Paul as returning to Jerusalem only to encounter an outcry against him as one who misleads Israel. As a consequence of that, Paul was arrested, held in custody for two years (from 58–60 CE), and taken to Rome where (for a further period of two years, from 60–62 CE) he waited for his case to be heard by the emperor himself (Acts 21–28).

What happened after that is not entirely clear. But what is clear is that one of the main threads weaving through Paul's life from about the years 53 to 62 CE is the collection for poor Jesus followers in Jerusalem and its aftermath. This should not be surprising since, as we will see momentarily, that collection was not an anomaly within Paul's mission or a mere appendage to the main currents of his theology. Instead, it was a concrete expression of his theology and gospel mission.

This is evidenced, for instance, by the way Paul speaks about the collection in 2 Cor 9:13, where he describes Corinthian contributions to the collection as "your obedience to the confession of the gospel of Christ" (*tē hypotagētēs homologias hymōn eis to euangelion tou Christou*). Alongside terms like "obedience," "confession," and "gospel," others of Paul's favored theological terms appear in his discussion of the collection in 2 Cor 8–9, including: "grace" (*charis*; 8:1, 6–7, 9, 19; 9:8, 14); "service" (*diakonia*, 8:4; 9:1, 12, 13); "fellowship" (*koinōnia*; 8:4; 9:13); and "righteousness" (*dikaiosynē*, 9:9–10), both the righteousness of God and of those who would be obedient to him. Evidently Paul understood the collection for the poor to be intricately intertwined with the gospel that he preached, a gospel about God's righteousness

---

3. When writing 1 Cor 16:3–4, Paul imagines that the collection will be delivered to Jerusalem through the use of emissaries from the various Jesus groups, with him accompanying the collection if that is necessary. But by the time he writes Rom 15:25–33, he knows that he himself must be involved in delivering the collection.

setting the world right, including in that project the transformed lives of his devotees, as demonstrated by their financial self-giving for those in need.

Scaling Poverty in the Greco-Roman World

We have seen some initial evidence indicating Paul's belief that, through the power of the gospel, Gentile Jesus followers would become transformed in their lives, including caring for the needy in ways that transcended the reputed norm of a general pagan indifference towards the poor. Further evidence demonstrating this will be highlighted below. In order to understand the full impact of those texts, we need first to recognize something of the dimensions of urban poverty of Paul's day.

Although not an exact science, certain data from the Greco-Roman world allow us to reconstruct a rough outline of the economic stratification of the urban environment in which Paul operated. I work with an "economy scale" that is largely indebted to the work of Steve Friesen (although I adjust his percentages somewhat).[4] The economy scale differentiates seven levels of economic stratification, from ES7 (economy scale 7) at its lowest point up to ES1 at its highest, allocating percentages of the urban population to each of those levels.

Economic Level	Basic Description	Percent of Urban Population
ES1 – ES3	The urban elite	3
ES4	The middling groups	15
ES5	Those with modest reserves	27
ES6	Those at subsistence level	30
ES7	Those below subsistence level	25

The following generalities indicate something of the differences between the various economic levels. The urban elite (ES1 through ES3) were enormously wealthy. They controlled the structures of the economy, and they used their privileged position to ensure that their privileges were maintained.[5] Those within the

---

4. Steven J. Friesen, "Poverty in Pauline Studies: Beyond the So-called New Consensus," *JSNT* 26 (2004) 323–61. My own interpretation of Friesen's helpful scale can be found in my *Remember the Poor*, 36–59 and 317–32.

5. According to Friesen's descriptors, ES1 comprises "imperial dynasty, Roman senatorial families, a few retainers, local royalty, a few freedpersons"; ES2 comprises "equestrian families, provincial officials, some retainers, some decurial families, some freedpersons, some retired military officers"; ES3 comprises "most decurial families, wealthy men and women who do not hold office, some freedpersons, some retainers, some veterans, some merchants." See "Poverty in Pauline Studies," 341.

middling groups (ES4) were relatively comfortable, often having control of large household estates and businesses of some kind.[6] Those in the top half of this level served the civic functionaries of the urban elite, and were well-placed to move into the lower levels of the urban elite, if fortune permitted. Those within ES5 operated small businesses or urban-related farms, and managed to store up some decent levels of reserves for themselves and their small households (i.e., the family and perhaps a servant).[7] Those at ES6 managed to get by on whatever resources they had available but were not able to accumulate many reserves, therefore being precariously placed in relation to utter destitution.[8] Those at ES7 were the utterly destitute, having to rely wholly upon others for the resources to sustain their life. Prolonged periods within ES7 would inevitably result in premature death, due to malnutrition or other physical ailments that characterized ES7 in particular.[9]

A model of this kind requires all kinds of qualifications about its utility and can be usefully employed only with caution. Nonetheless, as I have argued elsewhere, the dangers of using an economy scale of this sort are less significant than the dangers of not using one.[10] In fact, some of the most unfortunate debates in research about the early Jesus movement can be attributed to the fact that the participants in the debate failed to construct a well-informed heuristic tool of this kind in order to ground their discourse.

Poverty, Resources, and Generosity in Greco-Roman Urban Contexts

From the proposed economy scale it is evident that a high percentage of urbanites of the Greco-Roman world lived in conditions of near poverty (ES6) and utter poverty (ES7). Just over half of the urban population was extremely vulnerable to misfortune due to their economic situation. The "safety nets" to catch and protect those in

---

6. According to Friesen's descriptors, ES4 comprises "some merchants, some traders, some freedpersons, some artisans (especially those who employ others), and military veterans." I would add most *Augustales* and *apparitores* among their number. See "Poverty in Pauline Studies," 341.

7. According to Friesen's descriptors, ES5 comprises "many merchants and traders, regular wage earners, artisans, large shop owners, freedpersons, some farm families." See "Poverty in Pauline Studies," 341.

8. According to Friesen's descriptors, ES6 comprises "small farm families, laborers (skilled and unskilled), artisans (esp. those employed by others), wage earners, most merchants and traders, small shop/tavern owners." See "Poverty in Pauline Studies," 341.

9. According to Friesen's descriptors, ES7 comprises "some farm families, unattached widows, orphans, beggars, disabled, unskilled day laborers, prisoners." See "Poverty in Pauline Studies," 341.

10. See my *Remember the Poor*, 36–40, 231–35.

an economic downward spiral were virtually nonexistent. Consequently, not only were the poor numerous, their situation was virtually impermeable to alteration and correction.

There was generosity in the Greco-Roman world, but very little of it ever touched the lives of those in ES6 or ES7. No doubt some gestures of charitable giving were evident out on the streets, where coins might be tossed to beggars from passersby. But the Greco-Roman world was not awash with concerns to offset poverty and care for the poor and needy, and not many were in a position to do much about it anyway. For instance, those in ES5 were unlikely to do anything of real substance for those in poverty conditions, being all too conscious of how precarious their own economic position was. This means that roughly eighty percent of the population was poorly placed to undertake generosity in any meaningful fashion; generosity would have to emerge from those above ES5 through ES7.

The elite were well groomed in customs of generosity. Although they were enormously wealthy, they took great care to involve themselves in generous expenditures for the benefit of those most involved in civic life. Their generosity could take many forms including lavish banquets, sporting events, civic monuments, roads, water systems, public baths, arenas, and the like. The costs involved in these extravagant measures were usually huge. The elite undertook such massive expenditures willingly, although altruism was rarely a sole driving force in their motivation. Benefitting the public life of the civic community empowered their public and political prestige, enabling them to bolster their resources, which could then be used to enhance their political status further, in something of a never-ending loop.

This looped system of generosity and reciprocity worked well for all those involved. Usually, however, the ones involved were primarily the elite of ES1–ES3 and those most closely associated with them in the middling groups of ES4; on occasion some at ES5 might have benefitted, perhaps if they belonged to a Greco-Roman "association" of one kind or another. But for those at the bottom of the economic scale, the benefits of elite generosity were negligible. The generous exchange of resources marked out relationships at the top of the economic scale, but failed to "trickle down" to those in ES6 and ES7 whose lives dangled precariously by a thin economic string.

With great expenditures came the urgent need to replenish the coffers of the elite. With approximately eighty-five percent of the Roman imperial economy being dependent on agrarian produce, land ownership was an essential component of fiscal well-being. Consequently, the elite made it their business to acquire as much land as possible, often through less than respectable means. But one way or another, the majority of the society's resources made its way upward on a never-ending conveyor belt that enhanced the elite in their quest to capture honor through generous initiatives and opulent living. The poor of ES6 who worked in agrarian contexts usually played a key role in harvesting agrarian resources for the benefit of the elite, even though they themselves were not in any real sense the beneficiaries of elite generosity. Resources moved from the bottom to the top of the economic scale and then were redistributed among those at the top through to those at the middle. Those at the bottom simply did what they could to survive, their chances being enhanced if they could find a role within the economic machinery. Those at ES6 had a foothold within that machinery, but a precarious one. Those at ES7 were virtually expendable, having no place within the economic machinery and threatening to drag down the system in an unproductive mire.

If there is an exception to this, it is found in the practices of the Jewish people. The Jewish Scriptures and traditions placed care for the poor and vulnerable at the very heart of Jewish piety and practice. Among the various functions of ancient Jewish synagogues was the operation of "treasuries" for the poor. Members of the synagogues donated resources to the synagogue for distribution among the poor and needy, or they operated food distributions to those in need of basic provisions. Such initiatives were expressions of their devotion to God, for whom the weak and helpless were not to be despised as expendables but were, instead, considered worthy recipients of his covenant love and gracious benevolence.

Jewish care for the poor was, then, primarily an intra-Jewish phenomenon, with Jews caring for the very poor within their communities. There is little reason to think that Gentiles were frequent beneficiaries of support from synagogues (although Jews might certainly have offered charitable initiatives when passing beggars on the street). That was all about to change when a form of Judaism began to spread throughout the Mediterranean basin—the early Jesus movement. In the name of the one who had lived as a Jew from Nazareth and who they knew to be the exalted Lord, the early Jesus followers began to take the rich resources of Jewish thought and practice to the pagan Greco-Roman world, with Gentiles themselves as targets to hear and respond to the good news of their proclamation. In the process, caring for the poor would get a foothold in a wholly unprecedented manner.

Texts Illustrating Paul's Concern for the Poor

We have already seen why Paul himself should be included in this process in which Jewish sensibilities about caring for the poor were brought to the Gentile world.

The collection that Paul undertook for "the poor among the saints in Jerusalem" is a strong case in point, as Gentile followers of Jesus gave of their resources to care for poor Jewish followers of Jesus. Although Gentile followers of Jesus who belonged to the ES4 catgegory were probably strong contributors to his collection, Paul's instructions regarding the collection make it clear that he sought to enlist ES5 followers of Jesus as a necessary part of the collection effort (see, for instance, 1 Cor 16:1–4, advice that resonates on lower economic levels than ES4).[11]

While Paul's texts regarding the collection are important and notable, other passages are just as significant when compiling a full inventory of texts that pertain to caring for the poor. In what follows, ten of those texts are highlighted, six of which are from letters that are undisputedly authored by Paul, four of which are disputed, a point to which we will return.

Writing two chapters to the Corinthians about the collection, Paul nears the end of his discussion with this statement in 2 Cor 9:13 (one phrase of which has already been discussed): "Because of the genuineness of this selfless assistance, people will praise God for the obedience that transpires from your confession of the gospel of Christ—that is, for the generosity of your sharing with them and with all people." Paul cites selfless generosity as a reason why praise is given to God. But in a revealing phrase Paul speaks not merely of Corinthian generosity toward Jesus followers in Jerusalem ("with them," *eis autous*) but also of a much broader target of their generosity—that is, their sharing "with all people" (*eis pantas*). Although Paul's focus is not on generosity in general, in the last phrase of 2 Cor 9:13 we see how easily Paul can shift from talking about generosity towards specific Jesus followers in Jerusalem to talking about generosity towards the needy in general. Moreover, Paul speaks as if both forms of generosity are outworkings of the Corinthian "confession of the gospel of Christ"(*tēs homologias hymōn eis to euangelion tou Christou*).

A verse from Galatians is similarly indicative of Paul's theological interest in caring for the needy in general. The verse is Gal 6:10, but its significance needs first to be illustrated by its structural placement within the flow of Paul's discourse in Galatians. Throughout his letter Paul challenges the view that Gentile Jesus followers should become circumcised, an issue that he deals with largely in Gal 1–4. Paul hopes instead to focus the Galatians' attention on what it would look like if their lifestyle as Jesus followers was characterized not by the matter of circumcision but by the guidance of the Spirit, the Spirit of the self-giving Son of God, an issue he deals

---

11. The same is applicable to Paul's instructions in 2 Cor 8–9, although it would require more space than is affordable to demonstrate the point.

with largely in Gal 5–6. From Gal 6:11 through 18 Paul himself picks up the stylus and writes in "bold font" in order to recap and highlight the letter's central thrust. Just before that point, however, Paul includes an important sentence that begins in such a way as to emphasize its critical importance in Paul's overarching presentation. He begins Gal 6:10 with the doubly emphatic phrase "Therefore, then" (*ara oun*), which, understandably, is almost never translated fully in English translations. The verse reads: "Therefore, then, whenever we have an opportunity, let us work the good to all, and especially for those of the household of faith." According to Hans Dieter Betz, this verse "summarizes and concludes the parenetical section" of Galatians, and as such "sums up in a general way, and in the form of a final appeal, what the Apostle regards as the ethical task of the Christian community. Hence, it serves also as a definition of Christian ethics."[12]

For our purposes, what is most notable is that this "definition of Christian ethics" is framed in terms of "working the good," echoing and reinforcing the phrase "doing the good" on behalf of others in Gal 6:9. These terms must include the notion of supporting the economically vulnerable who were visible all around them.[13] As Ben Witherington notes, these exhortations "would surely at the very least include charitable works toward the needy and poor."[14] This view is strengthened by Bruce Winter's observation that the phrase "to do the good" is virtually technical terminology in the ancient world for bestowing material benefits on others.[15] As Tom Wright notes, the phrase "to do the good" was "in regular use in Paul's world, referring to financial contributions in civic and community life."[16] Accordingly, just prior to breaking off the flow of his thoughts, picking up the stylus and writing his concluding summary of the letter, Paul leads his discourse onto the high terrain of Gal 6:9–10, where it rings out with strong tones of economic urgency. The verse can be

---

12. Hans Dieter Betz, *Galatians* (Philadelphia: Fortress, 1979) 310. Cf. Richard N. Longenecker, *Galatians* (WBC; Dallas: Word, 1990) 282.

13. Paul has already introduced an economic dimension of "the good" in Gal 6:6, when exhorting those who are taught to "share all good things" (*koinōneitō . . . en pasin agathois*) with their teachers, i.e., support their teachers financially.

14. Ben Witherington, *Grace in Galatia: A Commentary on Paul's Letter to the Galatians* (Edinburgh: T. & T. Clark, 1998) 434. This injunction is not unlike that of Jesus, as recounted in Luke 6:32–36. After exhorting his listeners to love, to do good, to bless, and to "give to everyone who begs from you" (6:27–31), the exhortations of 6:32–36 repeat the prescriptions of loving, doing good (*agathopoieite*) and lending, where the phrase "do good" bears an economic dimension.

15. Bruce W. Winter, *Seek the Welfare of the City: Christians as Benefactors and Citizens* (Grand Rapids: Eerdmans, 1994) 11–40.

16. N. T. Wright, *Paul for Everyone: Galatians and Thessalonians* (London: SPCK, 2002) 79.

paraphrased in this fashion: "Therefore, the point I'm driving at is this: be generous to the needy—all the needy but especially the needy among Jesus followers!" Rather than focusing on whether male followers of Jesus should undergo circumcision, Galatian Jesus groups should be led by the Spirit to care for the poor within their orbit of responsibility.

Another of Paul's letters privileges key structural terrain as the place where care for the needy is admonished. Just before his farewells of 1 Thess 5:23–28, Paul offers a catalogue of exhortations in 5:12–22. Included in that catalogue is the charge to "encourage the faint-hearted, help the weak (*antechesthe tōn asthenōn*), be patient with all of them" (5:14). The word "weak" frequently has economic dimension in Paul's letters (see, for instance, 1 Cor 1:26–29; 1 Cor 8; 1 Cor 9:22), and the same is likely to be the case in 1 Thess 5:14.[17] The author of Acts imagines Paul to use the term "the weak" with economic significance; so in Acts 20:35 Paul speaks of helping the weak in accordance with the words of the Lord Jesus himself, who said "It is more blessed to give than to receive." If "the weak" bears something of the same significance in 1 Thess 5:14, that economic focus spills over into the following verse. There, just as in Gal 6:10, Paul includes in his final exhortations the charge to "pursue the good" (*to agathon diō*[set macron over o]*kete*), both in relation to the corporate community (*eis allē*[set macron over e]*lous*) and broader society in general (*eis pantas*).

If Paul included care for the poor as part of his instructions to communities of Jesus followers that he founded, his letter to Jesus followers in Rome indicates that he did the same when writing to Jesus groups founded by others in order to introduce his gospel to them. So he encourages Roman followers of Jesus to offset "the needs [*chreiais*] of the saints" (Rom 12:13). As Douglas Moo rightly notes, the needs mentioned here "are material ones: food, clothing, and shelter."[18] Here, then, Paul is exhorting Roman followers of Jesus to ensure that they make provision for others—"widows, orphans, strangers, and the community's poor in general."[19] The same economic dimension is probably in view in Rom 12:16, where Paul exhorts his audience to forsake human pride and conceit by "associating with the lowly" (*tois tapeinois synapagomenoi*). These exhortations fall in the paragraph amplifying his charge that Jesus followers should "Let love be genuine" (*hē agapē anypokritos*, Rom

---

17. Cf. Greg K. Beale, *1–2 Thessalonians* (Downers Grove: InterVarsity, 2003) 166.

18. Douglas J. Moo, *The Epistle to the Romans* (Grand Rapids: Eerdmans, 1996) 779. So too James D. G. Dunn, *Romans* (WBC 38A–B; Dallas: Word, 1988) 743. The term *chreiai* frequently connotes material needs; in Paul's letters, for instance, see Phil 2:25; 4:16, 19; Eph 4:28.

19. Dunn, *Romans*, 743. So too Moo, *Romans*, 779–80.

12:9). When outlining his proclamation of good news to Jesus followers in Rome, care for the needy finds an essential place in his theological essay on how "love" is to be effective within communities of Jesus followers.

We have been considering passages that illustrate something of Paul's concern for the poor from the letters that all agree were written by him. Other letters that are more controversial in terms of their authorship nonetheless demonstrate the same trace of theological DNA regarding care for the poor.

One passage of this kind is 2 Thess 3:6–13. Behind this passage lies a scenario in which some Thessalonian followers of Jesus were enjoying a situation of "idleness" (cf. 1 Thess 5:14). We can bypass the dispute about why some became "idle" and notice what is of primary significance for our interests, which is that some Jesus followers were able to assume that, despite their idleness, others within Thessalonian Jesus groups would provide them with economic support throughout their "idleness."

This situation alone is an extremely suggestive indicator of the economic dimension that was in place within Jesus groups in Thessalonica. With Jesus followers struggling to interpret the precise nature of their economic responsibilities to each other, the instructions of 2 Thess 3:6–13 seek to preserve the viability of Jesus groups as vehicles through which the weak are served. This is an expression of the corporate identity of Jesus followers. Paul assumed a differentiation between the truly needy and others who are not truly needy, and his instructions in 2 Thess 3:6–13 ensure that the resources of Jesus followers are not squandered in needless ways. Ultimately 2 Thess 3:6–13 is something of a case study in preserving a demeanor of legitimate generosity and care among Jesus followers. It is not surprising that the passage ends with this note: "Do not be weary in doing the good" (3:13), which is an exhortation that must include reference to "the material support the church had given to their fellow members in need."[20] Even in contexts where the corporate generosity practiced within Jesus groups has been taken advantage of by some Jesus followers, Paul still upholds the principle of caring for those who were truly in need. It is precisely on this note of economic generosity that the letter ends, prior to the final prayer (3:16), greeting (3:17) and benediction (3:18) that form the letter's conclusion.

A similar situation is reflected in 1 Tim 5:3–16. There, the Pauline author differentiates between needy widows, whom Jesus groups should continue to support, and others who should not be eligible for support of this kind.[21] The author's opening and closing instructions indicate his position clearly: "Honor widows who are

---

20. Abraham J. Malherbe, *The Letters to the Thessalonians* (New York: Doubleday, 2000) 458.
21. For more on this, see especially Winter, *Seek the Welfare of the City*, 62–78.

real widows ... Let the church not be burdened, so that it can assist those who are real widows" (1 Tim 5:3, 16). If corporate funds are to be used for the needy, the community must exercise discretion in determining who the truly needy are. In this way the fundamental character of generosity within the community will not be compromised. Notably, much like Galatians, 1 Thessalonians, and 2 Thessalonians, the text of 1 Timothy comes to a close with an emphasis on doing good works, with an emphasis on economic generosity: "do good, be rich in good works, be generous and ready to share" (1 Tim 6:18).[22]

The Pauline letter to Titus shares precisely the same structural feature, that is, the letter closes with an emphasis on doing good to those in need: "And let people learn to devote themselves to good works in order to meet urgent needs, so that they may not be unproductive" (Titus 3:14). As part of the author's concluding instructions before a verse of final greetings, these instructions "emphasize the theme of the epistle one last time": Jesus followers should be devoted to living in practical ways (cf. Tit 3:8).[23] The practical dimension that the author chooses to highlight is offsetting the needs of others. That an economic dimension is included in the author's instruction is further evidenced by the phrase "urgent needs" (*tas anagkaias chreias*), with the Greek noun commonly denoting the critical necessities of life (as noted above in relation to Rom 12:13).

Similarly in Ephesians, the Pauline author includes in 4:25–32 a list of actions of how Jesus followers are to live in order to demonstrate that they "no longer live as the Gentiles live" (Eph 4:17). The third entry in the list instructs thieves to give up stealing and work honestly in order to "share with the needy" (*hina echē metadidonai tō chreian echonti*, 4:28). It is unlikely that the author imagined that only former thieves would share with the needy. Instead, he seems to have imagined that former thieves would join with other Jesus followers in sharing with the needy. Here we are witnessing the expectation that Jesus groups in general will be marked out by caring for the needy. As Ernest Best has noted, this verse "provides some evidence for the continuance of communal sharing of possessions among the early Christians."[24] To

---

22. On the economic dimension of this exhortation, see Robert Mounce, *The Pastoral Epistles* (Nashville: Thomas Nelson, 2000) 367; Frances Young, *The Theology of the Pastoral Epistles* (Cambridge: Cambridge University Press, 1994) 31.

23. Mounce, *The Pastoral Epistles*, 458. Mounce reinforces the point (p. 459): Paul "wants to drive home the central thrust of the epistle: the practical necessity of good works (cf. Titus 1:16; 2:7, 14; 3:8)."

24. Ernest Best, *Ephesians* (ICC; Edinburgh: T. & T. Clark, 1998) 455. Cf. Ben Witherington, *The Letters to Philemon, the Colossians, and the Ephesians: A Socio–Rhetorical Commentary on the Captivity Epistles* (Grand Rapids: Eerdmans, 2007) 300.

that we might add that this corporate "sharing of possessions" must itself have been understood as a testimony of the transformation of Jesus followers by the divine grace given to them in Christ (cf. 4:32).

These instructions about caring for the needy from 2 Thessalonians, 1 Timothy, Titus, and Ephesians are not to be seen as incidental add-ons that simply and feebly fill the rhetorical space of the Pauline letter. They are better seen as standard features of Pauline exhortation. If these four texts were all written by Paul, they provide important resources for the reconstruction of Paul's own theology and expectations. All four suggest that Paul supposed that urban Jesus groups would care for the poor and needy.[25] If these letters were written pseudonymously, however, that would be even more significant, since these pseudonymous letters would then demonstrate the way that later authors (perhaps as many as four), seeking to apply Paul's voice in new situations, simply presumed that care for the genuinely needy was to be a hallmark of communities that he had founded.

This brings us to one of the most significant verses in the Pauline corpus on the issue of Jesus followers and poverty. It is also a verse that, in my view, has suffered from acute misinterpretation and, as a consequence, has been notably neglected. The verse is Gal 2:10, and the misinterpretation arises from the mistaken view that the term "the poor" in this verse refers to Jesus followers in Jerusalem. So when the verse describes Jerusalem apostles James, Peter, and John as stipulating that Paul and Barnabas should "remember the poor" as part of their apostolic ministry, interpreters almost unanimously have taken that verse to mean "send money to us here in Jerusalem" (not unlike, perhaps, what a televangelist might say). There are notable deficiencies with this view, and the best data suggests that the verse should be read along different lines, which I have argued for elsewhere and can only outline here.

The verse needs to be situated within the context of a debate among early Jesus followers, a debate about the extent to which Jesus followers should be uniformly identified and the extent to which diversity can be tolerated within their ranks. This debate is described by Paul in Gal 2:1–10, which features a meeting of Paul and Barnabas with the Jerusalem apostles concerning the practice of circumcision. Must all male followers of Jesus be circumcised, which is the case for all males within the people of Israel, or is diversity of practice permitted? The apostles all agreed that diversity is acceptable within the Jesus movement, a point that coincided wholly with

---

25. This is true even if qualifications were at times required to ensure that Jesus communities could continue to express generosity without unnecessarily draining their resources, as in 2 Thess 3 and 1 Tim 5.

Paul's own gospel. But Paul concludes his overview of the meeting by noting that, although the Jerusalem apostles added nothing to his gospel, they did stipulate that in the mission to the Gentile world Paul and Barnabas should "remember the poor." The point is *not* that Gentile followers of Jesus are required to send money to Jesus followers in Jerusalem. Instead, the point is that, as Gentile followers of Jesus care for the poor among and around them, the Jesus movement will exhibit uniformity across all of its sectors. Even if circumcision was not to be a pillar of uniformity across all the diverse Jesus groups, caring for the poor was to be precisely that, marking all Jesus groups, whether primarily Jewish or Gentile in character. The point is made to Paul and Barnabas only because they were leading the mission to Gentiles, and Gentiles did not have a reputation for caring for the poor, at least in comparison with Jews, whose reputation for caring for the poor was deeply entrenched within Jewish Scripture and tradition. On the assumption that Peter's mission to Jews would not compromise care for the poor, the Jerusalem apostles encouraged those leading the mission to the Gentiles to do the same as Jewish followers of Jesus would do, i.e., remember the poor who were to be found indigenously among their midst and in their locale. To this Paul adds a phrase that is best translated "I had already been actively devoted to this cause," a claim about which we should not be suspicious in light of the strong confirmatory data that we have already noted from his letters.[26] In its context Gal 2:10 has nothing to do with sending money to poor Jewish followers of Jesus in Jerusalem; instead, it has everything with the need for Gentile followers of Jesus to care for the poor within their own indigenous locations.

In Galatians Paul linked "remember the poor" to the overarching apostolic discussion about "the truth of the gospel," and this enables us to recognize the reasoning behind his concern and indignation when things went wrong with the economic configuration of the Lord's Supper among Corinthian followers of Jesus. It is a commonplace to understand the problem behind 1 Cor 11:17–34 as involving a socio–economic dimension. Most likely, some economically insecure Jesus followers were being disadvantaged in some fashion (and probably unintentionally) during the corporate gatherings of the community when the Lord's Supper was observed.[27] In Paul's view, if the poor are disadvantaged, the spiritual power inherent within

---

26. The phrase is usually translated "and I was eager to do precisely this," but this translation is problematic. For a full defense of the points made with regard to Gal 2:10, see my *Remember the Poor*, 183–206 (or even 135–206).

27. For a basic reconstruction, see James D. G. Dunn, *Beginning from Jerusalem* (vol. 2 of *Christianity in the Making*; Grand Rapids: Eerdmans, 2009) 814–16.

the Lord's Supper gatherings is short-circuited, with perilous consequences. Like a prophet of Israel, Paul links the serious offenses against the poor within Corinthian communities to the harsh realities of divine judgment, noting: "For this reason [i.e., offending the Lord's Supper in your treatment of the poor], many of you are weak and ill, and some have died" (1 Cor 11:30). Paul pulls no punches when seeking to enforce his view that real spiritual forces are at work in the Lord's Supper, and skewing the economic dimension of that supper involves a compromise of the good news. The equitable treatment of the poor at the Lord's Supper is required if communities of Jesus followers hope to articulate and enact the eschatological renewal of all things through what Israel's God has done in Christ.

To counter this disregard of the needy among the Corinthians, Paul simply reintroduced the narrative of the self-giving Jesus into their consciousness, expecting them to follow in the narrative's wake. Jesus' command to "do this in remembrance of me" (11:24-25) is rightly glossed as, "Do this community meal in such a way that you really become a community that supports one another,"[28] or as, "Do this, that is, give yourselves and your resources up for others, just as I am doing for you."[29] In doing precisely that (i.e., giving of themselves and their resources) and in rectifying the abuse of the poor within their midst, the Lord's Supper will again be eaten in a manner that "proclaims the Lord's death until he comes" (*ton thanaton tou kuriou katangellete achri hou elthē*, 1 Cor 11:26).

It is little wonder that Paul's ire towards Corinthian abuse of the poor spills so boldly onto the pages of 1 Cor 11. For Paul, caring for the poor is integral to the identity of Jesus followers, because it lies at the heart of the story of the Jesus who is proclaimed as Lord and at the heart of the story of the sovereign deity who judges all. For Paul, remembering the poor was indispensable to the eschatological identity of communities he had founded and was itself a practice fundamental to an embodied proclamation of the good news "until he comes."[30]

---

28. Terrence J. Rynne, *Gandhi and Jesus: The Saving Power of Nonviolence* (Maryknoll, NY: Orbis, 2008) 186.

29. Suzanne Watts Henderson, "'If Anyone Hungers...': An Integrated Reading of 1 Cor 11.17-34," *NTS* 48 (2002) 195-208, p. 202. The main proposal of this article, despite its attractions, is ultimately unconvincing.

30. In his helpful response to this essay, Aaron Kuecker rightly roots caring for the poor within Paul's participationistic theology. I have argued something similar, using Galatians as a test-case, in *Remember the Poor*, 207-19.

What We Are Seeking

Taking all this data into account, what is it that we are seeking? Four things are readily apparent.

First, we can see something about the place of the poor within Paul's theological interests. There is "multiple attestation" of concern for the poor in five of the seven undisputed letters of Paul (1 Thessalonians, 1 Corinthians, 2 Corinthians, Galatians and Romans), in four of the six disputed Pauline letters (2 Thessalonians, Ephesians, 1 Timothy, and Titus) and in the Lukan depiction of Paul in Acts (see Acts 20:35, which we have not had space to discuss here except in passing). These data are stable, regardless of whether the texts were written for specific communities or for a broader spectrum of communities. They are stable, whether those texts are written for communities founded by Paul or for communities founded by others, and they are stable across a period of approximately forty-five years (dating 1 Thessalonians around 50 CE and Acts around 95 CE). Within that data we can often note a fairly consistent structural pattern across a variety of texts in which curt but poignant economic challenges are embedded almost mantra-like toward the end of Paul's theological reasoning. This pattern has a strong foothold in the undisputed Pauline letters and has a strong presence in the disputed Pauline letters, the latter suggesting that for someone wanting to write in Paul's name closing a letter with a short gesture to care for the poor adds to the authenticity of the Pauline voice in that letter. The textual database also supplies cases demonstrating that Paul imagined the proclamation of the gospel to be compromised when economic relationships were skewed in unhealthy configurations (as in 1 Cor 11). The textual database includes the Thessalonian situation in which, it seems, those who chose to become idle could do so precisely because they could expect to be supported by the economic resources of local Jesus groups.

These data suggest that care for the poor was, in fact, deeply embedded within Paul's theological concerns. Exegesis and historical reconstruction are not, of course, about adding up how many verses Paul spends on this topic or that topic, but involve appreciating the consistent traces of "theological DNA" that show Paul to have been uncompromising in promoting care for the poor as integral to the practice and theology engendered within Jesus groups.

This strong and interconnecting evidence leads to the conclusion that Paul does not address issues of poverty all that much in his letters because the communities he addresses were generally getting it right. This is a deduction from strong data that supports it on every side.

We probably can go further and deduce that, although there is not much "length" to Paul's economic discussion within his letters, there is more to the situation than those letters indicate. Behind and beyond the letters is an apostle whose theological discourse is likely to have dealt with poverty alleviation at some length. I elaborate the point elsewhere, suggesting that Paul might have tried to attract Greco-Roman urbanites to his gospel by preaching on the streets and in workshops that the God of Israel would bless them as they cared for the poor.[31] If Paul used such rhetoric in 2 Cor 9:6, 8, and 10–11 to encourage the Corinthians to contribute to his collection for the poor in Jerusalem's Jesus groups, there is little reason to imagine that he would not have used the same promise of divine blessing to entice people to join Jesus groups in the first place. Consequently, we need to guard against being distracted by the often compact and general nature of Paul's exhortations to care for the weak and needy, seeing those exhortations instead as standing guard against any potential erosion of poverty-alleviation within the current practice of Jesus groups as Paul knew them.

Second, we see a form of Judaism expanding out into the Greco-Roman world and taking with it Judaism's deeply entrenched and heightened values about the necessity of caring for the needy. Although the impression is sometimes peddled that charitable initiatives were absent from the Gentile world of the first century, this is not wholly true. It is true that Jewish Scripture and tradition foregrounded concern for the poor as a central feature of Jewish identity, and it is likewise true that concern for the poor did not have the same kind of traction within non-Jewish traditions. With the spread of the Jesus movement, however, Judaism's rich traditions about concern for the poor intermeshed with lower grade forms of the same within the Greco-Roman world, resulting in a launch of an unprecedented period of concern for the needy in the ancient world.

Third, we see a concerted effort by early Jesus groups to move available resources to the bottom of the economy scale where those resources were most needed. In the ancient world every effort was made to move resources as efficiently as possible to the top of the economy scale, often at the expense of the well-being of those at the bottom. The elite would redistribute the wealth among themselves, their clients, beneficiaries selected by them, and the civic arena. By contrast, even if generosity within communities founded by Paul was unlikely to have amounted to a notable amount of fiscal outlay,[32] Paul nonetheless expected generosity toward the genuinely

---

31. See my *Remember the Poor*, 272–76.

32. I say this because of the extent to which poverty was experienced within Jesus groups themselves.

needy (i.e., those in ES6 and ES7) to be part of the lifeblood of communities of Jesus followers and, as such, to mark Jesus groups off as distinctive within their Greco-Roman surroundings.

Fourth, and finally, we see the reconfiguration of the honor of generosity. Whereas in the civic arena the elite were lauded for their civic-minded generosity, Paul seems to have imagined Jesus group benefactors—whether they be of middling or lower economic levels—to be vehicles of the generosity of Israel's God, who alone was worthy of praise and glory (see, for instance, the whole of 2 Cor 8–9). Although we have not been able to demonstrate the point here, Paul seems intent on ensuring that those who enjoy more economic security within Jesus groups are not deemed patrons of those groups, as if they are set apart as more honorable than any other member. This is probably why Paul places generosity within his extended lists of the various functions played by different members within the body of Christ (1 Cor 12:28; Rom 12:8).[33] Since money wields power in everyday life, Paul is careful to ensure that people who give generously within the eschatological arena of Jesus groups do not amass power and authority within those groups simply on the basis of their economic well-being and/or initiatives. Instead, they are to be perceived as any other member who, regardless of their economic standing, contributes to the community according to the way that they have been empowered to do so by Israel's God.

In the light of what has been shown above, there is little reason to think that Paul was in any way complicit in compromise when it comes to Jesus' concern for the poor. Whereas Jesus is remembered as one who brought good news to the poor who are blessed in the kingdom of God, Paul is to be remembered as one whose gospel included "remembrance" of the poor as an integral and necessary, but not sufficient, part of the proclamation about and embodiment of what Israel's God had accomplished through the life, death, and resurrection of Jesus.

---

33. It is probably for this reason that Paul chose to work with his hands instead of being supported by others in places like Corinth (see, for example, 1 Cor 9). By ensuring that he did not get embroiled in a patronal relationship, Paul ensured that his gospel was free from becoming hijacked by the interests of a patron. This situation also seems to inform Paul's discourse in the letter to the Philippians, where he engages in "thankless thanks" for the financial support of the Philippians, ensuring that they recognize that their financial support does not determine the shape of the gospel but permits the intact gospel to be spread further afield.

RESPONSE TO LONGENECKER

Aaron Kuecker

It is a real pleasure to respond to Longenecker's work on Paul, poverty, and wealth in the formation of early Christianity. Research that reexamines long and often uncritically held assumptions can be quite exciting and important. I am convinced that this work both helps us become better readers of Paul's writings and bears important ramifications for the life and witness of contemporary Christian communities. I am particularly grateful for the thread of identity transformation that is woven throughout this paper, with its contention that it is the generosity of Gentiles that bears witness to their Spirit-effected transformation. This generosity assuages anxiety about any tendencies toward antinomianism in Paul's allegedly "Law free" gospel.

One of the hallmarks of fruitful inquiry is that it unfolds toward further inquiry and dialogue. This is precisely what Longenecker's work has done with the issue of Paul and poverty, but also with the reconfiguration of the place of generosity within the early Christian church and the irreducibly eschatological nature of the act of giving to those who have need. I have imagined, as I have reflected on Longnecker's work, that we have been ushered into a great (perhaps Lewisian!) hallway lined with door after door. One suspects that some of these doors lead to new and exciting vistas, though it should be said that apart from exploring one does not know which doors lead to expansive rooms and which lead to cupboards. Longenecker points toward several of these doors, and in the majority of my response I will ask him to open a few of them with us in order to explore the ramifications of his work for the place of generosity within early Christianity and Pauline theology.

The major premise of the paper is that Paul's care for poverty relief is "not in any way complicit in compromise when it comes to Jesus' concern for the poor." As a faithful Israelite, Jesus cared for the poor. As a faithful Israelite, Paul cared for the poor. Longenecker hints that Paul's concern with generosity is connected to the "narrative of the self-giving Jesus" and that care of the poor is "at the heart of the story of the Jesus who is proclaimed as Lord." So while Longenecker points toward the relationship between Jesus and Paul, I suggest that the textual data show that Paul's interest in poverty relief is explicitly and essentially christological. Paul's connections to Jesus are, on this issue in particular, quite close. We can see this in two ways: more than a few of the texts examined by Longenecker bear either (1) close proximity and exegetical relationship to some of the clearer allusions to the teachings of Jesus in the Pauline corpus, or (2) bear a clear relationship between selfless giving and themes of *imitatio Christi*. I will point briefly to a number of these connections and will begin with Paul's allusions to the words of Jesus.

Paul's exhortation in Rom 12:13 to "Contribute to the needs of the saints; extend hospitality to strangers" immediately precedes a clear allusion to the teaching of Jesus: "Bless those who persecute you; bless and do not curse them" (Rom 12:14; cf. Luke 6:28). Moreover, as Longenecker notes, the exhortation to charity in 12:13 is one of the embodied expressions of the love called for in Rom 12:9–10: "Let love be genuine . . . love one another with mutual affection." What is not noted is that this charity-inspiring love is climactically described by Paul's allusion to Jesus' Torah-summarizing love command that appears in Rom 13:10: "Love your neighbor as yourself." In other words, the exhortation to generosity toward saints and strangers in Rom 12 is informed by Jesus' teaching about neighbor and enemy love. Likewise, Gal 6:9–10, a passage that Longenecker sees functioning as a summary of the parenesis of Galatians, stands structurally as the closing frame to the hortatory section that extends from 5:13 to 6:10.[1] The opening frame of this section is a call to freedom exercised as self-giving love, based once more upon Jesus' summary of the Torah that "You shall love your neighbor as yourself." In two cases, then, Paul's teaching on care for those who are in need is closely aligned with Jesus' notion of neighbor love (even for enemies) as the summary of Israel's law.

Moving in a different but related direction, the extended and challenging teaching about the Jerusalem collection in 2 Cor 8–9 is undergirded by the promise that the generosity of the God of Israel is the foundation upon which the generosity of the Christian community rests. "And God is able to provide you with every blessing in abundance, so that by always having enough of everything, you may share abundantly in every good work" (2 Cor 9:8). While this is not a quotation, it certainly bears close affinity with Jesus' teaching in the Sermon on the Mount where at every turn the challenge to give without reserve, even to enemies, is underwritten by the generosity of Israel's God who graciously provides for birds and flowers and people (Matt 6:25–34) and who gives good gifts to his children (Matt 7:9–11). Is it coincidental, then, that Paul appears to link his teaching on poverty issues very closely to

---

1. I am here following the macrostructure proposed by Hendrikus Boers, *The Justification of the Gentiles: Paul's Letters to the Galatians and Romans* (Peabody, MA: Hendrickson, 1994) 50.

some of the closest Pauline allusions to the teaching of Jesus in the entire Pauline corpus?

While these close connections to the teaching of Jesus are intriguing, there may be even stronger resonance with Paul's vision of the *praxis* of Jesus. At least four of the texts examined are suggestively related to *imitatio Christi* motifs. Returning to Romans, the extended discussion of the Jerusalem collection (15:25-33) is one expression of the *imitatio Christi* theme that closes the parenesis of chapters 12-15 in a breathtaking catena of texts (15:7-13) that show Israel's covenantal privilege extending outward to the Gentiles. Paul brings the fullness of the implications of the gospel to bear on his hearers when he says, "Welcome one another, just as Christ has welcomed you, for the glory of God. For I tell you that Christ has become a servant of the circumcised on behalf of the truth of God in order that he might confirm the promises given to the patriarchs and in order that the Gentiles might glorify God for his mercy" (15:7-9). Here it is Jesus' offering of himself for the sake of Israel and the Gentiles that stands as the prototype of Christian hospitality. Paul testifies that he is confident (15:14) his brothers and sisters in Rome are doing well in the Christlike hospitality that he uses to describe the gospel. This confidence in the other-centered hospitality of the Roman churches is then linked directly to the call to generous participation in the Jerusalem collection. Participation in the Jerusalem collection, in the arc of Rom 12-15, must be taken as a symptom of Paul's climactic call to *imitatio Christi* (Rom 15:7), here given shape as self-giving hospitality. This resonates well with 2 Cor 8-9, which places the *imitatio Christi* theme at the heart of Paul's concern for the collection. Paul says, "I am testing the genuineness of your love against the earnestness of others. For you know the grace of our Lord Jesus Christ that though he was rich, yet for your sakes he became poor, so that by his poverty you might become rich" (2 Cor 8:8b-9). Here again a life oriented toward generosity is in analogical relationship to the life of Christ. Finally, we should notice that in 1 Cor 11, the commendations (11:2-15) and condemnations (11:17-33) given to the community follow immediately upon the exhortation to "Be imitators of me, as I am of Christ" (11:1). In this instance Paul's own imitation of Christ is summarized as his unwillingness to seek his own advantage in social dealings. This is precisely Paul's concern regarding the economic injustice addressed in Paul's critique of the eucharistic practice of the Corinthian community.[2]

---

2. Though Longenecker does not discuss the economic teaching in Philippians, I would submit here that the Christ-hymn in Phil 2:4-11 is perhaps *the* central teaching connecting *imitatio Christi*, defined by self-giving love, to the economic concern stretching from the partnership named in ch. 1 to

The connection between poverty relief and overt calls to *imitatio Christi* is most dramatically evident in Eph 4:28, where thieves are exhorted to give up stealing in order to have something to share with the poor. This is located in a larger section that names greed as a characteristic of the former lives of these Jesus followers (and of Gentiles in general [4:17–19]). The ethical exhortations in this section find their center of gravity in the claim that the community is being clothed with the "new self, created according to the likeness of God" (4:24). This *imitatio Dei* theme is amplified in 5:1–2: "Therefore be imitators of God, as beloved children, and live in love as Christ loved us and gave himself up for us, a fragrant offering and sacrifice to God." Here Paul sets the *cruciform* life of Christ as the example for fully human life that results in, among other things, generosity to the poor. Moreover, the development in this section of Ephesians assures us that our own acts of generosity extend from the gift of the gospel. It is restoration of the irreducibly cruciform image of God that allows humans to participate in God-like concern for those who are in need.

I think that these close connections with the teaching and praxis of Jesus are highly suggestive, and I would like to invite Longenecker to reflect with us on the fully christological nature of Paul's concern for the poor. These close connections in the Pauline corpus also point toward at least two other significant potentialities for understanding Pauline theology and the place of generosity within the eschatological experience of the early Christian church. First, it has been a commonplace over the course of the past two centuries for voices of varying strength to posit multiple and competing Christianities with dogmatic flashpoints centered around disputes in the realm of soteriology in general, and justification in particular. So, for instance, scholars using theories of justification as the epicenter of Pauline, Jacobean, or Petrine theology have—whether rightly or wrongly—posited diverse and conflicting formulations of the nascent Christian faith. Longenecker's work shows promise in suggesting that those same sorts of reconstructions might unfold quite differently were we to take community-forming practices as a center of gravity.[3] If Paul, Peter, James, and, yes, Jesus see sustained charity as central to what it means to participate in the reign of Israel's God announced and inaugurated by Jesus, then perhaps giving greater attention to shared practices could open up fruitful new ways for consider-

---

Paul's navigation of reciprocity expectations in ch. 4.

3. It goes without saying, of course, that practices are not divorced from dogmatic claims about truth. I would contend, however, that the fundamental truth claim to which these practices of generosity bear witness is a claim about the identity of God. More particularly, it is a claim that the Creator God rules precisely as one who gives himself in love for the sake of creation.

ing the relationships between these early Christian "factions." Perhaps this can help us see that Jesus' kingdom proclamation *is* central to Paul's view and that unity in the early communities is maintained in significant ways through overtly eschatological practices like poor care that are a form of participation in the in-breaking reign of God in Christ.[4] If so, the unity of the early church is primarily located in its participation in Christ, in whom God is at work reconciling the world to himself and through whom good news has been, is being, and will be proclaimed to the poor.

Finally, I would ask Longenecker to reflect with us on whether we can locate Paul's concern for the poor more integrally within the deep structures of Pauline soteriology. Do the texts give us warrant for suggesting that, for Paul, poverty care is not simply an ethical imperative for communities of Jesus followers, but that the practice of care for the poor itself is a gift of the gospel that, by the power of the Spirit, unfolds its own benefits? It would seem that this coheres with Paul's insistence that generosity is deeply embedded in the "new self" enlivened by the Spirit which inspires patterns of corporate life commensurate with the apocalyptic liberation from "this present evil age."[5] For Paul, if care for the poor is closely connected to the apocalyptic arrival of the reign of God and the healing of the *imago Dei* within humans, then it must be said that a posture of generosity is not merely a thing we "have to do," but that it is also, and perhaps primarily, a thing we "get to do." It is in this practice and practices like it that communities and their members experience the fullness of salvation. Such people are conformed by the power of the Spirit to the

---

4. In favor of this suggestion, it would appear that an appeal to shared *praxis* is a strategy that Paul himself uses to mitigate the potentially schismatic effects of dogmatic dispute. In Rom 14, for example, rather than parsing out the dogmatic complexities of the celebration of holy days or the eating of meat sacrificed in temples, Paul preserves the unity of the church by appealing to the shared practice of cruciform hospitality.

5. The textual data interrogated by Longenecker hint that practices of poor care are eschatological gifts of the reign of God. The Spirit-led life envisioned by Galatians, which climaxes in charity (6:9–10), is available only because the church has been liberated from "this present evil age" (1:4). The exhortation to participate in the Jerusalem collection in 1 Cor 16:1–4 follows immediately on the heels of Paul's longest exposition of the defeat of death via the resurrection. In Ephesians generosity is explicitly connected to the restoration of the *imago Dei*. In 2 Thessalonians self-giving is contrasted with the self-indulgence of the mysterious "lawless one" (2:4; 3:6–14). In 1 Tim 5 the love of money destroys the sort of community created by the gospel (cf. 6:5–10). In Titus humans once enslaved are saved through renewal (3:4–7) which issues forth in good works that meet urgent needs (3:14) but are profitable for everyone (3:9). Indeed it would appear that generosity itself is a gift of the kingdom, not merely an ethical obligation.

image of God in Christ, the one who showed that one aspect of a truly human response to God was to leverage one's resources for the sake of those who are "other."[6]

Once more, I would like to thank Longenecker for this important and careful work on Paul and for the significant potential it holds. I commend to you his book *Remember the Poor*. This is the best sort of biblical scholarship: careful, informed, and relevant to the ongoing life of the church. I look forward to his engagement with the questions and ruminations in this response.

---

6. I suspect we can press further yet, and working from texts such as Phil 2 demonstrates that at a theological level it is fitting to see Paul's emphasis on caring for the poor through the generosity of the community as nothing less than participation in the life of the Triune God—Father, Son, and Spirit, who continually live toward one another in a relationship of self-giving love that overflows toward all creation.

A PATRISTIC VIEW OF WEALTH AND POSSESSIONS

Helen Rhee

When early church authors address or make references to wealth and possessions, it is directed to Christians who are already on the journey of faith and yet must persevere to the end. In an overall vision of salvation and Christian life in the early church, wealth, which is essentially granted by God but is fraught with dangers, temptations, and problems to souls and human relationships, presents Christians a unique challenge and opportunity to demonstrate their spiritual state and persevere in their salvation. Thereby they distinguish themselves from pagans. Money and possessions of Christians function as a critical boundary marker of Christian identity in the following four related aspects: heavenly wealth versus earthly wealth, salvation and wealth, Christian *koinonia*, and desire and display of wealth. I will deal with each aspect and will engage with a few particular texts from the second and third centuries while also providing general patristic voices from other available sources. In each of these areas the early Christian view(s) of wealth and possessions would conform to their overall vision(s) of Christianity as the specific manifestation of and testament to Christian identity, conduct, and reality in the pagan world.

The Contrast between Heavenly Wealth and Earthly Wealth

First of all, the early church viewed money and possessions within the eschatological dualism between heavenly and earthly riches. The *Shepherd of Hermas*, a second century text, has a parable of Two Cities (Herm. *Sim.* 1.1–11) that reflects concern for tension between this world and the world to come, a dualism that is both temporal and spatial. As dangers of wealth and possessions are overtly placed in this conceptual contrast and also in contrast between heavenly riches and earthly riches, the purpose of wealth is set in this perspective as well. Certainly in the NT the message of "laying up one's treasure in heaven" stands in tension with "laying up one's treasure on earth" (Matt 6:19–20), with the former giving a promise of eternal security and protection. The parable of the Rich Fool in Luke 12 highlights the imprudence of placing one's security in abundance of earthly riches as opposed to "being rich toward God" (12:21). The parable of the Two Cities in *Hermas* portrays Christian existence as a dual residence, one in a foreign country and one in the city of eschatological destiny, each governed by a law incompatible with the other. Accumulation of earthly riches in this temporary, foreign city through amassing fields, buildings, and other properties is a sure sign of foolishness and double-mindedness, for the lord of the foreign city will inevitably expel Christians who are subject to the law of their own city (Herm. *Sim.* 1.1–4).

Double-mindedness, a major problem in *Hermas*, prevents serving God with a pure heart and enduring in hope for the heavenly reward. Since Christians cannot keep the law of their own city by retaining their worldly possessions, it is in their best interest that they be self-sufficient (*autarkeia*), free, prepared to leave the land at any time, and "joyfully conform to the law" of their own city (Herm. *Sim.* 1.5–6). It is in this context that Christians should keep God's commandments (1.7): "Instead of fields buy souls that are in distress, as anyone is able, and visit widows and orphans, and do not neglect them; and spend your wealth and all your possessions, which you received from God, on fields and houses of this kind" (1.8). These divine commandments articulate the classic (Jewish and) Christian acts of charity as a way of converting earthly temporal riches into heavenly spiritual riches since it is God's intention and purpose for earthly wealth. God makes one rich for this reason, i.e., for performing "ministries" or "services" (*diakoniai*), and therefore "it is much better to purchase fields and possessions and houses of this kind" (1.9). Whereas earthly wealth brings grief and fear, heavenly spiritual wealth brings joy; earthly extravagance is unprofitable to the believer, but heavenly extravagance is salvific (1.10–11). This eschatological motif does not renounce material wealth but affirms it as God's gift, relativizes its earthly significance, and channels it to its proper use of amassing spiritual wealth through acts of charity/ministry.

The famous parable of the elm and the vine with its dualism of earthly and heavenly riches (Herm. *Sim.* 2.1–10) is to be seen in relation to this first parable. Earthly wealth is affirmed as God's gift, but God's specific intent of that wealth expressed in his commandments (Herm. *Sim.* 1.7–10) thematically leads to the second parable, which treats mutual cooperation and dependence between the rich and the poor in preparation for the world to come. The elm and the vine, representing the rich and the poor,[1] bear much fruit only when they are attached to each other and

---

1. Carolyn Osiek in her commentary, *The Shepherd of Hermas: A Commentary* (Hermeneia; Minneapolis: Augsburg Fortress, 1999) 163, makes a point that although the elm and the vine are traditionally understood as the rich and the poor respectively, this interpretation is not conclusive. According to her, the point of the parable is their interdependence, not exact correlation of symbols. See also C. Osiek, *Rich and Poor in the Shepherd of Hermas: An Exegetical-Social Investigation* (CBQMS 15; Washington DC: Catholic Biblical Association of America, 1983) 86.

function together, not on their own. The shepherd, the revelatory guide for *Hermas*, takes for granted the traditional notion that the rich are deficient in the things of the Lord due to their wealth and its attendant problem of distraction, while the poor are rich in intercession and praise with effectual power (Herm. *Sim*. 2.5; cf. Herm. *Mand*. 10.3.2). Therefore, the rich (should) "unhesitatingly" provide for the needs of the poor and the poor intercede for the rich; in this way they "complete" their work, which is "great and acceptable to God" (Herm. *Sim*. 2.6). This mutual partnership between the rich and the poor is spiritualized toward the end that both "will be enrolled in the books of the living" (Herm. *Sim*. 2.9). The thrust of this parable is that "the rich man understands about his wealth, works for the poor man by using the gifts of the Lord, and correctly fulfills his ministry (*diakonia*)" (Herm. *Sim*. 2.7). Those rich who fulfill their God-given ministry/service here and now and thus secure their heavenly riches are the ones who overcome double-mindedness and therefore survive the great tribulation (cf. Herm. *Mand*. 9.2, 4, 6; Herm. *Sim*. 2.7; 8.10.3; 9.24.2; 9.29.2). The parable concludes with the beatitude for the rich: "Blessed are the rich who also understand that they have been made rich by the Lord, for the one who comprehends this will be able to do some good service" (Herm. *Sim*. 2.10; cf. 1.9).

In *On Works and Alms* (*Eleem.*), which was probably written during the deadly and devastating plague after the first distressing empire-wide persecution by Decius (252–254 CE), Cyprian, bishop of Carthage in North Africa, capitalizes on the appeal of heavenly reward and the contrast between earthly and heavenly riches to entreat the rich members of his church. The Holy Spirit itself exhorts the practice of almsgiving for "everyone who is instructed into the hope of the heavenly kingdom" (4). And the Lord himself will be eager to distribute to their "merits and good works the promised rewards, to give heavenly things for the earthly, eternal things for temporal, great things for small" (26) for "those rich men . . . having pledged or scattered their [earthly] riches, yea, having transferred them, by the change of their possessions for the better, into heavenly treasures" (22; cf. 7; *Hab. virg.* 11). Quoting Tobit 12:8–9 Cyprian stresses the redemptive efficacy of almsgiving and connects it to the day of judgment (5, 9). There is a sense of serious urgency in Cyprian's tone as he urges the rich: "Let us, while there is time, take thought for our security and eternal salvation" (24). Furthermore, if one is truly concerned about leaving a secure future for one's heirs, there is no surer way than to "provide for one's pledges for the coming time," i.e., give alms, by "assign[ing] to Him your wealth which you are saving up for your heirs" (19). In proportion as Christians are rich in this world, they may become poor to God (13); if so, why would anyone amass their earthly patrimony for their own eternal punishment (cf. 13, 15)? The rich members should "make Christ a partner with [them] in [their] earthly possessions, that He also may make [them] a fellow-heir with Him in His heavenly kingdom" (13). If they are "lending to God" by giving alms to the poor, "there is no ground for any one preferring earthly things to heavenly, nor for considering human things before divine" (16).[2]

Salvation and Wealth

The dualism of heavenly and earthly wealth leads to the second, related theme for our discussion, that of salvation and wealth. Early Christian authors are emphatic that just calling Christ Lord will not save one but has to be accompanied by keeping his commandments (e.g., 2 *Clem.* 4.1–5; 6.7; cf. Matt 7:21). While the early church proclaimed the once-for-all and irreplaceable redemptive work of God through Christ (e.g., *The Epistle of Diognetus* 9.2–5), one cannot help but recognize nearly universal calls to almsgiving for the purpose of forgiveness of post-baptismal sins in the early church,[3] which reflects traditional Jewish piety and its Christian contextualization (in continuity with some Second Temple literature and NT passages, both implicit and explicit).[4] For instance, *Didache* at the turn of the second century commands the Christ followers, "If you acquire something with your hands, give it as a ransom for your sins" (4.6; cf. *Barn.* 19.10). Polycarp, the revered bishop of Smyrna in the mid-second century, exhorted the Philippians not to put off doing good (*benefacere*) when they were able, "since giving to charity (*eleemosyna*) frees a person from death" (quoting Tob 4:10).[5] In the ancient sermon called *2 Clement*, "renunciation" or "hatred" of the earthly things turns out to be none other than almsgiving: "almsgiving is good, as is repentance from sin. Fasting is better than prayer, while almsgiving is better than both, and 'love covers a multitude of sins' . . .

---

2. Based on Prov 19:17: "Whoever is kind to the poor lends to the Lord, and will be repaid in full." Cf. Luke 6:38. This notion is repeated in Cyprian, *Hab. virg.* 11; *Eleem.* 26; Clement of Alexandria, *Paed.* 2.13; 3.4; *Strom.* 3.6; *Const. Ap.* 3.1.4; 7.1.12.

3. Cf. G. A. Anderson, "Redeem Your Sins by the Giving of Alms: Sin, Debt, and the 'Treasury of Merit' in Early Jewish and Christian Tradition," *Letter & Spirit* 3 (2007) 68.

4. Patristic authors frequently cite passages such as Tob 4:10–11; 12:9; Sir 3:30, for scriptural support. Cf. Matt 6:19–21; 25:31–46; Mark 10:21 and parallels; Luke 16:9, 19–31; and 1 Pet 4:8–9. For parallels from rabbinic literature, see E. Ferguson, "Spiritual Sacrifice in Early Christianity and its Environment," *ANRW* 2.23.2 (1981) 1161–62; A. Cronbach, "The Me'il Zedakah," *Hebrew Union College Annul* 11 (1936) 511–49, especially 525–29.

5. Cf. Cyprian, *Eleem.* 5, 9.

almsgiving relieves the burden of sin" (16.4).[6] It is the first Christian text that explicitly links 1 Pet 4:8 to almsgiving and almsgiving to pardon of sin. Almsgiving is the ultimate antidote to love of money, the prime act of love and righteousness, and thus the surest way to get ready for the imminent judgment (cf. *2 Clem.* 12.1; 18.2). By the time of Cyprian, this notion of almsgiving contributing to eventual salvific effect for the givers would secure its place in a theological trajectory and practical ministries as we have seen above, and Cyprian would develop it further in relation to merit and penance that would sustain salvation of the rich. In the fourth century and onward this "redemptive almsgiving" would be one of the most consistent and traditional elements in the sermons and teachings of the church leaders.

Between the *Shepherd of Hermas* and Cyprian's *On Works and Alms* appeared a pastoral homily in the late second century by Clement of Alexandria, *Who Is a Rich Man That Is Saved?* This work is addressed to the affluent and cultured Christian audience in Alexandria[7] who could identify with the "rich young man" in Mark 10:17–31. Here salvation of the rich emerges as a considerable theological and social challenge that needs to be reinterpreted and reapplied. To the rich man's quest for eternal life, Jesus apparently demanded dispossession of his wealth and ultimately declared a virtual impossibility of the rich entering the kingdom of God *as the rich*. Is there hope for the rich? If so, how can they be saved? Clement approaches the salvation of the rich out of a pastoral concern and directs his message not to "those [rich] who are uninitiated in the truth" but to "the rich who have learnt of the Saviour's power and His splendid salvation" (2). From the outset, he acknowledges that salvation seems to be more difficult for the rich than the poor, but he wants to show the same *concerned* rich who *have already been initiated* into the salvation process "how that which is impossible with men becomes possible" (2)—with Christ's instruction of the truth and their good works in life-long perseverance (1). Clement first unfolds the "truth" of Christ's teachings in Mark 10:17–31 with his figurative interpretation and then guides the audience in how their good works would *secure* their salvation.

For Clement, the "truth" of Christ's instructions to the rich man lies in their "hidden meaning," which can be found with "an effort of mind" (5).[8] The funda-

---

6. Cf. Sir 3:30; Tob 4:10; 12:9.

7. For literary and inscriptional evidence of an "emergence of urban patron class" in Alexandrian Christian circles as Clement's probable audience and perhaps his own patron(s), see L. M. White, "Scholars and Patrons: Christianity and High Society in Alexandria," in *Christian Teaching: Studies in Honor of LeMoine G. Lewis* (ed. E. Ferguson; Abilene, TX: Abilene Christian University, 1981), 331–39.

8. E. A. Clark notes that Clement's figurative interpretation of the Markan passage offers a "classic example of how a 'spiritualized' reading might encourage a weakening of the ascetic rigor demanded

mental premise in understanding the Lord's truth is to submit oneself to reason as trainer and to Christ as master of the contest (*agōnothetei*), i.e., salvation (3). The Lord's truth is first and foremost to know God and the Savior (the greatest doctrine), which requires perfection beyond the observance of the Mosaic law; the rich man's fulfillment of the law was good but not perfect.[9] Eternal life is beyond the reach of the law, however; knowing the Savior and eternal life entails inner contemplation, not an outer act (6–10). Therefore, Christ's counsel of perfection to the rich man, i.e., to sell his possessions, does not mean any external act of divestment but rather inner detachment: "to strip the soul itself and the will of their lurking passions and utterly to root out and cast away all alien thoughts from the mind" (11). If the Savior's words were to be taken literally, they are no more than an extension of the law, which is external and therefore "no(t) life-giving" (9), and no more than a reiteration of what the Greek philosophers have already done prior to his coming (11). So Christ's teaching *must be* "more divine and more perfect," new and unique, superseding all human teachings before him (12). Thus, it *cannot* mean the literal renunciation of wealth, which points to mere, natural human capacity.

Clement then shows how the external acts of renunciation contradict Christ's other commandments such as making for ourselves friends with "mammon of unrighteousness" (Luke 16:9); storing treasures in heaven (Matt 6:20); feeding the hungry and giving drinks to the thirsty (Matt 25:41–43) and so on (13). All of these commandments presuppose personal wealth beyond bare necessities of life that a believer should share with the less fortunate, especially when the Lord threatens eternal punishment to those who have not obeyed them (13). Thus commandments like these reveal intrinsic neutrality and the necessity of wealth and correctly highlight its proper utility and instrumentality with right reason and judgment rather than its simplistic abandonment (14). In this context Clement, using Stoic vocabulary and principle, places wealth in the external realm of *adiaphora*[10]—things morally indifferent but potentially advantageous depending on their use[11] (15). Neither receiving inheritance nor saving wealth with frugality and investing property *prior to* conversion are morally suspect;[12] rather, he relates these kinds of wealth to the

---

by a more 'literal' exegesis." See her *Reading Renunciation: Asceticism and Scripture in Early Christianity* (Princeton: Princeton University Press, 1999) 94; for a fuller treatment, see 92–95.

9. Cf. *Strom.* 3.6.55.2.

10. See for example Seneca, *Ep. 87* (*On the Simple Life*).

11. Plutarch, a Greek moralist in the second century, examines this in *On Love of Wealth*, 527.

12. Cf. *Strom.* 3.6.56.1

gracious gifts of God, who in his providence distributes fortune to people (26). What is important is how the rich should *use* wealth to their spiritual advantage and for the benefit of their neighbors (14, 26). We will come back to this point a bit later.

Since Christ's truth regarding salvation "does not depend upon outward things" but upon the "soul's virtue" (18), purging oneself of the soul's passions is the key to entering the kingdom of God. The internal nature of salvation demands that people cultivate pure and passionless souls with God's help, not ridding themselves of external goods and possessions (cf. 18, 20). Cultivating pure and passionless souls is an essential part of the care of the self that involves continual vigilance, education, training, and discipline in curbing vices of desires, passions, and immoderation.[13] Elsewhere Clement presents Christian salvation more explicitly as a two-stage spiritual *and* ethical process of self-care: first, a struggle with and cure of pleasure, passion, and desire through purification and self-control (*autarkeia*) (*Strom.* 6.105.1),[14] eventually moving on to, second, a perfect state of passionless contemplation and imitation of God (*apatheia*) where the snares and traps of desire are no longer a danger to the soul (*Strom.* 6.7.1ff; 6.71.3–72.1).[15]

With baptism every believer embarks on a long, arduous, and upward journey of healing of the passions (*Paed.* 1.36.2.4; 1.43.1; 2.100.3), and an advanced baptized believer should grow and develop to reach the perfect gnostic[16] state. As Harry Maier aptly puts it, for Clement, "[t]he redeemed self is engaged in a life and death struggle [*agōn*] with the old sinful self of the passions" and cultivates freedom by applying the law and Christ's truth.[17] This struggle itself testifies to the salvation of the self.[18] So even the rich can "enjoy the object of their hope," i.e., salvation, with "settled purpose" and "hard training and exercises" led by Christ the Instructor and Guide (*Rich Man* 3). In this contest and race toward and of salvation, it is certainly possible for the rich to cast off inner lust and passions without literal dispossession. Clement says that because Christ does not envy their wealth only those who are controlled and overcome by their wealth should leave it (24). In fact, the literal

---

13. Cf. H. O. Maier, "Clement of Alexandria and the Care of the Self," *Journal of American Academy of Religion* 62 (1994) 725.

14. Cf. Maier, "Clement of Alexandria and the Care of the Self," 728.

15. Ibid., 734.

16. Clement uses the term "gnostic" in a sense of being "perfect" and "advanced," and his use is to be distinguished from "Gnostics" as Christian heretics.

17. Maier, "Clement of Alexandria and the Care of the Self," 732.

18. Ibid., 728.

renunciation of wealth does not actually cure the disease of the soul; instead, it could rather create a "double annoyance, the absence of means of support and the presence of regret," simply due to basic human needs (12). Therefore, it could result in false pretension of cure riddled with even greater passions and anguish. Both voluntary and involuntary poverty have no intrinsic value apart from attendant poverty of the soul, which is available for the rich as well as for the poor.

This internalization of salvation demystifies the traditional assumption of "the pious poor and the wicked rich" and spiritualizes wealth and poverty. As Clement deconstructs the pious poor and the wicked rich tradition, he constructs a model of the pious rich and the wicked rich on the one hand and the noble poor and the wretched poor on the other. The pious rich are the ones who are "rich in virtues and able to use every fortune in a holy and faithful manner" (19). They are contrasted with the "spurious rich" who are "rich according to the flesh" but pursuing the life of transitory outward possessions (19). Likewise, the genuine poor (*ptōchoi*) are the ones who are "poor in spirit" with "the inner personal poverty," whereas the spurious poor consist of the poor "in worldly goods, the outward alien poverty" but full of vices (19). Clement in this way connects the true, pious rich with the genuine, spiritual poor and shows how "the same man can be both poor and wealthy" (20).

Christ's call to "sell one's possessions" then is a universal call not only to the spurious, outwardly rich but also to the spurious, outwardly poor to detach themselves from the "alien possessions that dwell in [their] soul[s], in order that [they] may become pure in heart and may see God" (19). This is in fact what St. Peter exactly demonstrated in his life. When he said, "Lo, we have left all and followed [Christ]," he meant "by flinging away the old possessions of the mind and diseases of the soul that [the disciples] are following in the track of their teacher" (21). This is indeed how one follows the Savior: that "we seek after [the Savior's] sinlessness and perfection, adorning and regulating the soul before Him as before a mirror and arranging it in every detail after His likeness (*homoiōsis*)" (21).[19] Again, salvation in this paradigm is a continuous, upward progress toward perfection, which is passionless imitation of Christ,[20] overcoming the insidious inner persecutions—godless lusts and manifold pleasures, low hopes and corrupting imaginations, and covetousness (25). This is the life of a true gnostic, which is the costly result of the disciplined care of the self[21] and can never be achieved by a single act of external renunciation.

19. Cf. *Strom.* 2.131.5; 2.97.1.
20. Cf. *Strom.* 2.326.3ff.
21. *Strom.* 7.16.1.

Having established the truth of Christ's salvation, Clement shows how the rich can arrive at this state *using* their wealth. He first sets the theological ground for good works (almsgiving) in the greatest commandment of loving God (27). Just as knowing God is the foundation of Christ's truth, loving God is the foundation of Christ's love and our striving for good works (cf. 28). The second part of the greatest commandment is loving one's neighbor as oneself. According to Clement's interpretation of the parable of the Good Samaritan, our neighbor is none other than Christ himself, who showed us his mercy and heals our wounds of passions (29). How then do the rich love Christ as their neighbor as they love God? It is by loving Christ's disciples, fellow Christians in need. By giving relief to "one of those who have an eternal habitation with the Father" (31), the rich fulfill the Lord's injunction to make friends with unrighteous mammon for their eternal life (Luke 16:9) and secure their heavenly reward (31). In so doing, the rich should not just "yield to a request or wait to be pestered" but "should personally seek out men whom [they] may benefit" for their progress toward salvation, "men who are worthy disciples of the Saviour" (31). Thus, Clement champions the salvific effect of almsgiving in the following way:

> What splendid trading! What divine business! You buy incorruption with money. You give the perishing things of the world and receive in exchange for them an eternal abode in heaven. Compass the whole earth if need be. Spare not dangers or toils, that here you may buy a heavenly kingdom. (32)

Giving to the poor Christians promises a sure return of abundant reward and spiritual wealth to the rich to the extent that Clement freely uses an economic language of transaction and exchange, the notion already heavily featured in the *Shepherd of Hermas*. However, Clement qualifies this great exchange: the rich should see to it that "the Lord did not say, 'give,' or 'provide,' or 'benefit,' or 'help,' but 'make a friend'" (32); indeed, "a friend is made not from one gift, but from complete relief and long companionship" (32). Just as ridding one's soul of passions takes a continual struggle and training, making friends with one's wealth takes a sustained work and building relationships with the recipients of their alms. Furthermore, in doing so the rich should not try to distinguish the worthy from the unworthy poor lest they accidentally neglect the former and incur "eternal punishment by fire" (33). They are also not to take offence at the appearance of the needy or to gaze on them with contempt, for God and Christ dwell within the poor (33).[22] What is necessary

---

22. This identification of the poor with Christ, which is also seen in Cyprian (*Eleem.* 23), received particular attention and underwent significant development in the post-Constantinian period and beyond. A classic message based on Matt 25:31–45 and with universal application would be set for

and important for the rich is to find those among their recipients "who have power to save [them] with God" as they give to all who are enrolled as God's disciples, i.e., the Christian poor in general (33).

What is noteworthy is the fact that contrary to his earlier effort to deconstruct the tradition of "the pious poor and the wicked rich" in interiorizing and spiritualizing wealth and poverty, Clement presupposes and counts on that very tradition here in promoting redemptive almsgiving for the rich Christians. The pious poor's role is absolutely vital, and their spiritual services are both specific and comprehensive: "One is able to beg your life from God, another to hearten you when sick, another to weep and lament in sympathy on your behalf before the Lord . . ." (35). Clement loses no time to issue the clearest call to the rich:

> [E]nlist on your behalf an army without weapons, without war, without bloodshed . . . an army of God-fearing old men, of God-beloved orphans, of widows armed with gentleness, of men adorned with love. Obtain with your wealth, as guards for your body and your soul, such men as these, whose commander is God. Through them the sinking ship rises, steered by the prayers of saints alone . . . [and] the attack of robbers is made harmless, being stripped of its weapons by pious prayers. (34)

If the one-time renunciation would not be a solution for the salvation of the rich, the ongoing generous almsgiving is a palpable way to obtain their salvation. For redemptive efficacy of almsgiving is rooted in the reciprocal exchange of love among believers, which is in turn rooted in God's love and a reciprocal demand of Christ's sacrifice (37). In this sense almsgiving is a quintessential, positive *demonstration* of loving God and neighbor as well as of using one's wealth properly. Despite an unabashed appeal to the self-interest of the rich giver, a more fundamental appeal for almsgiving is love of God and love for God, without which no one can attain salvation (cf. 38). Because God receives and forgives everyone who turns to him in genuine repentance, almsgiving is an effective means of repentance and rooting out of the soul the post-baptismal sins leading to death (39).

For Clement then almsgiving becomes a necessary part of the care of the self, which is indispensable for the journey of salvation, the path to perfection. As such it

---

the rest of Christian history. In *every* poor person (regardless of one's Christian faith), Christ is fed, given drink, and welcomed as a guest. "Whatever is given to the poor is given to him [Christ]." The poor person identified with Christ is not just a Christian but can also be a non-Christian in light of the public interest the church is serving. It is significant that only in the post-Constantinian era with the public service of the church were non-Christians *explicitly* included as legitimate recipients of alms by the church.

constitutes an essential part of the Christian (perfect gnostic) sacrifice in God's sight (cf. *Strom.* 7.3.14.1; 7.7.49.5).[23] Make no mistake; Clement acknowledges that visible wealth is perilous, beggarly, transitory, and alien to the soul (cf. 30) and easily leads the soul astray to luxuries and fancy allurements (20). Therefore, if the rich know the truth of salvation, that it is internal and belongs to passionless souls and that it is God's love that calls them to love fellow believers, how could they hoard their worldly goods? They can only respond by properly channeling their wealth from the earthly to the heavenly realm, i.e., almsgiving (cf. 20). Through consistent and generous almsgiving, the rich cultivate inner detachment and freedom as the race to salvation takes laborious training and perseverance as in the case with athletes (3; 40).[24] They should even seek a special spiritual director as their "trainer" and "pilot"[25] to hold them strictly accountable and to beg for God's mercy on their behalf (41). The rich need and should utilize all the resources they can get to take care of their souls: "God's power, human supplication, the help of brethren, sincere repentance, and constant practice" (40). With all of those resources, "success is achieved" (40); the heavenly Father will give the earnest rich "true purification and unchanging life" (42). God helps those who help themselves with a given means.

Christian Koinonia and Wealth

This clear understanding of the purpose of wealth within the context of eschatological salvation entailed social responsibility in the present. Early Christians strove to bridge the social gaps and foster genuine fellowship by sharing material resources (*koinonia*) with the needy in their intracommunity and intercommunities over distant regions. The Great Commandments of loving God and one's neighbor led to two particular customs: the common fund (*koinos*) and the common meal (*agapē*), both influenced by the larger socio-cultural context. These two customs provided tangible, corporate ways of caring for the poor and the helpless in the communi-

---

23. *Strom.* 7.7.49.3–5: "For so, in the case of the Gnostic, who has unblameably and with a good conscience fulfilled all that depends on him, in the direction of learning, and training, and well-doing, and pleasing God, the whole contributes to carry salvation on to perfection. From us, then, are demanded the things which are in our own power, . . . possession, and use . . . And what? Does he [the gnostic] not also know the other kind of sacrifice, which consists in the giving of both doctrines and of money to those who need?"

24. Cf. *Paed.* 3.6.34–36.

25. According to White, "Scholars and Patrons," 334, these terms, trainer and pilot, "allude to two common metaphors for moral instruction among the philosophers."

ties and also symbolized intra-Christian solidarity among those in different social locations.

Tertullian, the North African theologian in the late second century, speaks of "the trust funds of piety" to which "everyone" brings "some modest coin" usually once a month or "whenever he wishes" according to one's ability entirely on a voluntary basis (*Apol.* 39.5). Its explicit purpose is "to feed the poor and to bury them, for boys and girls who lack property and parents, and then for slaves grown old and ship-wrecked mariners; and any who may be in mines, islands or prisons, provided that it is for the sake of God's school (*dei sectae*), become the pensioners of their confession" (*Apol.* 39.6). This results in sharing property not in a sense of abandoning private property but in terms of sacrificially benefiting and caring for the needy in their midst (*Apol.* 39.11; cf. Acts 2:44–46; 4:32–37).

Even the unsympathetic and ill-informed pagan observer Lucian of Samosata adds a further testimony to this practice in his *Death of Peregrinus*. Peregrinus Proteus, a religious imposter, took advantage of the gullibility and stupidity (from his perspective but certainly sacrificial, mutual love from a Christian viewpoint) of Christians who flocked around him when he was imprisoned in Palestine. Some of these Christians, having come all the way from cities in Asia (modern Turkey), were sent "from their common fund (*koinos*) to succor, defend, and encourage" him who quickly became "exceedingly wealthy" through receiving this money (12–13). In that way Christians demonstrated in Lucian's mind how "they despise all things equally and consider them a common possession," again in a sense of sacrificially meeting the needs of their fellow believers rather indiscriminately and recklessly (13). Their primary commitment was to (but not limited to) fellow Christians as the sharing—*koinonia*—was designed to cultivate a greater sense of Christian unity and harmony as well as to provide practical care for those within the local churches (cf. Cyprian, *Unity*, 26).

Another corporate way that early Christians experienced and expressed the Great Commandments was a "love feast," commonly called *agapē* (Jude 12). In the household setting Christians shared religious meals, typically in the late afternoon or early evening, which included the celebration of the Eucharist at some point. Contrasting it with pagan banquets of self-serving motives and "vile" and "immodest" table manners, Tertullian defines the nature of Christian *agapē* as a divinely inspired and therefore socially charitable *and* disciplined meal: "Whatever the cost, it is gain to spend in piety's name, for with that refreshment we help the needy ... because with God there is greater consideration for those of lower degree" (*Apol.* 39.16). Hence, Christians eat only so much as to satisfy hunger and drink as much as is beneficial to the modest as those who worship the true God (*Apol.* 39.18). The purity of *koinonia* at the *agapē* in its dual function of fellowship and charity had to be guarded and protected all the more with Christian propriety and orderliness. (This was apparently a persistent issue in various house communities.) The wealthier hosts might invite the poor, the sick, widows, virgins, or any of the needy members of the church to the supper (*Ap. Trad.* 23, 28) and send them home with small baskets full of leftovers (*apophoreta*) and even deliver food to those who could not be present (*Ap. Trad.* 28.2–3). Just like the reciprocal symbiosis between the rich and the poor in almsgiving, the invited recipients in the dinner were expected to pray for the wealthier hosts for their spiritual blessings in return. While Clement of Alexandria was concerned that some hosts might think that they could buy the "promise of God" with their dinners (*Paed.* 2.1.4.3), the third-century Roman document *Apostolic Tradition* was concerned that the poor guests would not show proper gratitude to the hosts and that their behaviors would become too raucous and rowdy (28.1). Therefore, it gives specific warnings against the guests' drunkenness, noise, and quarrels at the table, all of which disrupt Christian unity and *koinonia* (28.1, 4).

Besides the common chest and the common meal, Christian hospitality, which reformulated and transformed Greco-Roman hospitality, was manifested in five concrete shapes. First, Christian individuals and communities, with proper discernment, welcomed traveling ministers and fellow believers into their homes. These travelers often contributed to the spread of the gospel. The most famous and elaborate guidelines come from *Didache*, which assumes a regular flow of itinerant apostles, prophets, and teachers, as well as ordinary Christians (11–13), into its church community where local, resident leaders—bishops and deacons—are present (15.1–2).[26] Christians also received local strangers with physical nourishment and care. In the subsequent centuries clergy in particular were charged with special responsibilities and privileges of offering hospitality to visitors and traveling missionaries. Costs were taken from the common fund under the charge of bishops (Justin, *1 Apol.* 67.6; *Didasc.* 8–9).[27] Cyprian stressed the church's continuous support for the strangers in need along with the poor during the Decian persecution, even out of his own personal funds either in addition to or in place of the common treasury when it was unavailable (*Ep.* 7.2). Later the regional councils of Elvira (ca. 306), Arles (314),

---

26. A steady flow of traveling Christians is also evidenced in Cyprian's letters, such as *Epp.* 8.2; 67.5.

27. H. Chadwick "Justification by Faith and Hospitality," *Studia Patristica* 4 (1961) 283, specifies presbyters with this role.

and Antioch (341) confirmed and enhanced the episcopal authority of extending hospitality to strangers.[28]

Second, Christians saw to it that they provided decent burials for the poorest of their own through generous donation of private burial places by the wealthy members. Starting from the early third century, "Christian cemeteries" began to emerge in Carthage, Rome, and Alexandria as reported by Tertullian,[29] "Hippolytus,"[30] and Origen,[31] respectively. They most likely refer not to the common cemeteries owned by the respective local churches but to familial tombs owned by the wealthier members of the local churches made available for the deceased poor members without any means of private burials. (Roman law did not acknowledge corporate ownership by a legal entity, and, of course, Christianity was illegal during this time).[32] This eventually led to the church's management and practical ownership of those burial sites even when it was not legally allowed to do so. In Rome one of the well-known examples is the Catacomb of San Callisto on Via Appia Antica, administered by then deacon Callistus (later bishop) and commissioned by bishop Zephyrinus (c. 199–217 CE). As it was a common custom in Roman society to appoint supervisors to manage private tomb properties, the original catacomb of San Callisto might have been the family tomb of bishop Zephyrinus.[33]

Third, Christians tended to both physical and emotional needs of those who suffered for the sake of their Christian confession, those imprisoned and condemned to mines, exile, and death. These confessors also served the faithful as the inspiration and exemplars of faith. Many martyr acts report streams of Christian

---

28. Cf. A. Arterbury, *Entertaining Angels: Early Christian Hospitality in Its Mediterranean Setting* (Sheffield: Sheffield Phoenix, 2005) 128.

29. *Scap.* 3.1: "our burial fields."

30. *Ref.*, 9.12.14; cf. *Ap. Trad.* 40.

31. *Hom. Jer.* 4.3.16.

32. C. Osiek, "Roman and Christian Burial Practices and the Patronage of Women," in *Commemorating the Dead: Texts and Artifacts in Context: Studies of Roman, Jewish, and Christian Burials* (eds. L. Brink and D. Green; Berlin: Walter de Gruyter, 2008) 244; P. Lampe, *From Paul to Valentinus: Christians at Rome in the First Two Centuries* (trans. M. Steinhauser; ed. M. D. Johnson; Minneapolis: Fortress, 2003) 370–71.

33. P. F. Bradshaw, M. E. Johnson, and L. E. Phillips, *The Apostolic Tradition: A Commentary* (Hermeneia; Minneapolis: Fortress, 2002) 191; J. Bodel, "From *Columbaria* to Catacombs: Collective Burial in Pagan and Christian Rome," in *Commemorating the Dead: Texts and Artifacts in Context: Studies of Roman, Jewish, and Christian Burials* (ed. L. Brink and D. Green; Berlin: Walter de Gruyter, 2008) 203–5, 230–31; Osiek, "Roman and Christian Burial Practices," 246; Lampe, *From Paul to Valentinus*, 25–28, 369–72.

visitors attending their fellow believers in prisons even as they were waiting for their martyrdom. For example, Perpetua and her fellow confessors (d. 203 CE) were visited multiple times while in prison by the Carthaginian faithful. These visits were organized by their deacons (Tertius and Pomponius) (3.7). The deacons bribed the soldiers who then allowed the confessors to move to a better part of the prison for their refreshment for a few hours (3.7). Other Christians brought the confessors meals and provided for even an *agapē*, which the martyrs had as their last meal on the day before their bloody martyrdom (as a replacement of the pagan banquet) (16.4–17.1). Before Felicitas faced her martyrdom soon after her childbirth, one of the women visitors took Felicitas's new-born girl to raise her (15.7). Also, with the help of a sympathetic adjutant who allowed many visitors, confessors and visitors shared mutual spiritual and emotional comfort and encouragement (9.1). The care was extended as well to those confessors who were condemned to the mines and exile. While in exile at the initial stage of Emperor Valerian's persecution (257 CE), Cyprian sent a letter to nine Numidian bishops, presbyters, deacons, and other lay people who were condemned to the mines (*Epp.* 76–79). These confessors received both physical and spiritual refreshments through the lower clergy (a subdeacon and acolytes) when they delivered them food and contributions from a certain layman Quirinus and Cyprian, along with Cyprian's letter of encouragement (*Epp.* 77.3.1; 78.3.1; 79.1.1).

Fourth, Christians, whenever they were able, sought to ransom those confessors and Christian captives with money and other means. In North Africa, after the Decian persecution ceased and the outbreak of the plague subsided, barbarian raiders in Numidian hinterlands carried off a great number of Christians as captives, and a group of eight Numidian bishops asked Cyprian for financial assistance for ransoming them (c. 253 CE; *Ep.* 62). In his response Cyprian was particularly concerned about the fate of children, wives, and above all virgins who might be subject to abuse and prostitution and therefore lose their purity and honor (*Ep.* 62.2.3).[34] Like his appeal for almsgiving for the poor, Cyprian located biblical and theological bases of ransom of captives in the love and unity of the body of Christ (1 Cor 12:1f; 3:16) and in the Lord's promise of reward at the last judgment with the hope of salvation (Matt 25:34f). He saw Christ in the captive Christians as well as in the poor (*Ep.* 62.1.1–2.2; 3.1). Then he collected a total of 100,000 sesterces in cash from the clergy and laity in Carthage (62.3.2) and sent the money to those Numidian bishops, plus smaller sums collected from other African churches (62.4.2). Along with the

---

34. For Cyprian, virgins represent the collective purity of the church; see his *Hab. virg.*

donation, he also sent a list of contributors (62.4.2; this list is lost) so that the recipients could pray for them as well as instructions to write again if they needed more (62.4.1). The fact that Cyprian mentions a list of individual contributors indicates that the money, indeed a substantial sum, did not come from the regular common fund but consisted of large donations from the limited number of the wealthy.[35] This remarkable collection bears witness not only to Christian readiness to assist but also to "the size, relative prosperity, and financial resilience of the Christianity community in Carthage," especially when one realizes how large this sum was. It was the same amount minimally required for the rank of provincial elite (Decurion). It was the rough equivalent of "the average monthly rations of some 3,000 unskilled workmen (which had) been collected [30 sesterces per laborer per month]—enough, therefore, to provide one month's food for their (average) family of four, or sufficient for keeping alive 12,000 people for a month."[36]

Fifth, Christians visited and took care of the sick, not only of their own but also of the larger society, especially during the recurring epidemics. Several contemporary accounts from Carthage and Alexandria enlighten us with what the contemporaries endured and how Christians provided for care while they were also suffering. The deadly plague, which had originated in Ethiopia in 250 CE, spread quickly throughout Egypt, North Africa, and from there to Italy and the West (as far as Scotland). This pandemic lasted fifteen to twenty years with intervals.[37] The civil authorities called on the traditional gods by making sacrifices and customary supplications, but they did hardly anything tangible to alleviate the situation.[38] Classical society lacked any organized program for the treatment of the sick on either a regular or an emergency basis.[39] The Christian churches, on the other hand, established a rather systematic care of the sick under the leadership of bishops who directed relief efforts. Cyprian in Carthage gathered his people for the whole city and gave them the theological grounding of their works of charity and mercy. Based on Christ's examples and Scripture, their care of the diseased and the dying would gain merit with

---

35. *The Letters of St. Cyprian of Carthage* (trans. and annotated by. G. W. Clarke; Ancient Christian Writers 46; New York: Newman, 1986) 3:285 n. 12.

36. *The Letters of St. Cyprian of Carthage*, 3:284–85 n. 11.

37. Sage, *Cyprian*, 269; G. B. Ferngren, "The Organisation of the Care of the Sick in Early Christianity," in *Actes/Proceedings of the XXX International Congress of the History of Medicine* (eds. H. Schadewaldt and K.-H. Leven; Düsseldorf: Vicom KG, 1988) 193.

38. G. B. Ferngren, "Medicine and Compassion in Early Christianity," *Theology Digest* 46 (1999) 318.

39. Ferngren, "Medicine and Compassion in Early Christianity," 319.

God and should be extended to Christians *and* non-Christians alike (Pontus, *Vita* 9). Cyprian instructed them to go beyond the practice of the "publican or heathen" and to seek perfection "by overcoming evil with good and by the exercise of a divine-like clemency, loving even [their] enemies, and by further praying for the salvation of [their] persecutors, as the Lord advises and encourages" (*Vita* 9). As Christians of all different social ranks assembled to help, their cares were given "according to the nature of the men and their rank" (*Vita* 10). Many on account of their poverty could not contribute wealth for the poor but provided their own precious labor while the wealthy donated money (*Vita* 10). Under Cyprian's effective leadership there was the generosity of works overflowing for all people, both Christians and non-Christians (*Vita*, 10), and these activities of looking after the victims of the plague continued until Cyprian's exile during Valerian's persecution five years later (258 CE) (*Vita* 11).

In all these ways of showing Christian *koinonia*, the faithful were exhorted to be generous and described as sacrificial. Particularly wealthy Christian women, though often unrecognized and unnamed, significantly contributed to the tangible care of the afflicted and the poor. By virtue of the Christian love commandments, loving God through loving one's neighbor was not an option but an obligation. The acts of mercy, which imply supererogatory and superfluous acts with blessings and reward attached, were in reality the acts of justice, which suggest necessary and mandatory acts with warnings and punishments accompanied when not followed (cf. Cyprian, *Eleem.* 1, 17). The very nature of the way the Christians understood and assumed their community responsibility "made wealth 'for the common good' a practical necessity."[40] Thus, the local churches and clergy regularly tapped into the common funds as these works of mercy and justice became more and more elaborate and extensive. As the charitable works and economic activities of the church became institutionalized, the clergy, especially bishops, took greater control of the common funds and patronage and came to function as "the lover and governor of the poor" in the subsequent centuries.[41]

---

40. D. E. Groh, "Christian Community in the Writings of Tertullian: An Inquiry into the Nature and Problems of Community in North African Christianity," Ph.D. diss., Northwestern University, 1970, 61.

41. P. Brown, *Poverty and Leadership in the Later Roman Empire* (Hanover, NH: University Press of New England, 2002).

Denunciation of Desire and Display of Wealth

The last theme in our discussion of the patristic view of wealth has to do with denunciation of love of money and possessions. This was not at all unique. Greco-Roman and Jewish moralists characteristically condemned the twin vices of love of money and luxury. Nonetheless, Christian authors constructed the problem of avarice ("love of money": *pleonexia, philargyria, avaritia, cupiditas*) essentially as idolatry (i.e., a theological problem even more than a moral problem, though they are usually intertwined; cf. Col 3:5). Thus avarice was something intrinsically antithetical to Christian identity. *Second Clement* warns that "when we desire to acquire these [worldly] things, we fall away from the way of righteousness" (5.7). In line with the dominical sayings on the impossibility of serving both God and money (cf. Luke 16:13; Matt 6:24), it goes on to put these two in an opposing relationship (6.1–5). Polycarp also admonishes the Philippians that unless they avoid avarice, they will be "polluted by idolatry, and will be judged as one of the Gentiles, who are ignorant of the Lord's judgment" (Pol. *Phil.* 11.2). Origen likewise repeats this close link between avarice and idolatry (*Hom. Jud.* 2.3; *Hom. Ex.* 8.4).

In the context of addressing Christian patience in the face of many ills in life, including the loss of property, Tertullian frames his argument after the dominical example of indifference toward money (*Pat.* 7.2). The Lord "has set disdain for wealth ahead of the endurance of losses, pointing out through His rejection of riches that one should make no account of the loss of them" (*Pat.* 7.3). Tertullian interprets the familiar maxim "the desire [*cupiditas*] of money [as] the root of all evils" (cf. 1 Tim 6:10) to mean that desire of money here refers to "the desire for that which belongs to another" and "even that which seems to be our own belongs to another" since God is the owner of all things (*Pat.* 7.5). Thus, if Christians fret and are impatient for their material loss, they "will be found to possess a desire for money, since [they] grieve over the loss of that which is not [their] own" (*Pat.* 7.6). When a Christian is unable to bear his or her material loss, s/he sins against God himself and behaves like a pagan by confusing a priority of heavenly goods over earthly ones (*Pat.* 7.7, 11). Consider to what extent the pagans go in order to pursue wealth: "they engage in lucrative but dangerous commerce on the sea; . . . they unhesitatingly engage in transactions also in the forum, even though there be reason to fear loss; they do it, in fine, when they hire themselves out for the games and military service or when, in desolate regions, they commit robbery regardless of the wild beasts" (*Pat.* 7.12). In contrast, in view of Christian identity, it fits Christians "to give up not our life for money but money for our life, either by voluntary charity or by the patient endurance of loss" (*Pat.* 7.13).

Avarice, idolatrous and irrational lust of money or wealth, goes hand in hand with luxury, an idolatrous and irrational display of one's wealth. Clement of Alexandria, addressing his cultured audience, indulges in describing a "disease" of avarice and outrageous and even comical displays of luxury among the refined elites, from clothing, food, vessels, crowns, shoes, to jewelries and ornaments (e.g., *Paed.* 2.3, 8, 11–13). Christians who are serious about salvation must understand and settle the first principle in their minds "that all that we possess is given to us for use, and use for sufficiency, which one may attain to by a few things," whereas those with love of money, "the stronghold of evil," "take delight in what they have hoarded up" from that greed (*Paed.* 2.3.39). The latter will "never reach the kingdom of heaven, sick for the things of the world, and living proudly through luxury" (*Paed.* 2.3.38). Clement highlights the unnatural and thus degenerate nature of avarice and luxury: "Love of wealth displaces a man from the right mode of life, and induces him to cease from feeling shame at what is shameful" (*Paed.* 3.7.37). A Christian who lives in luxury (which itself is an oxymoron) commits not only a "sin of commission" (avarice, vanity, self-love, and attachment to the world; cf. *Paed.* 3.6.34–36), but also a "sin of omission" by neglecting the commandment of loving one's neighbor (*Paed.* 2.13.120). "It is monstrous for one to live in luxury, while many are in want. How much more glorious is it to do good to many [i.e., giving alms], than to live sumptuously!" (*Paed.* 2.13.120). The very existence of the many needy and poor testifies to an outrage against luxury, especially in its social ramification. God created all things for all people. For the rich to hoard and appropriate an undue share of goods and wealth beyond what is necessary and useful is to oppose God's very purpose and intent for creation (*Paed.* 2.13.120). Thus avarice and luxury cause and result in the eternally damning consequences in both the vertical relationship with God and the horizontal relationship with humanity.

Note further how Clement's argument for common use of property as a principle against avarice and luxury is informed by his doctrine of creation:

> God created our race for sharing (*koinonia*) beginning by giving out what belonged to God, God's own Word (*logos*), making it common (*koinos*) to all humans, and creating all things for all. Therefore all things are common (*koina*). . . . To say therefore, "I have more than I need, why not enjoy?" is neither human nor proper to sharing (*koinonikon*). . . . For I know quite well that God has given us the power to use; but only to the limit of that

which is necessary; and that God also willed that the use be in common (*Paed.* 2.13.120 PG; trans. Gonzalez).

The purpose of God's creation of humanity is for sharing, which is demonstrated first by God's sharing of the divine logos. What makes us human is our sharing in this logos; hence, for anyone not to share with others what is meant to be shared, i.e., "all things" created, rebels against the very *koinonia* which is the foundation and principle of our creation.[42] Although we are created for a higher order than mere material things of the world that are transient, God has made them for our use, and *all humans* are given access to these material things as means of necessary sustenance (*Strom.* 4.13). Thus, our "right" of property is limited by the legitimate use made of it—i.e., meeting our needs *and* the needs of fellow humans—"avoiding all excess and inordinate affection" (*Strom.* 4.13; cf. *Rich Man* 14, 26).[43]

The corollary to this understanding of avarice and luxury was the notion that business and commercial activities were motivated by unnatural greed. The extant Christian texts are almost unanimous in disapproving and warning of the dangers of business affairs that were thought to obscure Christian identity and responsibilities. Tertullian clearly sees the fundamental motive of trade as covetousness (*cupiditas*; *pleonexia* in Greek), which is the root of all evil (1 Tim 6:10; cf. 1 Tim 1:19) and also called idolatry (Col 3:5) according to the Apostle Paul (*Idol.* 11.1). If covetousness, which is accompanied by mendacity and perjury, disappears, Tertullian asks, "[W]hat is the motive for acquiring? When the motive of acquiring ceases, there will be no necessity for trading" (11.1). *Hermas* also censures especially those who are "absorbed in business" (Herm. *Sim.* 4.5; 8.8.1; 9.20.1)[44] and those "who became rich" (Herm. *Sim.* 8.9.1), probably through business ventures. To these very ones who are guilty of "desire for gain" and hypocrisy, (one-time) repentance was offered (Herm.

---

42. Cf. the fourth century apologist Lactantius who acknowledges the Golden Age (with the rule of Saturn) as the time of worship of one true God, where people lived in harmony and contentment and shared the God-given land in which "all need was met in common" as intended by God (*Inst.* 5.5.5, quoting Virgil). However, for Lactantius, justice and *aequitas* that marked the Golden Age did not do away with private property or social distinction but led to voluntary sharing of goods by the rich with the poor (*Inst.* 5.5.7–8).

43. Cf. Peter of Alexandria, *On Riches* 14: "He [God] did not give it [wealth] to you [a rich man] for you to revel in it with worthless men and frivolous people or mocking theater performers. Nor did he give it to you so you could hide it in the earth, nor did he give it to you so you could spend it on large houses beyond the standard of life of the men of old. But he has given it to you so you (could) eat and give to the poor with it and those who are in need."

44. In Herm. *Vis.* 3.6.5–7 the rich and those who are preoccupied with business are the identical group.

Sim. 8.8.2; 9.19.3). While many heeded the commandments and repented, others "fell away completely . . . for on account of their business affairs they blasphemed the Lord and denied him" (Herm. *Sim.* 8.8.2). In times of peace their "excessive involvement in business" pulls them away from the church community and the Lord (Herm. *Sim.* 4.5), leading them to helpless self-absorption with riches and evasion from due service to their own Lord, i.e., avoiding almsgiving and sharing with the poorer members in the community (Herm. *Sim.* 4.5). In times of persecution they are especially prone to apostasy "because of their riches and their business affairs" (Herm. *Vis.* 3.6.5). Thus, those involved in business "a great deal" sin "a great deal" (Herm. *Sim.* 4.5). Much like the seeds that fell on the thorny soil in the Gospel parable (Mark 4:7, 18–19; Matt 13:7, 22; Luke 8:7, 14), their concerns in "business affairs and wealth and pagan friendships" prevent their minds from understanding the truth and "the parables about the Deity," choke their faith, and leave them in spiritual barrenness and ruin (Herm. *Mand.* 10.1.4).

This triad of business affairs, wealth, and pagan friendships, which forces them to commit hypocrisy out of "desire for gain," is indicative of how powerful and critical the social connections are for the social climbers and the rich addressed here. The way to stay afloat in their social circle and business and to climb up the social ladder through accumulating riches, if possible, is by connecting with and maintaining "the right company" through patronage. Those preoccupied with business and wealth avoid offending their pagan friends (which is interpreted by the author of *Hermas* as hypocrisy) and end up following "the desires of sinful men," i.e., their pagan friends (*Sim.* 9.19.3). They want to have the goods of both worlds and yet are incapable of attaining the heavenly good due to their double-mindedness and murky and distracted state of the soul (cf. Herm. *Sim.* 9.20.1). They are always on the verge of sliding back to the world until they get rid of enough wealth and put aside business activities (Herm. *Vis.* 3.6.5–6; 3.9.5–6; Herm. *Sim.* 4.5) on the one hand and "do some good with that which was left to them" (Herm. *Sim.* 9.30.5) on the other, i.e., share with those in need (Herm. *Vis.* 3.9.4; Herm. *Sim.* 2.5, 10; 10.4.2). Note that the way for the rich to be useful to God is to cut away their wealth (Herm. *Vis.* 3.6.7) though not entirely, but just enough to make them "fit for the Kingdom of God" through removing "the vanities of their possessions" (Herm. *Sim.* 9.31.2) while keeping them enough to "seek out the hungry until the tower is finished" (Herm. *Vis.* 3.9.5).

Overall, as Christianity moved up the social ladder in this period, the Christian texts repeatedly disapproved of business affairs and commercial activities. The texts linked these activities to the inordinate acquisitiveness of the (Christian) rich and *those who tried to be rich*, i.e., the middling group who could have had hope and chance of upward social mobility through those engagements.[45] The messages of not envying the rich and not seeking to gain wealth that accompanied disapproval of business and avarice (e.g., Clement of Alexandria, *Rich Man* 2; Peter of Alexandria, *On Riches* 55) and the tendency to assume positions of honor and power as involving un-Christian activities and disposition (e.g., Tertullian, *Idol.* 18) would have discouraged social mobility.[46] There could have also been a reaction against the social reality of many socially mobile people in local Christian assemblies.[47] For Christian leaders wealth itself is morally neutral (though clearly dangerous), and, following the cultural understanding, inheritance is superior to trade or business as a way to acquire wealth, which reveals their idea about socio-economic order (cf. Eusebius, *Hist. eccl.* 8.14.10). Indeed, while Christianity attracted the socially mobile groups, upon becoming Christians they would have to give up aspirations for upward social mobility through accumulation of earthly fortunes. While this implicit and explicit message against social mobility was not likely followed by those who were capable of moving up, the leaders' vision of society was largely conservative and static and assumed that people's stations were ordained by God (e.g., *1 Clem.* 38.2; Clement of Alexandria, *Rich Man* 3, 26; Peter of Alexandria, *On Riches*, 66; Cyprian, *Epp.* 3.1.1; 8.1.1; cf. 12.1.1; Tertullian, *Apparel* 2.9.1) and even that all the worldly powers and honors were to be rejected as the enemies of God (Tertullian, *Idol.* 18.8). Thus, "there was an irreconcilable incompatibility between social mobility and Christian community—between the opportunities and status of human community and the commitment to divine community."[48] Ironically, while Christian identity was partially and indirectly associated with social immobility, Christianity of this period penetrated into the circles of the socially prominent and elite in unprecedented ways.

Summary and Conclusion

This paper has shown the Christian affirmation of almsgiving and charity as positive markers of Christian identity and life and the denunciation of avarice and luxury as their negative markers with regard to the God-given gift of money and posses-

---

45. Those who put confidence in "the [business] transactions that have made them rich" are condemned in *On Riches*, 37, attributed to Peter of Alexandria in the early fourth century.

46. Cf. R. M. Grant, *Early Christianity and Society* (San Francisco: Harper & Row, 1977) 123.

47. This kind of message would be repeated by the bishops throughout the Late Antiquity; e.g., John Chrysostom, *Hom. 1 Cor.* 15.6.

48. Groh, "Christian Community in the Writings of Tertullian," 69.

sions. On the one hand, early Christians associated the desire for and acquisition and display of wealth with the worldly passion for self-exaltation and status, items dangerous and destructive for Christians. Wealth in this way disrupts the relationships with God, fellow humans, and the self. On the other hand, they acknowledged and advised the constructive use of wealth for the works of charity—almsgiving and sharing—which is in fact the only redemptive purpose of wealth for Christians. Wealth in this way demonstrates and confirms the life-long salvation of its possessor who must persevere to the end. Early Christians in general did not admonish divestment of wealth but voluntary restraint in pursuit and display of wealth, a restraint necessary for curbing immoderate desire for wealth, which is idolatry.

When Constantine seized the imperial power in the West with the power of the Christian God (312 CE), the church had been functioning as a formidable social and economic institution with a substantial operation of charity. Constantine's unprecedented imperial patronage of the church did not prompt a brand new theological base for the work the church had been doing, which by then had been securely established, but it transformed the scale, way, and impact that the church's charity and wealth had on Roman society. Although in the measures of religious freedom, financial subsidy, and clerical exemption Constantine did not necessarily go beyond extending to Christian churches the privileges that the official cults of the empire enjoyed, with further "pro-Christian" policies before and after his sole reign of the Empire in 324 CE, their overall impact was nothing less than revolutionary.[49] With the dawn of a new era of peace and prosperity for the church under Constantine and his successors, the church had to deal with a new reality of imperial patronage and favors. Aside from other political reasons and purposes, with imperial largesse Constantine made the church not only officially visible (much more so than before) but also accountable to the public for the very public gifts it received. Now, in the words of Peter Brown, "by a slight but significant shift of emphasis, traditional Christian charity to fellow believers within the Christian community came to be

---

49. Constantine's joint edict of toleration with Licinius (the so-called the Edict of Milan, 313 CE) officially acknowledged what had been a *de facto* reality of church ownership of buildings, cemeteries, gardens, and other movable and immovable properties throughout the third century by ordering their restoration (Lactantius, *Mort.* 48; Eusebius, *Hist. eccl.* 10.5.9–11). Then he granted the churches and bishops financial assistance (3,000 *folles*) that would turn into regular support (cf. Eusebius, *Hist. eccl.* 10.2.2; 10.6) and clerical exemption from all compulsory public services and personal taxes so that they could devote themselves to worship their God on behalf of their communities and the empire (Eusebius, *Hist. eccl.* 10.12; *Cod. theod.* 16.2). He exempted church lands and other properties, which would keep growing from pious endowments, from the taxation, and in fact, he himself endowed lands in Italy, Africa, Crete, and Gaul that produced more than two hundred pounds of gold a year (Grant, *Early Christianity and Society*, 152).

regarded as a public service, as a more general 'care of the poor' performed in return for public privileges."[50] With this shift Christian identity was all the more linked to the church's care of the poor in Roman society, both Christians and non-Christians, as "the rich must assume the secular obligations and the poor must be supported by the wealth of the churches" (*Cod. theod.* 16.2.6). Bishops as the guardians and protectors of the poor were now obligated to care for the poor of the church *and* of the society in view not only of the eschatological judgment but also the imperial judgment. In this new context, the church leaders continued to exhort the faithful to almsgiving and charity with the familiar, foundational themes. Those themes continued to appear in the writings of the Latin, Greek, and Syriac Fathers with further theological augmentation now viewed as the established church tradition (e.g., Ambrose, Jerome, Augustine, Basil the Great, Gregory Nazianzen, Gregory of Nyssa, John Chrysostom, and Ephrem the Syrian). This tradition emphasized heavenly wealth versus earthly wealth, almsgiving as effecting atonement for sin and pious lending to God, the symbiotic exchange between the rich and the poor, the pious poor and the wicked rich, God's creative intent of common use for humanity, and identification of the poor with Christ.

From the limited topics addressed in this chapter, I hope I have shown that early Christian texts and practices concerning wealth and poverty still offer us relevant and illuminating frameworks, principles, perspectives, and practices for our contemporary dealings with wealth and poverty and their attendant opportunities and challenges, notwithstanding the enormous historical and socio-cultural distance and "otherness" involved.[51] Just as early Christians consciously constructed their self-definition(s) using wealth, responding to poverty, and understanding the responsibilities of the rich and the poor in light of God's creative purpose, Christians today are inescapably called to and have been forming and reforming Christian identity(-ies) in relation to our attitude, use, and distribution of wealth and dealing with poverty for the common good, individually and corporately.

Appendix: Monasticism, Poverty, and Public Service

The Constantinian reformation not only brought about a new era of peace, privilege, and responsibility for the church but also ushered in organized monastic movements

---

50. Brown, *Poverty and Leadership*, 31.

51. Despite P. Allen, "Challenges in Approaching Patristic Texts from the Perspective of Contemporary Catholic Social Teaching," in *Reading Patristic Texts on Social Ethics: Issues and Challenges for Twenty-First-Century Christian Social Thought* (eds. J. Leemans, B. J. Matz, and J. Verstraeten: Washington, DC: Catholic University of America Press, 2011) 30–42, 40.

against the backdrop of imperial Christianity—a mixed bag of opportunism, nominalism, coercion, and genuine spiritual and ecclesiastical growth and influence on society. With the unprecedented development and popularity of the monastic lifestyle and movement, a new group of "the poor" emerged: the ascetics who practiced voluntary poverty by renouncing one's private property and social and familial ties and/or sharing possessions in common with monastic colleagues in communities.

Ascetics were not a new group of Christians in the time of Constantinian peace, but they constituted a "new" formidable Christian elite who came to be both entitled to alms and dispensers of alms, at times in complement and competition with the clergy.[52] While these monks individually renounced all worldly attachments, including possessions, many, if not most, cenobitic monastics could count on sufficient shelter, clothing, regular meals, and "excellent" health care for the rest of their lives due to the economic stability of monastic communities.[53] The monastic brotherhoods were usually engaged in local enterprises of various goods, for example, the production of oil in northern Syria or around Bethlehem.[54] According to Egyptian papyri the monks were involved in extensive economic activities with the secular world they were supposed to leave behind, and they kept a close contact with local elites.[55] In addition, semi-eremitical monks clustered around particular *abbas* in northern Egypt (Nitria, Kellia, and Scetis). They supported themselves with self-managed finances through farming and crafts.[56] Even "radical" hermits living in the Egyptian deserts and remote areas ("Desert Fathers" and "Desert Mothers") also survived by similar labors of trade, gardening, and agriculture, however rudimentary they might have been. Their solitude and separation from village or town were "only relative."[57] Moreover, the Sayings of the Desert Fathers (*Apophthegmata*

---

52. It should be noted that from the mid-fourth century and on, an increasing number of bishops (e.g., the Cappadocian Fathers, Augustine, and John Chrysostom) would have experienced monastic life and come from the monastic ranks, thus leading to greater cooperation between clergy/church and monks/monasteries.

53. D. Brakke, "Care for the Poor, Fear of Poverty, and Love of Money," in *Wealth and Poverty in Early Church and Society* (ed. S. R. Holman; Grand Rapids: Baker Academic, 2008) 76.

54. E. Patlagean, "The Poor," in *The Byzantines* (ed. G. Cavallo; trans. T. Dunlap, T. L. Fagan, and C. Lambert; Chicago: University of Chicago Press, 1997) 22.

55. See E. A. Judge, "Fourth-Century Monasticism in the Papyri," in *Proceedings of the Sixteenth International Congress of Papyrology* (Chico, Calif.: Scholars, 1981) 613–20.

56. Cf. Brakke, "Care for the Poor, Fear of Poverty, and Love of Money," 77.

57. Patlagean, "The Poor," 22. Speaking of the social and economic interaction of the monk and the world, J. E. Goehring [*Ascetics, Society, and the Desert: Studies in Early Egyptian Monasticism* (Harrisburg, PA: Trinity, 1999) 41] says, "Such interaction was not only possible; it was inevitable. The

partum) and other sources contain references to monks owning servants, books, garments, and vessels, as well as references to hospitality, thieves, charity, wages, bakeries and wine-presses, which indicate private resources and business activities of even anchorite and semi-anchorite monks.[58]

The model hermit, Anthony portrayed by Athanasius, despite earlier divestment of his property, eventually practiced economic self-sufficiency through producing his own bread and vegetables. He repeatedly and throughout his life provided alms for the poor and hospitality for his visitors (*Life of Anthony*, 50.4–6). Thus, whether one was an anchorite, semi-anchorite, or a cenobitic, a monk did not necessarily live in destitution with "total" renunciation of private property, although other wandering monks in Syria lived off of begging and did choose a life of destitution and severe economic vulnerability. The monastic poverty in reality was more patterned after economic self-sufficiency than destitution.

On the one hand, a monk's relative security and the latitude permitted regarding personal possessions and finances complicated one's attitude and relationship to possessions and poverty.[59] The fact that another famous semi-anchorite, Evagrius Ponticus, often advised the monks to renounce possessions is telling. Avarice (*philargyria*) and vanity were consistent points of concern in the Sayings of Desert Fathers and other monastic literature, including Evagrius's works.[60] The ideal monk, whether a hermit or cenobitic, should *possess* just enough to support oneself and from however small a surplus to give alms to the economic poor, since almsgiving was a monastic obligation. At issue was how to balance wealth and charity in light of and in relation to their voluntary poverty and freedom from worldly concerns and passions. However, due to the business affairs in which they were engaged as a way to support themselves, monks were just as vulnerable to love of money, which precipitated repeated teachings against avarice and vanity. In case of avarice creeping in under the pretext of having money to distribute to the poor, Evagrius admonishes, "Do not desire to possess riches in order to be able to make donations to the poor, for this is a deception of the evil one, and often leads to vainglory" (*Foundations of*

---

desert in Egypt, while sharply distinct from the inhabited land, was not remote."

58. S. Rubenson, "Power and Politics of Poverty in Early Monasticism," in *Prayer and Spirituality in the Early Church: Vol. 5, Poverty and Riches* (eds. G. D. Dunn, D. Luckensmeyer, and L. Cross; Strathfield, Australia: St. Pauls, 2009) 91–110, 96.

59. Brakke, "Care for the Poor, Fear of Poverty, and Love of Money," 77.

60. See *Evagrius of Pontus: The Greek Ascetic Corpus* (trans. R. E. Sinkewicz; Oxford Early Christian Studies; Oxford: Oxford University Press, 2003); *The Desert Fathers: Sayings of the Early Christian Monks* (trans. Benedicta Ward; London: Penguin, 2003).

the Monastic Life, 4). For these reasons there was also a certain ambivalence with regard to monastic almsgiving and even reluctance to give to the poor out of fear that charity might take a priority over prayer and knowledge of God.[61]

On the other hand, on account of institutional (i.e., communal) wealth and financial revenues and individual freedom from worldly attachment, at least in theory, the monks acted as key players in serving the poor of the society. They lived "the life of an angel" here on earth due to their spiritual disciplines and voluntary poverty and therefore emerged as new "mediators of salvation through alms and intercession."[62] While their spiritual prowess made them impervious to their own needs but particularly sensitive to the needs of the poor (cf. Cassian, *Conlat.* 21.33 [CSEL 13.609–10]), charity for them was also a means to fight against passions such as avarice and irascibility and to display their inner freedom.[63] The monks and the poor had "mutual attraction." While monks liberally and "cheerfully" reached out to the vulnerable, the sick, and the poor by establishing hostels for lodging, hospitals for care, and regular distribution of food and clothing, the able-bodied poor also migrated to the cities and the regions of monastic developments, especially the Holy Land and northern Syria.[64] Indeed, the theological construction of the poor person as Christ in disguise and charity as the imitation of Christ reinforced this mutual attraction.

Thus, the voluntary poverty of the monks in general rather conformed to the classical ideal of noble self-sufficiency coupled with generosity, and was meant to be clearly distinguished from the economic destitution of the involuntary poor.[65] Even for ascetics it was not poverty in itself that was praised or considered a virtue; rather, it was what poverty signified and made possible—freedom, prayers, and charity.[66] Hence, the ascetic rule of thumb was once again the twin principles of self-sufficiency and charity, similar to the general rule of thumb for Christian life, but ascetics actually embodied that rule with much greater success for which they were praised and admired, though not imitated, by a vast majority of the faithful.

61. Brakke, "Care for the Poor, Fear of Poverty, and Love of Money," 84–86.

62. Patlagean, "The Poor," 24.

63. Evagrius, *Chapters on Prayer* 17; *To Monks* 30; cf. Rubenson, "Power and Politics of Poverty in Early Monasticism," 106–7.

64. Cf. Patlagean, "The Poor," 21, 24.

65. W. Mayer, "Poverty and Generosity toward the Poor in the Time of John Chrysostom," in *Wealth and Poverty in Early Church and Society* (ed. S. R. Holman; Grand Rapids: Baker, 2008) 140–58, 151, 154; Rubenson, "Power and Politics of Poverty in Early Monasticism," 104.

66. Rubenson, "Power and Politics of Poverty in Early Monasticism," 104.

RESPONSE TO RHEE

Bradley Nassif

There are two subjects I would like to focus on in response to Helen Rhee's paper: method and *phronēma,* the "mind" of the early church. The most important one is the latter. I have selected these two subjects because they call attention to the criteria by which one may discover the "enduring relevance" of patristic views of wealth and possessions for contemporary life.

Method

I commend the research methods employed in this study. It is an outstanding model of descriptive historical analysis. As Rhee herself stated, her task was to explore money and possessions in the church of the second and third centuries to see how such attitudes became markers of Christian identity. She explored the themes of wealth and poverty along four lines: heavenly versus earthly wealth, salvation and possessions, Christian fellowship, and the desire and display of possessions. Those four themes summarize the broad economic values of the Greek and Latin traditions. In each of these categories Rhee displayed an exceptional competence in historical analysis. The primary and secondary sources she interprets were some of the most influential Greek and Latin texts of the second and third centuries.

While we are indebted to Rhee for explaining the meaning of these four features in the works of selected writers, perhaps there is a more important question that remains unanswered. How did those four features of wealth and poverty manifest themselves in the broader ongoing life of the Christian church? How normative were they then and now? Although no one can be expected to say everything about this subject in early Christianity, we might have been able better to see how those four areas became imbedded in the wider tradition of the church and not just in these selected writers. More specifically, we may have had a greater sense of the enduring values of these four categories if Rhee had applied them to a different corpus of writings, namely, primitive monastic texts of the third and fourth centuries in Egypt, Palestine, and Syria. Each of these regions made its own contribution, but together they impacted the wider life of the church in both the Greek and Latin traditions, as well as the Syriac, Coptic, and other linguistic families of the eastern Mediterranean.

For example, in the *Life of Anthony* (written by Athanasius in Egypt in 356), we gain insight into primitive monastic views on wealth, possessions, justice, and care for the poor and needy. The *Life of Anthony* became a literary model for later Christian biographies as well as serving as a spiritual model for all would-be monks. Next to the Bible, it was the most widely read book in the ancient and medieval worlds for nearly one thousand years. That in itself privileges the text above the works Rhee consulted in her study. It attracted literally thousands of early Christians to divest their possessions in exchange for a life of prayer and voluntary poverty. The *Life of Anthony* became so influential that Athanasius tells us that by the middle of the fourth-century "the desert was made a city by monks."[1]

The ascetic posture towards wealth and possessions eventually made its way into the liturgical life of the wider Christian community at that time and in subsequent centuries. Ascetical ideals shaped the liturgical services, fasting practices, and ethical values of the worshipping communities of Eastern and Western Christianity. Then, as now, Christians who worship in Byzantine, Syriac, Latin, Coptic, and other ancient liturgies are indebted to monastic ideals for the church's continuing emphasis on almsgiving and self-sacrifice for the poor and needy, the sick and suffering, and those in prison. Nowhere is this social emphasis more readily seen than in the liturgical texts prayed during the fifty days of Great Lent. The constant Lenten exhortations for Christians to fast, pray, and give alms are astonishing. Due largely to monastic influence, the Great Fast became a time of great austerity and serious physical hardship for the sake of God and fellow humans. So I think Rhee's presentation could have been more complete had she included the impact of early monasticism on the liturgical and spiritual life of the church.[2]

---

1. Athanasius of Alexandria, *The Life of Anthony* (trans. Tim Vivian and Apostolos N. Athanassakis; Kalamazoo, MI: Cistercian, 2004) 93. For inspirational reading of the lives and teachings of the desert fathers and mothers see Bradley Nassif, *Bringing Jesus to the Desert* (Grand Rapids: Zondervan, 2012); for scholarly work on selected monastic texts in Eastern Christianity see *The Philokalia: A Classic Text in Orthodox Spirituality* (eds. Brock Bingaman and Bradley Nassif; Oxford: Oxford University Press, 2012).

2. Patristic scholars in the past two decades have begun to widen their perspectives on the early church by focusing on the neglected field of Syriac studies. The subject of wealth and possessions in the Syriac tradition has recently received more attention. See Susan Ashbrook Harvey, "The Holy and the Poor: Models from Early Syriac Christianity," in *Through the Eye of a Needle: Judeo-Christian Roots of Social Welfare* (ed. Emily Albu Hanawalt and Carter Lindberg; Kirksville, MO: Thomas Jefferson University Press, 1994) 43–66; and Robert Doran, *Stewards of the Poor: The Man of God, Rabbula, and Hiba in Fifth-Century Edessa* (Kalamazoo, MI: Cistercian Studies, 2006).

Phronēma: The "Mind" of the Church

The second observation I would like to make is an extension of the methodological issue just raised. It is more in the form of a question than a critique of the content of Rhee's very fine paper. It is a question with which all "Christian" historians and theologians should be concerned in their study of the early church, namely, What is the role of early Christianity in shaping the life and faith of the Christian church today? How may historical and theological inquiry serve the needs of *both* rigorous academic study *and* contemporary church life? I think Rhee's paper answers the first part of that question very well. Her rigorous academic study on wealth and possessions has done an outstanding job of informing our understanding of some of the key players of second and third-century Christianity. But what are we to make of these teachings when applying them to contemporary church life? *What is the mind of the church and how can we acquire it?*

This is not an easy question to answer. A satisfactory reply requires a great deal of historical knowledge and sophistication. The topic of our conference, however, is a good test case for this question. Is "the mind of the church" acquired simply by obtaining second and third century information on a given topic? If so, Rhee has given us the answer we seek by simply providing us with the four points of her paper. However, I do not think even the church fathers she studied would have agreed with that way of discerning the mind of the church. One does not acquire the church's faith and practice simply by analyzing a given set of thinkers in an isolated period of time, whether it is the time period of the authors Rhee has examined or a monastic text such as the *Life of Anthony*.

In his book *Bible, Church, Tradition*,[3] the late Fr. George Florovsky explored the patristic expression "following the Holy Fathers." This expression was used to introduce major doctrinal statements such as the opening lines of the Chalcedonian definition of faith at the Fourth Ecumenical Council in 451 CE. At the Seventh Ecumenical Council in 787 the fathers also introduced their decision concerning holy icons by saying, "Following the divinely inspired teaching of the Holy Fathers and the Tradition of the catholic church." Virtually all seven Ecumenical Councils (325–787) made similar claims to consistency and continuity with the past. Such expressions as these were much more than just an "appeal to antiquity." Antiquity, in and of itself, was never adequate proof of the true faith or "the mind of the church."

---

3. George Florovsky, *Bible, Church, Tradition: An Eastern Orthodox View* (Nordland: Belmont, 1972) 105–12.

Just because something was old did not make it right. Antiquity as such may simply be old error! So when we seek to evaluate a given conclusion such as wealth and possessions, it is not enough to report the past and hand it on as eternal truth. On the contrary, to "follow the Holy Fathers" involves much more than quoting lines and sentences from Christian antiquity. To "follow the Holy Fathers" is an appeal first and foremost to the apostolic faith. It is an appeal to Holy Scripture and the witness of the apostolic documents preserved and passed down in the worshipping life of the church.

So for the church fathers and mothers, the apostolic faith is embedded in the church's tradition. It is preserved and passed on through the life of the Holy Spirit in the church. This was the point of Irenaeus in the second century in his refutation of the Gnostics. Tradition is a living reality. It is the ongoing witness of the apostolic faith in the church's "rule of faith," its ministerial succession, and its biblical canon. That is why it is a dangerous habit to quote the fathers outside the concrete setting in which they have their full and proper meaning. "To follow the Holy Fathers," as the Ecumenical Councils were accustomed to saying, does not just mean to quote their sentences and phrases. On the contrary, "to follow" the fathers means to acquire their "mind," their *phronēma*. That "mind" can only be known by pursuing the fullness of the church's tradition, i.e. the fathers, councils, creeds, hymns, saints, and worship. It requires much knowledge, great patience, and sustained exposure to the organic life of historic Christianity.

When it comes to the study of Christian antiquity, therefore, we may profitably ask whether the conclusions of our research truly reflect "the mind of the church" or merely the mind of a particular patristic author or group of authors? That, I believe, is the most profitable question regarding "wealth and possessions" in Christian antiquity. To know the thoughts of a particular author or group of writers provides us with essential information about a given time and place in history. Helen Rhee has served us well in this area, but perhaps the church's mission can be more effectively accomplished today if we move beyond the methodological confines of historical particularity. If we widen our vision so that our scholarship may grasp "the mind of the church" regarding "wealth and possessions," we may be better able to discover the enduring ethical principles that apply in every time and place of the church's earthly pilgrimage.

BLESSINGS, CURSES, AND THE CROSS[1]

Kelly Johnson

Pastor Joe Nelms became an internet sensation for his invocation, partly inspired by a scene from *Talladega Nights*, before a NASCAR race in Nashville. He gave thanks for the blessings of "GM performance technology and the RO7 engines. Thank you for Sunoco racing fuel and Goodyear tires that bring performance and power to the track. Lord, I want to thank you for my smoking hot wife tonight, Lisa, and my two children. . . . Lord, I pray you bless the drivers and use them tonight. May they put on a performance worthy of this great track. In Jesus' name, boogity boogity boogity, Amen."[2] Christians in the United States talk a great deal about blessings and apparently pray quite regularly. Robert Putnam and David Campbell's study of religion in America notes that forty-four percent of Americans say grace (or the prayers appropriate to their tradition) before meals regularly, giving thanks for blessings and/or asking God's blessing on their meal.[3]

Bart Simpson, on the other hand, once prayed, "Dear God, we paid for this stuff ourselves, so thanks for nothing." If about half of Americans commonly pray grace, about another half rarely or never do. In Christian talk about stewardship, which is the major if not only language used within the church to discuss possessions, the central concern is getting people like Bart to consider their possessions (including their "time and talents") to be blessings given by God so that they will then recognize an obligation to use those blessings in a way pleasing to God.

Some fine work—as well as some rather poor work—has been done to that end. Many commentators have tried to enrich stewardship into a spirituality that integrates gratitude, generosity, and responsibility before God into the whole of a community's life. The United States Catholic bishops, for example, have tried to enrich stewardship thought by counting among the gifts of God to be cared for and used responsibly, not only personal wealth, but the environment, one's vocation,

---

1. Wes Arblaster, Jana Bennett, Maura Donahue, Brad Kallenberg, and Jonathan Wilson-Hartgrove all provided helpful comments on earlier drafts of this paper.

2. http://www.youtube.com/watch?v=1TZckKSxAS4&feature=related

3. *American Grace: How Religion Divides and Unites Us* (New York: Simon and Schuster, 2010) 10.

and the church itself. In fact, they have so emphasized these other gifts that the area of personal wealth is not specifically named in their own summary of the teaching.[4] Throughout the history of stewardship work, pastors have called Christians more generously and more creatively to use their power and wealth to do good.[5]

I remain one of those, however, who find that tradition on the whole quite theologically thin. Given that the right use of wealth is a deep concern to many Christians and a morally complex matter (though not always as complex as we would like it to be), it is a significant problem that such important and widely-used theological language for addressing the issues remains merely a vague way of indicating God's relation to things we judge to be good, safe enough to serve nicely in a joke at a NASCAR event, general enough to cover all possessions. I hope in this paper to explore ways an attentive study of Scripture on the topic of blessing could challenge us to enrich ordinary thinking and daily prayer about possessions. In particular, I want to attend to ways blessing can be understood in light of the stories of Israel and Jesus, rather than as a generality about creation understood to stand apart from redemption and eschatology.

"Blessing" in the Pentateuch

What does the language of "blessing" mean in Scripture?[6] We will be wise not to search for a single, univocal sense of blessing across all of Scripture, but in its most basic and continuous sense, blessing is the gift of God, typically a gift which allows life to flourish more fully. The first blessing spoken in Genesis is God's blessing on the living creatures of the water and the air, that they be fruitful and multiply, and the second is the similar statement to the human creatures. Progeny is, it seems, the principle example of God's blessing as well as the subject of God's commandment in these texts, and the presence of blessing is seen in fruitfulness.[7] The third blessing

---

4. "To Be a Christian Steward: A Summary of the U.S. Bishops' Pastoral Letter on Stewardship," in *Stewardship: A Disciple's Response* (Tenth Anniversary Edition; Washington, DC, 2002).

5. For historical analysis of stewardship and a fuller development of my critique, see chs. 3 and 5 of *The Fear of Beggars: Poverty and Stewardship in Christian Ethics* (Grand Rapids: Eerdmans, 2007).

6. This discussion is deeply indebted to Scott Bader-Saye, "Fear in the Garden: The State of Emergency and the Politics of Blessing," *Ex Auditu* 24 (2008) 2–6.

7. The same blessing is given to Noah and his family in Gen 9, and Gen 24:60 shows Rebekah's relatives blessing her that she might be the mother of "thousands of ten thousands"; in Gen 28:3 Isaac wishes for Jacob God's blessing of descendents and land for them. God's blessing of Sarah results in her becoming the mother of nations in Gen 17. God blesses Abraham after he does not withhold Isaac, saying he will have descendants as numerous as the stars of heaven (22:17).

spoken in the first creation account is the blessing of the Sabbath day. Blessing is not simply about productivity but about the fullness of life which includes rest, particularly rest that God's people share with God. The Sabbath is blessed and hallowed—"blessing" making it fruitful and joyous, "hallowing" giving it a share of God's own fullness already achieved and yet still overflowing.

Within the Pentateuch land is also a key example of blessing, although it is conjoined to the blessing of progeny and wealth. During a time of famine God tells Isaac that he will bless his descendants with the land promised to Abraham (Gen 26:3); family, land, and food are connected in one promise of that full life that Scripture calls peace or *shalom*. In Gen 49:25 Jacob says God will bless Joseph "with the blessings of heaven above, blessings of the deep that couches beneath, blessings of the breasts and of the womb." The land is not a blessing on its own, but a land to be filled with descendants who will work it, enjoy its produce, and use it to provide still more descendants. Nevertheless, the land is essential to the blessing because land creates the possibility for the growing family to live together in peace. God's blessing does not only touch individuals; it creates communities who care for each other, networks of reciprocity and gift that ripple out among creatures.

Take, for instance, Gen 32:26–30, the story of Jacob's demanding a blessing from the one with whom he wrestles. Jacob tricked a blessing out of his father and then during twenty years living with Laban's family built up his own household. When his herds begin to cause jealousy in Laban's household, he leaves, makes a covenant of peace with Laban, and sends word to Esau that he is returning. The messengers return with word that Esau is coming to meet him with four hundred men. The night before he faces Esau again, fearful for the safety of all that he has gained, Jacob wrestles with, the text says, a man, although in the end of the episode, Jacob names the place Peniel: "For I have seen God face to face, and yet my life is preserved" (32:30). The one he wrestled injured him when he saw he could not win. Jacob still refuses to let go, however, and demands a blessing. He does not receive God's name, as he asks, but he does receive a blessing.

What is this "blessing"? No specific content is named, but that morning, limping, Jacob goes to see Esau and finds him welcoming, not resentful. In fact, Esau runs to greet him and refuses all the bribes that Jacob had sent ahead to soften him up. Jacob insists on giving them as gifts, saying that seeing Esau is "like seeing the face of God, with such favor you have received me" (33:10).

The blessing of God, given the night before, was not identified with anything specific. Jacob already has children and wealth. The immediate surprise, however, is that Esau welcomes him, easing Jacob's quest for his own land by making peace. Esau becomes God's blessing to Jacob—an end to fear and enmity, fraternity, and a place for all to dwell. Jacob insists all the more on giving his gift to Esau, no longer as a way of buying safety but now because God has been gracious to him. Esau, on those terms, accepts it. The blessing, given by God, bears fruit as it creates and spreads peace—not just an absence of conflict, but fullness of human life—among humans.

Blessing opens up an economy of blessing, as its gift is fertile or is to be passed on rather than hoarded or settled by a payment in return. More precisely, it is not the one gift that is passed on, but a new event arising from the original gift but now coming from the one who was blessed by that original gift in a new way. It draws together those who are different, even those who might be enemies, as between Jacob and Esau. Blessing is the life that binds creatures to each other, a movement originating in God, a gift paid forward "even, perhaps especially, to those who in conventional terms have not earned it."[8]

While embodied and social flourishing describe the major examples of blessings given, it would not be right to say simply that they constitute the meaning of blessing in Scripture. Consider, for example, the gift of the law. It is interesting that in the Pentateuch the law itself is not called a blessing, but the Wisdom literature repeatedly refers to the one who follows the law as blessed. Does this simply mean that God rewards those who obey with gifts such as progeny, land, prosperity, security from enemies? It is a common understanding of the covenant to say that it is conditional; blessings will be given *if* Israel obeys the law (e.g., Deut 28:1–2, 15). Indeed, for the Deuteronomist, looking at Israel's exile, it seems clear that failure to obey the law did result in loss of blessings. But as important as the blessings (and curses, which will be addressed below) are, they are not merely extrinsic rewards for obedient behavior. The blessings are not simply gifts to be gained by pleasing God. Rather, as the late chapters of Exodus make painfully clear, the question is whether God will be with the people. The punishment of exile is not merely the loss of land, as important as that is. It is the loss of God's presence, of the temple, of the ark so joyously and painstakingly constructed to be God's presence. Note the Aaronic blessing of Num 6:24–26:

> The Lord bless you and keep you;
> The Lord make his face to shine upon you, and be gracious to you;
> The Lord lift up his countenance upon you, and give you peace.

---

8. Bader-Saye, "Fear in the Garden," 3.

God's being gracious and giving gifts is paired with God's shining gaze, God's fellowship with Israel. This is not an equal relationship; Israel cannot gaze on God to see this face. What Israel will see is God's graciousness, which is *shalom*. Nevertheless, the blessing is not only in the results that Israel and its neighbors can see. The blessing is in God's faithful attention, God's not turning away. Blessings, by definition, are most fundamentally a sharing in God's joyous life.[9]

The move in the Psalms and Proverbs to declare that the blessed are those who love God's law, trust in God, and fear God is not a rupture from the Pentateuch's attention to material blessing but a development of it. The God who chooses a particular family to bless (for the sake of all) blesses people as humans, as family, as bodies that get hungry and tired. But food, land, and progeny can only amount to *shalom* when they are ordered by God's law, as part of a life that returns in worship to God. Blessings are never mere "stuff"; if they are blessings, then they are part of an unfolding relationship with God and God's people. Blessings are blessings, rather than mere wealth or children, because they draw people further into God's work.

Therefore those formulations which describe blessing even in the absence of progeny and prosperity must be heard as part of Israel's ongoing discovery of the meaning of God's blessing. Most notably, given the importance of children as a blessing, is Wisdom 3:13–14:

> For blessed is the barren woman who is undefiled, who has not entered into a sinful union; she will have fruit when God examines souls. Blessed also is the eunuch whose hands have done no lawless deed, and who has not devised wicked things against the Lord, for special favor will be shown him for his faithfulness and a place of great delight in the temple of the Lord.

Notice that this does not spiritualize the problem away. If the barren woman is to be called blessed, then she must eventually have her role in this unfolding of full life. Nevertheless, it does not say only that she *will be* blessed with fruitfulness; she is blessed, even in her present barrenness, because she has kept the law. Likewise the recognition in Habakkuk and Job that the appearance of poverty does not simply equate to evidence that God has turned away or has failed to do good complicates thinking about God's blessings. These voices caution against a simplistic claim that blessings of prosperity follow from justice (or that the affliction of poverty results from God's curse). Blessing is about being drawn into God's life.

---

9. Christopher Wright Mitchell, *The Meaning of brk "to bless" in the Old Testament* (Atlanta: Scholars, 1987).

At the risk of synthesizing too neatly what is clearly a complex and not entirely univocal tradition, we can say that while blessing is God's giving to creatures their fullest lives so that they can share that fullness in dynamic networks of gift with others and enjoy it in rest with their God, still the core of blessing is that it is an element of ongoing relationship with God. Mere possession of prosperity is certainly not to be equated with blessing.

Curses and Filthy Lucre

Blessing is a rich and complex category in the OT, but if we are going to be faithful to the tradition, we have to talk about curses as well. In Genesis and Deuteronomy, blessings and curses often stand together. The modern sensibility which presumes that God's goodness is incompatible with punishment can blind us to a biblical vision which speaks frankly about curse as the corollary to blessing.[10]

As Scott Bader-Saye points out, drawing on Barth, curses are the flip side of blessings, because they are the result of God's continuing to engage with creatures even when they have rejected blessings. The curses of Gen 3 do not revoke life or creativity, as would happen if God simply withdrew, but they do endow it with misery, making labor into toil, childbirth into unavoidable pain, and the movement and nutrition of the serpent into humiliation.[11] The humans and animals and earth now no longer share blessings but become enemies, fearful and hostile to each other's well-being. In Augustinian terms, we could say that the evil that arises in the curses is not a substance, but the twisting of blessings as they lose their orientation toward God. They cease to be blessings but they remain, nevertheless, good creatures made by God.

Bader-Saye's point seems to be born out in Gen 12:3, where God says he will bless those who bless Abram and curse those who curse him and make him a blessing to all. How can he be a blessing to all if the result of meeting him will be a curse to some? Although God gives a blessing to all, such blessings can, when people reject or abuse them, become curses.

What we learn from considering the proximity of curses to blessing is that the encounter with blessing is perilous. Would we truly want God's face to shine on us? Can we bear to be seen in that gaze? Deuteronomy 11:26 does not say that Israel's

---

10. I recognize that there are serious reasons for shying away from talk of curses. The history of appeals to the curse on Noah's son as justification for the enslavement of Africans, for example, is enough to make one cautious about any use of biblical curses.

11. Bader-Saye, "Fear in the Garden," 5.

options are to receive a blessing or be ignored by God, but to receive a blessing or a curse. There is no neutral option. The gifts given for the abounding of human life can be used for that purpose, or they can be used against it. Anyone who thrills to the blessings God promises would do well to ponder Deut 28, where the blessings take up fourteen verses and the curses run on for fifty-three lengthy and gruesome verses. Israel's blessings of land are, in fact, the site of greatest grief when idolatry and injustice pervert those good gifts. Although "Woe to you rich" is in only one Gospel, warnings about the dangers of personal wealth appear throughout the NT, echoing the prophets' denunciation of luxury at the expense of those in need.

Moreover, given that injustice is not all that uncommon, it should be obvious that not everything people have is given to them by God. Yet this matter tends to be ignored in conversations about "the blessings God has given us," which operate on the presumption that whatever is in a person's possession is presumed to be given by God. Scripture—both OT and NT—provides many examples of ill-gotten gain. We read of wealth taken in battle contrary to God's command (Josh 7:15–26), gained by oppression of the poor (Naboth's vineyard in 1 Kgs 21 and throughout the prophets), cheated out of buyers by use of false scales (Mic 6:10), and so on. Usury, understood as wealth gained through taking advantage of someone's need, is consistently condemned through the Scriptures. Proverbs repeatedly warns against wealth gained unjustly (see 1:19; 10:2; 21:6; and 22:16).

A particularly forceful condemnation of ill-gotten gains can be found in James 5.

> Come now, you rich, weep and howl for the miseries that are coming upon you. Your riches have rotted and your garments are moth-eaten. Your gold and silver have rusted and their rust will be evidence against you and will eat your flesh like fire. You have laid up treasure for the last days. Behold, the wages of the laborers who mowed your fields which you kept back by fraud cry out; and the cries of the harvesters have reached the ears of the Lord of hosts. You have lived on the earth in luxury and pleasure; you have fattened your hearts in a day of slaughter. You have condemned, you have killed the righteous man, he does not resist you. (James 5:1–6)

Such holdings of property work against the logic of blessing. Rather than establishing a ripple effect of more full life, these possessions arise when people deny that life to each other. They are not blessings gone wrong and turned to curses; wealth earned in an unjust way was never a blessing as it was not given by God.

Ched Myers and Eric DeBode have proposed a reading of Luke 19 that provides a striking example of how rarely Christian talk about wealth pauses to ask whether someone's wealth is in fact a blessing.[12] In this chapter Zaccheus's conversion results in his agreeing to make restitution to those he has defrauded. He recognizes and confesses that his wealth is ill-gotten gain, and so he acts not as a good steward but as a penitent, redistributing what he has taken in order to restore justice. After that, as people "supposed that the kingdom of God was to appear immediately" (19:11), Jesus tells the parable of the Pounds, the parable that is central to contemporary claims about our need to be good stewards of the blessings God gives to us.

Myers points out that in this version of the parable, the king who entrusts wealth to his slaves is not a likely figure for God but one who has to gain his power from a distant authority, one who "gathers where he did not scatter, reaps where he did not sow." This ruler sounds more like Herod or Pontius Pilate, an imperial underling who uses violence to extort wealth for himself from colonized people. Once we entertain the idea that this nobleman is not an image of God, we can pause to consider whether his expectations of his slaves are in fact in keeping with God's law. While the law certainly does not forbid doing business, it is full of requirements about how business is to be done. One of the best known is the prohibition of usury. Yet this ruler demands that his slave have at least, if nothing else, lent the money at usury, so that it would have made a profit. The slave is punished because he did not violate Israel's law. The result is that the rich get richer and the poor get poorer (19:26, paraphrased). Then those who had tried to convince the distant power not to appoint this tyrant are slaughtered.

DeBode and Myers argue that this story is about how those in power act when confronted with justice, and it is intended to temper the optimism of those who think that Zaccheus' conversion means that the struggle is over. This is, in Luke, the last parable before Jesus' triumphant entry into Jerusalem. The parable serves then more as a prediction that Jesus will be rejected than as a general call for people to use wealth to make material or spiritual profit.

This reading is not common in the tradition. In fact, in my unscientific searches in the history of exegesis, I have never found any treatment of this text which reads it as Myers and DeBode do. Yet this reading is at least worthy of consideration and all the more notable because it points out how easily we can pass over the question of whether all gain in wealth is to be counted blessing.

---

12. Eric DeBode and Ched Myers, "Towering Trees and 'Talented' Slaves," *The Other Side*, May–June, 1999.

Blessing and Jesus

Myers' reading of Luke 19 brings us to what is the most difficult part of scriptural thinking about blessing: the relation of blessing to Jesus and especially to the cross. Directly following the parable of the Pounds, Jesus goes to Jerusalem, and the crowds cry out, "Blessed is the king who comes in the name of the Lord!" (Luke 19:38). Jesus is recognized and acclaimed as the blessed one. This is surprising, given the Pentateuch's account of blessing, because he is at this point homeless, childless, and riding on a colt. Soon he will be condemned, tortured, and executed. What does Christ as the blessed one have to do with creation or with Abram or Jacob?

The problem of blessing in the Gospels as compared with blessing in the Pentateuch is most obvious in the Beatitudes.[13] Luke's "Blessed are you poor, for yours is the kingdom of God" (6:20) strikes a discordant note in much talk about the blessings God gives us. Certainly the Beatitudes can be read as expanding the wisdom tradition that associates blessing with faithfulness (to be rewarded later) rather than with present material gain, and in the case of the rewards promised to those who are persecuted wrongly, this connection seems quite clear. The most difficult point to reconcile with the earlier tradition on blessing is the first beatitude, where the verb is in present tense. Rather than entering into the centuries-long exegetical arguments over this passage, I want to reflect on the Lukan version in the context of the many references to poverty within Luke and Acts, not simply to reconcile this understanding of blessing with earlier texts but to see how the Gospel's account of blessing can illuminate the development of the whole tradition.

The blessing named in the first beatitude is not poverty, but the kingdom of God, and yet inevitably some connection between poverty and that blessing is being named. In Luke, this beatitude is addressed particularly (though not necessarily exclusively) to the disciples. Luke 10 sheds light on that connection, when Jesus says privately to his disciples, "Blessed are the eyes that have seen what you have seen." What they have seen is Jesus himself, of course, but in the context, they have just returned from being sent out in pairs, poor and unarmed, to all the towns Jesus intends to visit. What they saw there was this: welcome in Israel for wandering strangers; healing of the sick and demons subject to Jesus' name; or in a word, the kingdom coming near. The blessed are those who see the in-breaking kingdom. They are not to rejoice in the power they have in his name over demons but to rejoice that they

---

13. *Makarioi* is not translating *bārûk* but *ʾašrê*. Nevertheless, *ʾašrê* refers to a person who has been blessed. While *brk* has a wider range of application and meaning, *ʾašrê* is a synonym in its particular contexts. See Mitchell, *The Meaning of brk*, 180.

are citizens of that kingdom. He himself rejoices, thanking God for revealing "these things" to the little ones rather than to the wise.

This passage suggests something about how being blessed, receiving gifts from God, relates to wealth, but particularly to wealth as power. The disciples rejoice because they have found power in Jesus' name to give victory over every evil. Yet they find this when they are sent out without purse, bag, or sandals, depending on the faithful of Israel who will care for the stranger. They are blessed because they witness not simply the power of God to defeat all opposition, but the peace of God, which comes barefoot and without cash, unarmed. It is precisely when the vulnerable disciples are welcomed that the cycle of gifts overflows in healing and triumph over evil spirits. As Gerhard Lohfink put it in a commentary on Luke 10 and Matt 10, "The renunciation of staff and sandals led to defenselessness and entailed nonviolence; it had to become a demonstrative signal of absolute readiness for peace."[14] The readiness for *shalom* initiates a cycle of *shalom*, as a blow can initiate a cycle of violence. Jesus teaches the disciples that God's peace and God's power are not at odds with each other. The kingdom is proclaimed by messengers who arrive with power not to dominate but to invite into peace.

Unlike those blessed in the Pentateuch with progeny, wealth, and land, these blessed, the disciples, are still homeless, still a minority, and still headed for Jerusalem. Yet the blessing the disciples receive in seeing the kingdom can also be understood to be about material well-being: Jesus tells them that those who leave family and land get them back a hundredfold (and eternal life), as Israel is called back to God (Luke 18:29–30). Blessing, as different as it may look here, is still about the fullness of human life. Rather than being given homes and lands and families for their individual ownership, however, the disciples are given all this because God's peace is breaking out among the people of Israel. What is given to them is not individual security of possession or a power they can own to use either for good or ill. They are taught to enter as supplicants and in that way to initiate a cycle of gift giving which provides them will all they need. They seek shelter; when it is given, they offer their peace. They accept food, offer healing, and proclaim the kingdom. This is the pattern of blessing as we have seen it from the beginning; it is not a static gift but a gift which opens out into cycles of fuller life, drawing creatures into networks of mutuality.

To be blessed and in a position of sharing God's blessing with others is not to be in a position ordinarily recognized as power. While the disciples have power in

---

14. *Jesus and Community: The Social Dimension of the Christian Faith* (Philadelphia: Fortress, 1984) 55.

Jesus' name over demons and all that would harm them, they do not have food for tomorrow or weapons or money. They have gifts, the greatest of gifts, to give, but they must also receive. They are practicing what political theorist Rom Coles has called "receptive generosity."[15] They are not givers who come in strength to deliver to passive recipients. Such a relationship can all too easily become domination. They give their gift but in the context of a relationship in which they also must receive. The blessing of God comes not as power or wealth that the blessed one must deliver to passive others. Rather, it creates relationships of giving as it creates full life. That can only happen when the blessed ones are also vulnerable ones.

It makes sense then that Jesus the blessed one, God's beloved to whom all lands and all people are given, is also the one who comes in poverty, meekness, riding on an ass. His poverty initiates a cycle of gift-giving. Family expands, property serves its function of providing for God's people, and the land becomes a sign of God's peace—not because God has showered wealth and power on good people who cared for it and used it responsibly but because God has sent the blessing of a vulnerable one, asking for shelter, for welcome, bringing gifts of peace. Even when these messengers of peace are not welcomed, when they are left hungry and grieving, they should still rejoice. Promises that they will be full, that they will laugh, are not only rewards for them but encouragement that God does not cease to offer blessing, even—particularly—by means of messengers who come in weakness. Blessing does not eliminate vulnerability but heightens it as the vulnerable are sent to make peace.

Given the contemporary uses of "blessing" to name wealth and power which must be administered responsibly and used to make good come about, it is useful to consider what happens as Luke's story continues in Acts, in the community to whom the greatest of God's gifts, the life of the Spirit, has been given. Peter and John have no gold or silver (Acts 3:6) and no political power. But when a lame beggar asks them for alms, they are able to heal him, only to be led then into giving testimony about the blessing God offers to Israel in Jesus, a testimony that gets them arrested so that they can offer further testimony with the result that "all people praised God for what had happened" (Acts 4:21). What they have is not any resources or influence but the Spirit of Jesus which calls all people into reconciliation, if they will hear. The text continues after that episode to tell us that the whole community used their wealth not as an endowment to be prudently administered, but as something to be put at the disposal of the community, laid at the feet of the apostles. They use wealth

---

15. *Rethinking Generosity: Critical Theory and the Politics of Caritas* (Ithaca, NY: Cornell University Press, 1997).

to meet needs, but they do not mistake its ownership for a blessing that rests on an individual or a kind of power to be treated with reverence. Rather, they claim nothing as their own. The building up of community requires a vulnerable trust in each other of the sort that Ananias and Sapphira were unwilling to embrace.

All of this ought to cause us again to approach blessings with both joy and a healthy fear of the Lord. Consider Elizabeth's claim that Mary is "blessed among all women" and Mary's own claim that "all generations will call me blessed." God's favor and gift to her, given after waiting on her consent, is to bear a child, which is hardly unusual as blessings go. But this child becomes the cause of her near-divorce, her homeless labor in Bethlehem, her having to leave home to seek shelter in Egypt, and the greatest pain a mother could know, watching her child be tortured and executed. Blessing is not safe or easy.

Blessing is still the gift of God for full life, and Mary is the queen of heaven who, as the traditional antiphon says, rejoices that "the son whom she merited to bear, Alleluia, has risen as he said, Alleluia." But the triumph given in this blessing is not about safety, comfort, or power, as we would ordinarily conceive it. Being blessed by God sets her off on a road of uncertainty. Luke gives to Simeon a blessing over the holy family that tells us much: "This child is destined for the falling and rising of many in Israel, and to be a sign that will be opposed so that the inner thoughts of many will be revealed and a sword shall pierce your own soul too" (Luke 2:34–35). The blessing, when rejected, can become a curse and it does not give security. Rather, it draws Mary into the vulnerability that is God's way of working in the world. Blessing is no guarantee of certainty or security. Jesus says, "Blessed are those who have not seen and yet have come to believe" (John 20:29).

Back to the Beginning

From this angle we can revisit the Pentateuch to see how this understanding of blessing in the Gospels could illuminate the blessings there. This is particularly important because in the common use of "blessing" in our churches, whether in graces or in stewardship appeals or in prosperity gospel materials, it is the OT that provides the major scriptural warrants. In offering blessings or advising people on responsible use of their "blessings" texts from Genesis or Proverbs are more commonly used than the Beatitudes. But if we begin from understanding how blessing is related to Jesus and his living and calling his disciples into a trusting vulnerability, what might we recognize anew about blessing in the Pentateuch? We have already seen that the blessing of God, as described in the Pentateuch, does not end a story, but opens it out to new participants and new circles of life. But does the blessing of God, on its way to fostering *shalom* throughout the world, arrive in power and strength, or does it come in patience and vulnerability? Is there any sense in which the poor are blessed in the Pentateuch, or is that asceticism only a Christian innovation?

This is in many respects a matter beyond my competence and surely a topic on which Jewish-Christian dialogue might be very fruitful. Nevertheless, without denying that Scripture holds a multitude of voices and a tradition of argument and development, I will make a few suggestions on how Christians may see the one Word of God at work in both Genesis and Luke.

We might note, for example, that the mighty gifts of creation come through the peaceful word of God, and the blessings of fertility and Sabbath are gifts which demonstrate God's power by making room for others to live, which leaves God's work vulnerable, for humans can—and do—abuse them. Such blessings draw humans into the full life of God's *shalom*, but they neither guarantee nor control it. Moreover, the peace of God's rest is a promise and hope to humanity, but it is also practice which demands Israel accept a certain weakness. That is, they not only do not have to work; they may not work on the Sabbath. They learn in the difficult Sabbath training of the wilderness manna that keeping the Sabbath is about trust in God and each other, not simply possession of time off. To become God's own people, they must become little ones or lose themselves, not as an end in itself but because God's power is shown in human weakness.

Similarly, regarding the blessing of progeny, Adam and Eve are not the only parents who can reflect that the adventure of parenting is no easy and safe possession of joy but always a cause of new vulnerability and new relationships in which trust may be returned or may not. The gift is a call into an unfolding and uncertain venture, a gift that waits to see what return the child will or will not make. We can reflect as well that Jacob's blessing leaves him wounded, and all of his attempts to parade his wealth as bribes to his brother do not achieve what he desires—peace. In fact, peace is given in a way beyond his control and only when he is face-to-face, at the mercy of his brother's understandable anger. The blessing that Jacob sees when he sees God's own face in Esau does not come to him because he was given the strength or wealth to turn the meeting to good but as a surprising gift given to him in his fear of the unknown.

The origins of Israel lie in the story of God's blessing Abraham with progeny and land. That blessing, again, comes not as secure possession to be administered for the good of others. Being blessed by God does not grant Abraham power and strength to use to promote the worship of God. Instead, it comes with a call to abandon home and to enter into trust. That trust eventually demands that Abraham even sacrifice the child of the promise, that he claim in his blessing no security, no guarantee of home and safety, and that he cling to a promise because the one who made the promise is to be trusted.

God's blessings in Scripture are about full life, but they are not about a comfortable life. Most importantly, they are not gifts which grant to some people power which they must use responsibly for the sake of others. Rather, they are gifts that leave us limping, vulnerable, and therefore calling for peace and inviting trust from others.

Conclusion

This survey, quick as it is, leads to a number of conclusions about how Christians could improve talk about "blessings." First, not all wealth is a blessing. Searching questions that discern the difference between blessings for which we should thank God and ill-gotten gain for which restitution should be made and penance performed must be part of our ordinary Christian talk about wealth. To praise God for ill-gotten gain is not only irreverent and dishonest but also scandalous, as it encourages others likewise to neglect examination of conscience and repentance for wrong-doing.

Second, blessings are given to initiate cycles of gift that promote well-being for all. They create dynamic communities rather than static individuals. In Scripture the particularity of blessings on a person, a household, or a nation refers to beginnings of such economies of blessing and ought not be taken as warrant for claiming blessing in a way that would serve, for example, American exceptionalism. The blessings given to Israel in Scripture are given that they may become blessings for all; Jesus is the fulfillment of that blessing for all nations.

Third, curses and woes have a role in talk about blessings. God's presence does not disappear when gifts are used to impoverish, dominate, or shut out the needs of others. Even goods which begin as blessings can become the source of curses when they are not rightly used. Although "Woe to you rich" is in only one Gospel, cautions about the dangers of wealth abound in the NT. Insofar as receiving blessings may put one into a position of power, clinging to that power or claiming it as one's own inverts the logic of blessing. Nothing in Luke's story suggests that the wealth of the rich man who neglected Lazarus was ill-gotten. But his using it for his own comfort and neglecting the needs of the poor man at his door means that only a fool would call that wealth a blessing. One of the great problems in the use of "blessing" to talk about wealth is its banality. Restoring a proper sense that blessings are, as Bonhoeffer might put it, free but not cheap will be one part of the work of disciplining that language.

Fourth, those who would share the blessing of God's *shalom* must do so through a vulnerable, receptive generosity, initiating cycles of peace by arriving in trust. That means that bearing blessing into the world is not the triumphal march of strength battling against evil but the trusting and risky confidence of lambs sent out in the midst of wolves to meet up with those God wants to call into the fullness of peace. Blessing is not safe; it can, and according to the Gospels will, lead to the cross.

By way of highlighting the significance of such reflections, I would like to consider a particularly influential view of blessing among United States Christians: *The Prayer of Jabez*.[16] I select this work because it is has been very influential and because it attempts to be a particularly biblical reflection on what God's blessings are. The comments that follow are not meant to deny that many people may have been challenged by the book to enter more seriously into their callings. God can use many tools. Nor is it meant to single this work out as though its claims were unusual. In fact, it seems to me that much of my critique of *The Prayer of Jabez* could also apply to the United States Conference of Catholic Bishops' pastoral letter on stewardship, although the faults there are considerably less flamboyant and paired with some admirable strengths. At any rate, the problem is not the one book, but a discussion of the one book can display much about the problem.

The Prayer of Jabez resonates at a number of points with my analysis. Wilkinson is quite clear that blessing is not a tame category. God's blessings "sweep you forward into the profoundly important and satisfying life He has waiting" (15). Blessing is not static but dynamic and growing, ever-reaching out to touch more people. Receiving God's blessing involves not merely receiving a gift but entering into a profound relationship of "trust in God's good intentions" (23). Wilkinson's treatment of the prayer that God would "expand my territory" in particular leads to reflections on the growth implicit in God's blessings and the sometimes terrifying challenges that come with that, challenges which lead us to understand our dependence on God. That is, blessings lead us not to independence but to further humble dependence on God, even as the blessings draw us out into further adventures.

---

16. Bruce Wilkinson, *The Prayer of Jabez: Breaking Through to the Blessed Life* (Sisters, OR: Multnomah, 2000).

There are, however, as many before me have noted, significant problems that cause even those good insights to go awry. In relation to the reflections I have just offered, it is clear first that this book (like most discussions of blessing) lacks attention to problems of ill-gotten gains. In the United States economy the history of genocide against Native Americans and enslavement of Africans is a fundamental question that any account of wealth as blessing must confront. In much more direct and recent ways, the global economy complicates questions of the innocence of wealth dramatically. To discuss praying that God would bless a business with expansion as long as "you're doing it God's way" (30) without entering into any discussion of what that would and would not mean in our day is to undercut any validity of the language of blessing. I wish that we could take for granted that "doing business God's way" would include discussions of workers' rights, environmental responsibility, moral investment practices, and production of products and services that promote genuine human well-being. I do not think that we can.

Second, this prayer lacks the ironic sense of power and vulnerability so important to the NT account of blessing. As we have seen, particularly in the NT and also in the OT as read through Christ, blessing flourishes when those initiating God's outpouring of gifts arrive in vulnerability and need, inviting others to join in a cycle of giving. Wilkinson treats dependence as a quality one needs to have toward God, but when it comes to other people, ambition and boldness to draw on God's strength are what is called for. When Wilkinson says, ". . . for the Christian, *dependence* is just another word for power" (59), he seems to mean we should depend on God mentally and expect therefore to be socially and materially powerful.

This is a crucial difference. In both the OT and NT time and again those who are blessed by God appear in the world as weak, small, unimportant, and poor. Their power to bless by drawing others into God's peace arises within that position of vulnerability. It is when they gain armies and palaces that things are much more likely to go awry. While *Jabez* speaks of trust, dependence, and humility, those are spiritual attitudes oriented toward God. What blessing looks like externally, however, is large numbers, larger influence, more power (including more money) to be used to advance the march of the good news. That is, blessing looks pretty much like any other material success.

Perhaps the most surprising point of contrast between "blessing" as I have been exploring it and as Wilkinson develops it is that his account is more "spiritual" than mine. The content of blessing, when named explicitly by Wilkinson, is growth in ministry and success in preaching or counseling. Because Wilkinson does not explicitly distance himself from the presumption that "blessing" refers to personal property, and because of passages such as the one affirming prayer that business should expand, he can certainly be read as implying much about blessing and wealth, but his specific illustrations are about blessing as expansion of ministry. Given the nature of blessing in Scripture, my attention has been drawn much more to material prosperity.

In fact, I would argue that the tendency to spiritualize questions about blessings (and stewardship) is not a way to make such questions more in tune with the tradition. Rather, it can allow us to sidestep the concrete questions about possessions, wealth, and the power they give. Thinking about the blessings of land, food, wealth, and family makes us much more aware of the danger—or the reality--that such blessings become woes. In our hands they do not serve their function of building up networks of gift that promote the full life of all, giving room for others to grow together and share in the expansion of God's *shalom.*

To be clear, I am not suggesting that Wilkinson lacks a sense of sin. He recognizes that "blessedness is the greatest of perils because 'it tends to dull our keen sense of dependence on God and make us prone to presumption,'" (63), and he even warns that people can easily be misled and deceived about the nature of blessedness: "We're steeped in a culture that worships freedom, independence, personal rights, and the pursuit of pleasure. We respect people who sacrifice to get what they want. But to be a living sacrifice? To be crucified to self?"(69). But because these cautions are presented as a matter of internal struggle, with examples relating to episodes of doubt and the temptations of pornography, the crucial questions about how material goods will be used so that they are part of God's economy of blessing never gets raised. Neither, then, do the scriptural accounts of how wealth can become curse.

God's blessings bear fruit in the peaceful interchange of gifts, in welcome and thanks, and in requests for help and generous material sharing to provide it. Such blessings are powerful, and all of them are rooted in the great blessing, the Word who became flesh as a poor man in a dominated nation. This blessing may be frightening, especially for those of us who have personal wealth that seems to provide us independence and security. God's way of blessing the world shows the strength of his arm by bringing down the powerful from their thrones and lifting up the lowly. The challenge is that we let our sense of blessings and stewardship be shaped by the sense of the gospel that characterizes Bonhoeffer's famed 1934 speech at Fano.

> There is no way to peace along the way of safety. For peace must be dared, it is itself the great venture, and can never be safe. Peace is the opposite of

security. To demand guarantees is to mistrust, and this mistrust in turn brings forth war. To look for guarantees is to want to protect oneself. Peace means giving oneself completely to God's commandment, wanting no security, but in faith and obedience laying down the destiny of the nations in the hand of Almighty God, not trying to direct it for selfish purposes. Battles are won, not with weapons, but with God. They are won when the way leads to the cross.[17]

---

17. Renate Bethge, *Dietrich Bonhoeffer: A Brief Life* (trans. K. C. Hanson; Minneapolis: Fortress, 2004) 31–32.

MONEY AND POSSESSIONS: A BIBLICAL PERSPECTIVE

Jonathan J. Bonk

My interest in the subject "Money and Possessions" may be traced to the social context in which I was reared. As a child of missionary parents, my most formative years were spent in Ethiopia, where, until I reached my later teens, I unconsciously absorbed the values and assumed the entitlements of material and social privilege. The boarding school that I attended was unapologetically a bastion of privilege. Ethiopians were permanently relegated to kitchen, laundry, garden, and custodial duties. Tinkle the small bell on the dining room head table and a bare-footed servant would patter in from the kitchen, apron scarcely concealing his own threadbare clothing. The school was surrounded by a chain-link fence, intended to keep us in and the Ethiopians out. Aware that we were members of a privileged superior class, we accepted, expected, and sometimes demanded the obsequious deference shown to us by Ethiopians, even adults. In our play and discussion Ethiopians were subjects of curiosity, sometimes the butt of ridicule, and on occasion even admired for their incorrigible bravery in the face of persecution, but they were seldom friends and never social peers.

After going to Canada to complete my education, I did not return to Ethiopia until fourteen years later (1974)—this time as a missionary with the Sudan Interior Mission. My wife and I were assigned to work in Tigre Province to lead a sixty-five member multinational relief and development team working with survivors of the terrible famine that would precipitate the collapse of Ethiopia's ancient monarchy and the murder of its venerable last emperor, Haile Selassie. By now a convinced egalitarian, thanks to my natural instincts, my Mennonite orientation, and my somewhat critical view of the *modus operandi* of traditional mission societies, I insured that each member of the team—an eclectic mix of medical doctors and nurses, hydrologists and water engineers, agriculturalists and mechanics, drivers and cooks, evangelists and interpreters—received an equal portion of the financial pot. We worked and lived together both in the field and at the home base. I regret to recall that my not-always-subliminal attitude vis-à-vis other missionaries bordered on that of the infamous Pharisee in our Lord's parable whose self-consciously conspicuous piety compared so unfavorably with that of the wretched tax collector who prayed nearby (Luke 18:9–14).

With the deposition of the venerable emperor came a palpable shift in the way that foreigners were portrayed in the public media. The country was in a state of relative euphoria, as its military junta (the *Derg*) proceeded to move the country from oppressive feudalism to enlightened socialism. For the first time in several millennia, peasant farmers could contemplate the prospect of owning and reaping 100 percent of what they sowed, since absentee landlords were a thing of the past. Millions faced the happy possibility of learning to read and write as the country's students poured into rural Ethiopia to teach literacy and socialism. Students, in turn, would learn to respect the peasantry and hard manual labor.

After completing our work in Northern Ethiopia, my wife and I were assigned to Kaffa province in the south, the birthplace of coffee. Here we worked with established congregations scattered across the province. Our primary role was to lend support to the work of evangelists sent by the Kale Heywet (Word of Life) Church. The church, seeing the emerging stress on literacy as an ideal opportunity, sent Christian teachers and their families to assist in congregational and community literacy in the hinterlands of the province. Poverty-stricken local communities were encouraged to construct simple single-room schools for which the mission would provide roofing tin and a blackboard and the Kale Heywet Church would provide the teacher. As the presumably neutral foreigner, residing not far from a small town that boasted a post office and a telephone, I was to serve as communications and finance conduit between the Kale Heywet Church and their employees, the evangelists and the literacy teachers. The monthly stipend for each family was roughly equivalent to twenty dollars U.S., while my net monthly income was approximately twelve hundred dollars. To this was added such benefits as medical insurance, a semi-furnished house, travel funds, and educational opportunities for my children. None of this was available to my Ethiopian colleagues.

I derived quiet satisfaction from what I perceived to be my ability to work in a fraternal, nonpatronizing way with these wonderful men and women. Our home was as open to them as theirs was to me when I would visit them each month to deliver their meager monthly wage (unless it failed to arrive, which frequently happened) and their mail. Although I was vaguely disquieted by the conspicuous material inequities that marked our lives, I did not know what could be done about it. There was an unwritten code among foreign missionaries that obliged one to toe the line when it came to wages and other forms of fiscal reward. If one of us were to break rank by being overly generous with our Ethiopian colleagues, not only would this set a dangerous precedent, it would put enormous pressure on the Kale Heywet denomination to do the same and would probably "spoil" the Ethiopian evangelist or teacher to such an extent that they would no longer be satisfied to work for such a modest amount.

Shortly following the departure of our senior missionary colleagues, government schoolteachers held a national strike. Although our teachers did not join them, several of them were detained by the police. They were required to show proof that they were legitimately employed by a recognized organization and not—as suspected—illegally striking government teachers. Since this was an emergency and the Kale Heywet Church headquarters was hundreds of miles away, where its leaders were dealing with myriad Marxist-revolution-related challenges of their own, I obliged by providing the teachers with identification cards on which was clearly marked the name of the mission society with which I served. To add emphasis to the fact that they were in good standing as teachers, at their request I provided them with receipts indicating the amount and dates of their monthly reimbursement. The receipt, like the identification card, bore the imprimatur of the Sudan Interior Mission. They returned to their posts more secure and apparently relieved.

Three weeks later the local bailiff served me with a twenty-three point indictment, brought against me by the very seven Ethiopian colleagues to whom I had so recently rendered service. Charging that I was a "running dog capitalist and exploiter of the people," the document then went on to enumerate my misdemeanors and reached its climax with the accusation that I had consistently defrauded them of half of their contracted wages. When I protested that the teachers were not in fact employed by me, but by their denomination, they declared flatly that I was a liar, presenting their identification cards and pay receipts as proof. Stamped on both was the name of the mission society with which I served. When I then offered to show the officials the individual contracts that each of the teachers had agreed to with the Kale Heywet Church, which were kept in a filing cabinet in the central office of the elementary school, they responded that there were no contracts and that I was lying. An inspection of the filing cabinets revealed that they were right; the contents of the file drawers had disappeared. Mission policy clearly stipulated that Ethiopian employees be reimbursed a minimum of what was then the equivalent of forty U.S. dollars per month, yet according to the Sudan Interior Mission receipts signed by me, these men had been receiving only half of that amount. I was guilty as charged. The only recourse open to me was to compensate them for their back pay and damages.

This and several similarly distressing experiences drove me from Eden. Acutely and humiliatingly exposed to a reality that had been long evident to Ethiopian fellow believers, the gross asymmetry marking our supposed fraternity—until then passively ignored—was no longer possible to conceal. The standard rationalizations and denials of the social consequences and theological implications of gross economic and social inequity in close social proximity proved to be pitifully threadbare. Having contentedly chosen to see these things through a glass darkly, I was blinded by the merciless clarity with which they now pierced my conscience. I understood as never before why the rich live apart from the poor, if possible, and why, when circumstances force them to live in close physical proximity, the rich must protect themselves and their possessions with walls, bars, dogs, armed guards, the society of the similarly privileged, and, if necessary, lethal violence or even war. This experience provided me with an opportunity to view myself from the vantage of the poor among whom I lived and worked, and the more closely I looked the less I liked what I saw.

My ruminations eventually resulted in the book *Missions and Money: Affluence as a Western Missionary Problem*, which was drafted during a 1987–1988 Yale sabbatical.[1] The argument of my book may be summarized as follows:

1. For the past two hundred years, and especially the last fifty years, missionaries from the West have tended to be materially wealthy in relation to a majority of so-called "mission field" peoples among whom they serve. This affluence is a byproduct of historical and social factors which cannot (and should not) be replicated by the poor today.

2. Since Scripture is understood and applied parochially, it follows that what the Bible says *to* and *about* the rich, it says *to* and *about* Western missionaries. If *wealth* and *poverty* were not such pervasive themes in the Christian Scriptures, we could be forgiven for meekly acquiescing to our culturally derived sense of material entitlement.[2]

---

1. *Missions and Money: Affluence as a Western Missionary Problem* (American Society of Missiology Series 15; Maryknoll, NY: Orbis, 1991). After fifteen years and eleven printings, a revised edition, now in its third printing, appeared. See *Missions and Money: Affluence as a Missionary Problem . . . Revisited* (rev. ed.; Maryknoll, NY: Orbis, 2006). The book was translated into Korean by Hu Chun Lee and published by the Christian Literature Society of Korea in 2010.

2. See Jim Wallis, "A Bible Full of Holes," *The Mennonite* (November 21, 2000) 6–7.

3. This material entitlement is based on ideologically incontrovertible proof that life—at least that proportion of it worth fighting and dying for—*does* consist in the abundance of possessions and that all good citizens should defend this ideology at home and enforce it abroad. While gross economic inequity in close social proximity poses profound relational, communicatory, and strategic challenges for missionaries, more serious are the complex questions of ethical integrity that challenge us as wealthy followers of Jesus in contexts of profound poverty.[3]

4. Since missionary training and on-the-field orientation do not adequately prepare missionaries to see themselves as those who in St. Paul's words *"peddle the word of God for profit"* (2 Cor 2:17) in contexts of poverty, it is important that the institutions and agencies responsible for training missionaries and facilitating mission work begin to address the issue directly, deliberately, persistently, and biblically through training, mentoring, and policy.

Missionaries and the Abundance of Possessions

When Western missionaries discover themselves to be materially wealthy relative to most people in the so-called "mission fields" in which a majority of them serve, they should understand that their good fortune is at least partially due to factors which cannot be replicated by the poor today. While the statistical data informing both the first and second editions of my book is now out of date, the integrity of its central argument seems to have been reinforced in the twenty years since it first appeared. More than twenty years ago I reported that throughout the period often referred to as the "William Carey Era" of modern missions the per capita gross national products of the developed and underdeveloped worlds widened from a factor of less than two to one in 1792 to three to one by 1913 and seven to one by 1970.[4] Since then, the situation has actually deteriorated for more than 20 percent of the world's population. According to recent World Bank figures, approximately 1.5 bil-

---

3. The data assembled by Richard Wilkinson and Kate Pickett in *The Spirit Level: Why Greater Equality Makes Societies Stronger* (New York: Bloomsbury, 2009) provides convincing proof that almost every modern social problem—poor health, violence, lack of community life, teen pregnancy, mental illness—increases in direct proportion to socio-economic inequities.

4. "Missions and Mammon: Six Theses," *International Bulletin of Missionary Research*, 13.3 (July 1989) 174–81. See E. J. Hobsbawm, *The Age of Empire, 1875–1914* (New York: Pantheon, 1987) 15.

lion people subsist on less than one dollar per day, while some 2.8 billion live on less than two dollars per day.[5]

Missionaries from Western lands, on the other hand, reflecting the culturally prescribed material entitlements of aggressively consumer cultures, grow ever more rich by the standards of a majority of the world's population. As recently as August 17, 2005, the "basic support" of a missionary family—good friends of mine who were en route to South Africa with a well-known faith mission—was pegged at $4,344 per month. An additional estimated $600 in monthly "ministry funds" would also be needed, on top of "outgoing funds" in excess of $19,000.[6] However inadequate $60,000 per annum might be for sustaining a North American family at levels of minimal social and material entitlement in a bicultural, intercontinental ministry, it guarantees them a place among the privileged in the social hierarchy of South Africa. How easily accustomed we become to our escalating scale of material entitlements, with one generation's luxuries mutating into another generation's needs. Peter C. Whybrow observes that "As America's commercial hegemony has increased and our social networks have eroded, we have lost any meaningful reference as to how rich we really are, especially in comparison to other nations."[7]

Obscured by the lofty ideals and economic ideology to which we attribute a way of life that is the envy of the world lies a more sinister history which cannot be legitimately replicated by our would-be emulators: centuries of brutal slavery that emptied Africa of an estimated sixty million of its inhabitants, genocidal conquest of three continents that issued in the obliteration of an estimated 90 percent of their incumbent populations, a two-ocean moat and a century of relatively cheap national defense, and maintenance of a privileged position through both the actual and threatened use of nuclear and chemical weapons of mass destruction. Such instruments of development are not available to the poor today.

---

5. Stephen C. Smith, *Ending Global Poverty: A Guide to What Works* (Basingstoke: Palgrave Macmillan, 2005), 1–8, passim.

6. In an e-mail dated August 17, 2005. This support would cover salary, administration, health care, and pension.

7. Peter C. Whybrow, *American Mania: When More is Not Enough* (New York: Norton, 2005) 38–39. Whybrow is the Judson Braun Professor of Psychiatry and Bio-behavioral Science and the director of the Jane and Terry Semel Institute of Neuroscience and Behavior at the University of California in Los Angeles. George Packer's appended opinion piece ("When Here Sees There," *New York Times Magazine*, April 21, 2002) is a poignant reminder of the global impact of media inundation of poor countries with pictures of America's "glittering abundance and national self-absorption."

While factors such as these do not mitigate the inherent economic and social advantages of a democratic way of life based on law and the protection of private property, they should at the very least induce a profound humility in those of us who consciously serve as exemplars of Christianity or development in the "underdeveloped" populations of our world. It is difficult to imagine what the lands of old Christendom would be like today if virtually the entire populations of the Americas, Australia, and New Zealand—together with large segments of South Africa and Israel—were packed into what is today known as greater Europe.

The political-economic ideology in which America places its trust is built on the assumption that is uniquely and manifestly entitled to perpetual economic growth and that such growth is possible, desirable, and necessary. In the two decades following World War II, "the expectation of plenty . . . became the reigning assumption of social thought."[8] The word which perhaps best sums up the plethora of secular values which influence all North Americans—including missionaries—from infancy throughout life is *consumerism*, the way of life established upon the principle that the necessary goal of human life and activity is more things, better things, and newer things, in short, that life *does* consist in the abundance of possessions.

On the other hand, new consumer cravings had to be discovered and created. Nothing could be more economically destructive than an outbreak of widespread contentment. Were a majority of North Americans to remain content with last year's shoes, hats, clothes, cars, furniture, electronic gadgets, breakfast cereals, detergents, perfumes, hair styles, and houses, the "good life" would sputter to an end. "To bring into being wants that did not previously exist" became the great mission of advertising and salesmanship, a process compared by economist Galbraith to a humanitarian who, while impressing upon would-be donors the urgent need for more hospital facilities, inadvertently overlooks the fact that the local physician is running down pedestrians to keep the hospital fully occupied! As Galbraith laconically comments, "Among the many models of the good society, no one has urged the squirrel wheel."[9] In North America we have come close.

President George Bush's urgent appeal to Americans to go out and buy things as a patriotic response to 9/11 was both appropriate and predictable. The slump in consumer confidence in response to the American sub-prime mortgage fiasco and sub-

---

8. See David E. Shi, *The Simple Life: Plain Living and High Thinking in American Culture* (New York: Oxford University Press, 1985) 248. Chapter 10, "Affluence and Anxiety" is worth reading in this context.

9. John Kenneth Galbraith, *The Affluent Society* (2nd ed.; Boston: Houghton Mifflin, 1969) 124–28.

sequent Wall Street crash brought America to its economic knees. Economists and politicians continue to wait hopefully for the day when large numbers of American consumers will once again rise to the occasion by living beyond their means, stretching the thin façade of prosperity over the dangerously fragile superstructure of personal indebtedness.[10] Only this will redound to the glory of the financial and political plutocracy that has long ruled in the United States.

Theoretically, of course, American Christians do not countenance such a reductionist view of life. Yet, like frogs swimming in a gradually heating pot of water, we find ourselves caught (or should I say, cooked!) in a way of life that our own Scriptures refer to as "idolatry" (Col 3:5).[11] Greed—*the insistence on more than enough in the full awareness of many who have less than enough*—is idolatry.

The culture in which most North American missionaries are born and bred has instilled within them the "need" for far more than their nineteenth and twentieth-century counterparts dreamed possible. Nurtured in and supported by churches which, for the most part, have long since succumbed to the "spirit of the age" that engulfs them, the Western missionary enterprise has not been markedly resistant to the "Laodicean" phenomenon at either personal or institutional levels. Perhaps too much criticism of the status quo would cost prophetic missionaries the financial support of a wealthy and self-satisfied church. More likely, the frog has been in the kettle so long that it can no longer get out, even though the water temperature is now dangerously high.

We are now haunted by distressing indications that for most of our fellow human beings, there neither *is* nor *can be* any possible road to our way of life, with its visions of ever increasing levels of comfort and consumption. The stark truth is that the dwindling natural resources of our planet are sufficient to support "developed" life for only a tiny fraction of its human population. This is the only economic gospel that we Westerners can authentically proclaim, since it is the one that we personally model. It is within the context of such considerations that missionaries are obliged to fulfill their commission to "make disciples of all nations . . . teaching them to obey everything I have commanded you" (Matt 28:19–20).

---

10. See James V. McTevia, *The Culture of Debt: How a Once-proud Society Mortgaged its Future* (Ortonville, MI.: MB Communications, 2010). This book tells how the United States drove itself to the brink of an unparalleled debt crisis. See also Carmen E. Reinhart and Kenneth Rogoff, *This Time Is Different: Eight Centuries of Financial Folly* (Princeton: Princeton University Press, 2009).

11. See Brian S. Rosner, *Greed as Idolatry: The Origin and Meaning of a Pauline Metaphor* (Grand Rapids: Eerdmans, 2007).

In *The New Faces of Christianity: Believing the Bible in the Global South*,[12] Philip Jenkins implies that the widening rift between the Episcopal Church and the wider Anglican Communion was not only inevitable but probably unbridgeable. A key element in his argument posits that while American and African churches appear to be using the *same book*, they are in fact reading quite *different Bibles*. Decades ago, the perspicacious Lesslie Newbigin said as much in his frequently reiterated recognition that for the West the Enlightenment is the final revelation, and everything, including the Bible itself, must be subordinated to it.[13] Enlightenment thinking does not infuse the hermeneutics of most majority-world Bible readers. The rift within the world Anglican Communion over the issue of church response to homosexuals shows how cultural conditioning significantly affects our understanding of Scripture.

African Anglicans, to take a well-publicized recent example, with their strong evangelistic impulse, surging memberships, and overwhelming social challenges tend to read the Bible *evangelically*, not only understanding its teachings to be authoritative in all matters of faith and life, but its words to be the *verbal plenary* revelation of God. Theirs cannot be a comfortable post-Enlightenment "Yea hath God said?" hermeneutic, encouraging believers to adjust their sails to the shifting winds of current cultural predisposition. The prevailing winds in Africa and in most of the majority world are, at least for now, blowing in a different direction. That American and African bishops should have reached an impasse is little wonder. The Tanzanian primates' ultimatum to the Episcopal Church on February 19, 2007, and Archbishop Peter J. Akinola's dramatic installation on May 5 of Bishop Martyn Minns as a "missionary bishop" for the Nigerian church's American outpost were in some ways not only predictable but may serve as a harbinger of growing rifts between Western and non-Western Christianities.

---

12. New York: Oxford University Press, 2006.

13. In her superb essay, "Defining the Indefinable West," Sasha Abamsky explores "the West" as a concept. She observes that in contrast to the "isms" that defined the savage conflicts of the last century, it is a "vague and spectacularly imprecise intellectual organizing tool," the cognitive equivalent of trying to touch the image of a hologram. "[It] means" in her words, "a state of mind more than a distinct plot of land." In the end, she concludes, "perhaps the only three constants in Western history are the totemic power of the phrase 'the West'; the flexibility of the definition and boundaries as it morphs to meet changing intellectual and geopolitical realities; and an assertive self-confidence, a haughty sense of its own infallibility and righteousness. In truth, because we *think* there is a West, as a result there *is* a West, and it *does* somehow encompass both the Inquisition and the Enlightenment; it *does* have room for both Marx and Dante; it *does*, in the information age, even have room to expand into lands formerly considered the heart of the East." See *The Chronicle of Higher Education* (March 23, 2007) B6, B7, and B9.

A Biblical Perspective on Money and Possessions

Readers of the Scriptures in most parts of the world will not exempt Western missionaries from biblical teaching on money and possessions. It is possible to envisage this teaching as comprised of two streams: a *narrow stream* that reassures the rich and distresses the poor; and a *broad stream* that reassures the poor and distresses the rich.

Old Testament Teaching that Reassures the Rich

Private property is not wrong. Encouragement of generosity and prohibition of theft assume the sanctity of personal ownership. Injunctions against stealing and covetousness, on the one hand, and provision for the protection of one's possessions, on the other, make sense only if ownership is presumed (Exod 20:15, 17; 22:1-15; cf. Deut 5:19, 21).

Wealth can bring happiness and prosperity. Although personal or socially systemic envy may incline to the comforting notion that the wealthy are miserable, in fact they are often supremely happy, secure in the present, and unworried about the future (Eccl 5:19-20). While economic calamity is sometimes a result of righteousness, there is a current of teaching in the Old Testament that promises tangible rewards to right-living people (Ps 128:1-6; Prov 3:9-10; 10:4; 13:4, 11; 20:4, 13; 1:5, 6; 28:19-20).

Poverty is not romanticized. Descriptions of famine in 2 Kgs 6-7 and Jer 52 make it clear that extreme poverty is something to be avoided (cf. Prov 14:20; 13:23; 22:7; 19:4, 7; Eccl 4:1-2; Isa 32:7; 41:17; Lam 4:9–10). The poor are sometimes to blame for their own poverty (Prov 6:6-11).

New Testament Teaching that Reassures the Wealthy

In the New Testament there is a corresponding strand of teaching that can serve to ease the conscience of persons of economic and material advantage.

Private property is legitimate. The followers of Jesus were encouraged to loan freely to the poor—an action that presupposes ownership, although the prescribed terms are not conducive to personal wealth creation (Matt 5:42; cf. Luke 6:34–35). Similarly, Jesus urges his followers to give to the poor. Since giving away what belongs to someone else is theft, the legitimacy of private property can be presumed

(Matt 6:2-4; cf. Luke 6:30). Simon owned a house in which Jesus was a frequent quest (Mark 1:29; Luke 4:38).

In those instances where Jesus challenges people such as the rich young ruler to part with personal wealth, he is not denying the right of his followers to own property per se. On the contrary, he challenges these aspiring disciples to forego this right for his sake—presenting them with a moral choice, rather than establishing a biblical principle (Matt 19:21; Luke 12:33; 14:33; 18:22).

Jesus' followers included several who were wealthy. The magi, for instance, were among the earliest to acknowledge and worship Jesus as the Christ (Matt 2:1–12); Nicodemus, a member of the Jewish ruling council, was a person of some means (John 3:1; 19:39), and Joseph of Arimathea was the rich disciple who made arrangements to bury Jesus in his own new tomb (Matt 27:57–60).

The legitimacy of private property is also implied in numerous parables (the parables of the talents, Matt 25:14–30; the unjust steward, Luke 16:1-8; and the pounds, Luke 19:12–27). These parables feature the use of money without any suggestion that it is intrinsically evil.

Old Testament Teaching that Distresses the Wealthy

Material possessions are not to be a primary goal of life. See Deut 8:3-5; Eccl 2:10-11; 4:13; Jer 9:23-24; Job 1:21; Pss 37:16; 39:5-11; 49:12-13, 16-20; 68:5-6, 10; Prov 11:4; 15:16-17; 16:8, 16, 19; 17:1; 22:1; 23:45; 28:3, 6.

Rights associated with personal property and possessions are not absolute. This is true for several reasons. First, God is Lord of all creation and all creatures (Gen 1–3). God's people are frequently reminded of this fact and its attendant implications. "The foundations of the earth are the Lord's," the grateful Hannah acknowledges in dedicating her firstborn son (1 Sam 2:8b). As Moses descended with the tablets the second time, he reminded the Israelites that obedience was the only sensible response to the One who "set his affection on your forefathers and loved them," for "To the Lord your God belong the heavens . . . the earth and everything in it" (Deut 10:14–15). The creator and Lord of all things laid out the ground rules for acquiring and using property and possessions (cf. Deut 10:1–22; 1 Chron 29:14-19; Job 41:11; Ps 24:1-2; Prov 22:2).

Second, rights associated with acquiring, using, and disposing of personal wealth are subordinated to an obligation to care for poorer, weaker members of society. That this was a primary concern in the OT is evident in the regulations that were to govern community life. The Jubilee year seems to have been designed to have a leveling effect. Its practice meant that any economic advantage gained by one person over another could not be legitimately sustained indefinitely or across generations. Jubilee was a time of fresh beginnings for both the land itself and for the economically unfortunate. Faithful compliance with the spirit of this provision made the permanent and unlimited accumulation of properties impossible (Lev 25; Exod 23:10-11; Deut 15:1-11). Perusal of the prophets makes it clear that the wealthy found ingenious ways to annul or at least circumvent any provision that impinged upon their presumed entitlements. Interestingly, chronic failure to implement these sabbatical provisions resulted in the demise and exile of an entire nation, as the chronicler's recounting of the fall of Jerusalem suggests (2 Chron 36:15-21).

Third, the triennial tithe was to be stored for the use of aliens, fatherless, widows, and Levites. In effect, giving to God and giving to the poor were inseparable (Deut 26:1–15; 14:22-29; Exod 22:29-30; 23:19).

Fourth, regarding loans, interest, and collateral, benefits accruing from the lending of money were strictly curtailed. Interest could not be charged on money loaned to a fellow Israelite. The rules governing collateral were deliberately designed to protect the borrower, rather than secure the lender (Exod 22:25-27; Lev 25:35–38; Deut 23:19-20; 24:6, 10-13, 17-18; 15:1–11). What seems to be a sound business principle—refraining from high risk loans—is dismissed as a "wicked thought" (Deut 15:9).

Fifth, harvesting was not to be so efficient as to leave nothing behind for the poor to glean (Lev 19:9–10; 23:22; Deut 24:19-20; Ruth 2).

Sixth, debts were to be routinely cancelled on a seven year cycle, ensuring that neither poverty nor blatant wealth would become a structurally reified, intergenerational phenomenon (Deut 15:1-11).

Seventh, employers were not to take advantage of poor employees. The poor employee was to be compensated "each day before sunset" (Deut 24:14-15; cf. Lev 25:35–43; Deut 15:12–18; Prov 14:31; 19:17).

Eighth, strictures were placed on the wealth of royalty. A king was not allowed to "accumulate large amounts of silver and gold" (Deut 17:14-17). Sadly, Solomon's disregard of these instructions resulted in the oppression of the poor and in the demise of his kingdom. It took seven years to build the magnificent temple, but thirteen years to construct his far more grandiose personal palace (1 Kgs 6–7; cf. 1 Kgs11:1-6).

Wealth is inherently dangerous spiritually. Wealth induces forgetfulness or defiance of God (Deut 8:1-20; 9:4-6; 31:19-20; 32:15; 1 Kgs 6-7; 11:1-13; Ps 119:36-37;

Ezek 28:4-5; 13:31-32; Hos 13:6). Wealth fosters a false sense of security, spawning pride in one's imagined personal accomplishments or entitlements and generating self-delusion that derails repentance (Ps 30:6; 49:5-6; Prov 10:15; 11:28; 18:11-12; 28:11; Eccl 5:8-15; Isa 5:7-23; 22:12-13; 30:9-11; 56:9-12; Jer 6:13-15; 8:10-11; 17:11; 49:4-5; Ezek 28:4-5; Hos 2:8; 9:7; 12:6-8). Wealth is frequently associated with overindulgence, gluttony, and greed. As noted, Solomon's unabashed self-indulgence set in irreversible motion a set of events that would result in the obliteration of his kingdom. One of the grandest and most famous despots of ancient times, he failed to heed his own vaunted wisdom, ending his reign as a tragic old hypocrite (1 Kgs 6-7; 10:14-29; cf. 1 Kgs 11:1-6; 12:1-24). Ecclesiastes, perhaps with King Solomon in mind, portrays the utter futility of a possessions-absorbed life. The wealthy frequently abuse personal power by their mistreatment of the weak and their contempt for the poor. This is the record of numerous kings in the Scriptural record (2 Sam 11-12 on David and Uriah; 1 Kgs 10:14-29, cf. 1 Kgs 12:1-24 concerning Solomon and Rehoboam; 1 Kgs 21:1-16 concerning Ahab and Naboth; see also Exod 23:6; Job 12:5; and Ezek 16:49). Greed, gluttony, and covetousness—sins that are ethically and morally disastrous at every level of human life—frequently underlie human acquisitiveness and self-indulgence. Recognizing this, early Christian theologians included these among the "deadly" or "root" sins (Deut 5:21; cf. Exod 20:17; Prov 30:11-14; Isa 57:17-21).

Further, if godliness with contentment is great gain, discontentment is at the root of the overindulgence that in modern times is promoted and celebrated as "consumerism." God's people are to be content, even with little. If Israel's response to crises involving critical shortages of food and water during their flight from Egypt was entirely appropriate in human terms (Exod 14-17), God's assessment raises serious questions about contemporary recourse to discontentment as an engine of economic growth (Ps 95:10-11). It is possible not only to have too little but too much (Prov 30:8-9).

Personal indulgence and deference to the wealthy compromise the integrity of those who claim to speak for God. As in the case of Balak and Balaam (Num 22), the rich frequently reject God's teaching about property and possessions, hiring teachers who for a price are willing to reassure them (Isa 30:9-11; Jer 6:13-15; 8:10-11; 14:14-16; 23:14-17, 25-32; Ezek 34:1-5, 17-24; Mic 2:6-11; 3:1-11; 7:1-3).

Wealth and prosperity are frequently the tangible symbols of brutality, disobedience, and endemic injustice, rather than signs of God's blessing as a reward for personal or national righteousness. The biblical text remarks on both the prosperity and the wickedness of Noah's contemporaries (Gen 6:1–8) and of the Tower of Babel builders (Gen 11:1–9). The prosperity of Egypt was built on slavery. The inhabitants of Canaan, a land flowing with milk and honey, were notoriously wicked (Num 13:26–29; Lev 18:24–28; 20:23–24). Sodom and Gomorrah, bywords for decadence of the most appalling kind, were affluent (Gen 13:13; 18:16–29; Ezek 16:49). Rulers of Israel and Judah were materially and politically prosperous yet often notoriously wicked: Baasha (1 Kgs 15:33–16:7); Omri (1 Kgs 16:21–28); Ahab (1 Kgs 16:29; 22:40); Jehoram (2 Kgs 8:16–24); Ahaziah (2 Kgs 8:25–29); Jehoahaz (2 Kgs 13:1–9); Jehoash (2 Kgs 13:10–25); Jeroboam II (2 Kgs 14:23–29); Menahem (2 Kgs 15:17–22); Pekah (2 Kgs 5:27–31); Ahaz (2 Kgs 16:1–20); Manasseh (2 Kgs 21:118); Amon (2 Kgs 21:19–26); Jehoahaz (2 Kgs 23:31–35).

One of the most perplexing theological conundrums has always been the question of how, if God is omnipotent and just, the wicked prosper while the righteous suffer (Job 21:7–14; Pss 10:2–6; 37:14–17; 52:7; 73:2–17; 92:7; 109:1–16; Prov 11:16; Eccl 5:8–15; Isa 1:10–23; 2:6–9; 3:15–24; 5:7–8; 56:9–12; Jer 2:34; 5:26–29; 12:1–4; 17:11; 22:13–19; 44:15–18; Hos 10:1–2; 12:6–8; Amos 5:4–7, 11–15, 21–24; 6:4–7; 8:4–7; Hab 2:4–12; Zech 11:4–6). The rich are often actively or passively to blame for the plight of the poor. "A poor man's field may produce abundant food, but injustice sweeps it away," Solomon observed and probably exemplified personally (Prov 13:23; Eccl 5:8–15; Isa 32:7). Preoccupation with material advancement signals spiritual bankruptcy, rendering profession of faith a hollow sham. Lot's fatal decision to choose the best for himself revealed his fundamentally hedonistic orientation to life. When at the last moment he took the angels' warning of pending doom seriously, his sons thought he was joking (Gen 13:10–11; 19:14). Eli made obedience to God a secondary concern, thereby forfeiting both his sons and his posterity (1 Sam 2:12–36). Religious orthodoxy without a passion for justice is a hollow sham. Oppression or neglect of the poor leads inevitably to judgment. Proactive concern for the poor leads just as inevitably to reward (Isa 1:10–20; 10:1–4; see also Prov 29:14; 2 Chron 36:15–21; Prov 28:22–27; Isa 3:15–24; Jer 7:3–7; 14:11–16; 22:13–23; Mic 2:1–2; Hab 2:6–12; Zech 7:8–14).

God is consistently aligned with the poor and oppressed. This theme infuses the story of the people of Israel, beginning with their enslavement and subsequent exodus from Egypt, and continuing throughout their history when the rich among them became their oppressors (Exod 22:21–27; Lev 25:39–43; Deut 10:14–20; 15:7–18; 27:19; Job 5:8–27; Pss 9:9, 12, 18; 10:17–18; 12:5; 18:27; 22; 35:10; 37:10–11; 68:4–6; 72:2–4, 12–14; 103:6; 107:9; 109:31; 112:9; 113:7–8; 136; 138:6; 140:12; 146:7–9;

147:6; Prov 14:31; 15:25, 27; 16:8; 17:5; 19:17; 21:13, 17; 10:1–4; Isa 11:1–4; 26:3–6; 29:13–21; 41:17–20; 53:1–12; 57:15; 61:1–8; Jer 20:13; 49:11; Hos 14:3).

The biblical record is unsparing in its criticism of those who either oppress or neglect the poor. Job, portrayed as righteous rich exemplar par excellence, evidently took an active interest in the well-being of the poor around him (Job 29:11–17; 30:24–25; 31:26–28. See also Pss 37:21–28; 41:1–3; 74:21; 94:1, 3, 6; 112:5; Prov 25:21; 31:8–9; 31:18–20; Jer 22:3, 16–17).

Righteousness (justice) always manifests itself in practical concerns with the well-being of the poor (Amos 8:4–7; Zech 7:8–10. See also Exod 23:6–7; 1 Sam 15:22–23; Job 30:24–25; 31:16–28; Ps 40:6–8; Prov 3:27–28; Isa 1:10–23; 29:13–21; 58:1–11; Jer 7:3–7, 21–23; 21:11–14; 22:3; Ezek 16:49; 33:31–32; Amos 5:4–24; 6:4–7).

True repentance involves economic reformation and justice (Isa 58:1–11; see also Neh 5:1–12; Isa 1:10–23; Jer 7:3–7, 21–23; Hos 4:7; 8:2; Mic 6:6–16; Zech 7:8–10).

Economic repentance is costly and rare. The wealthy usually deal with prophetic criticism by doing away with the prophet and engaging the services of those more tolerant of both their excesses and the unjust means used to gain and maintain material advantage (e.g., Isa 30:9–11; Ezek 18:5–23). A rare OT account of economic repentance by the powerful is found in Neh 5:1–12. Another is found in the book of Jonah. The wealthy, including those who are professionally religious, are seldom portrayed as repentant.

New Testament Teaching that Distresses the Wealthy

New Testament teaching about money is annoying, meddlesome, and distressing to those who are rich.

The pursuit of wealth and the accumulation of possessions are not worthwhile goals in life. Societies organized on the principle of steadily increasing consumption subvert Paul's teaching in 2 Cor 4:7–18.

Personal property is a trust, to be utilized for the good of others. Sharing of possessions was a significant characteristic of the earliest community of believers. Freedom from love of money and contentment with one's possessions mark the faithful believer (Matt 5:42; Mark 8:34–38; Luke 14:12–14; Acts 4:32–35; see also Luke 6:27–36; 10:25–37; and 16:19–31).

Prosperity is generally not an indication of righteousness, but proof of greed. Conversely, poverty and hardship, far from being indications of God's displeasure, are often inevitable consequences of obedience. Paul's hardship was directly attributable to his persistent obedience to his calling as a follower of Jesus and an apostle of the Good News (2 Cor 11:16–12:10; see also 1 Cor 4:1–17; 2 Cor 4:1–18; 8:9; Acts 20:22–24; 21:10–14). Zacchaeus was wealthy precisely because he was corrupt (Luke 19:1–10). Repentance for him involved giving away half of his possessions and making four-fold restitution to anyone he had cheated.

Christ pronounced woes on the wealthy, observing that it was virtually impossible for a rich person to inherit eternal life. To be both "wealthy" and a "disciple" was, with rare exceptions, an oxymoron. Freedom from the love of money and contentment with what one had were defining marks of Christ's true followers. In the Sermon on the Mount it is the poor who are blessed (Matt 5–7). For the rich, discipleship on Jesus' terms is especially costly (Matt 19:16–24; Mark 10:17–31; Luke 14:25–33; Heb 13:5–6).

Sins to which the rich are especially prone—greed, gluttony, and contempt for the poor—are closely associated with idolatry, impurity, and immorality. Even in a son's seemingly legitimate desire to share in his family's inheritance Jesus detected greed, warning his followers to be on guard against "all kinds of greed" (Luke 12:13–21). Paul urged Corinthian believers to be as wary of the greedy as they were of swindlers (1 Cor 5:9–11). St. Paul labels *greed*—the insistence on more than enough in contexts where others have less than enough—as *idolatry*, part of the futile way of thinking characterizing godless societies (Eph 4:17–5:7; Gal 5:16–25; Col 3:1–6).

Wealth and prosperity are inherently dangerous spiritually. Where one's treasure is, there one's heart will be also (Luke 12:32–34). Wealth is the natural culture in which pride and a self-deluding sense of security best flourish. It is usually fatal to the virtues of humility and meekness (1 Tim 6:6–19). Wealth deludes both individuals and societies regarding the relative worth of persons, coloring and distorting one's perspective on life itself (Matt 18:1–9). Despite the repeated insistence of Jesus that there is little room in his kingdom for the great and the powerful and the fact that most injustices can be traced to the greed of those who already have more than enough (Luke 22:24–30), his followers have always been tempted to favor the rich. Not personal ambition but the needs of others should be each Christian's paramount concern (Phil 2:1–4; James 2:1–7; 5:1–6).

Wealth dulls the sense of personal spiritual need, fosters alienation from God, and masks spiritual sterility. The Laodicean church evidently lacked nothing materially but had no room for Christ himself (Matt 13:22; Luke 12:13–21; Rev 3:14–22; see also Luke 16:19–31; 2 Tim 6:6–19; James 5:1–6; and 1 John 2:15–17). Wealth chokes the word, rendering it unfruitful (Matt 13:22; Mark 4:18–19; Luke 8:14).

Wealth comes into conflict with the demands of the kingdom. In response to the implausible financial advice from someone as parochial as Jesus, the Pharisees—many of them comfortably well established—sneered. This highly impractical man seemed to be out of touch with their reality (Mark 10:17–31; Luke 16:13–15; Matt 10:5–10; 10:37–39; 13:44–46; 16:24–28; 19:16–24; Luke 14:15–35; 17:32; 18:18–30; 1 John 2:15–17).

The New Testament holds out scant hope that select groups of disciples might somehow embrace wealth and remain resistant to its baneful effects. Wealth tends to produce alienation from one's fellow human beings (1 Cor 11:17–34; James 2:1–13; 5:1–6). Preoccupation with self, money and pleasure is a "last days" symptom of a way of life on the brink of destruction (2 Tim 3:1–5).

Christ identified with the poor, coming for the poor and as one of the poor. Jesus' first recorded public words in Luke related to the poor (Luke 4:18–30). He made it clear that God's kingdom was not intended for the rich but for the poor. While he came to liberate both rich and poor, it was nevertheless as a poor man—born in a stable (Luke 2), out of wedlock, subservient to Roman political and military power—that he identified himself with the human race. Judging from the circumstances of his presentation at the Temple, his parents were poor (Luke 2:22–24; cf. Lev 12:1–8). Not surprisingly and as predicted by the prophet Isaiah, his mission was to the poor, not to the rich (Luke 4:16–19; cf. Isa 58, and 61, especially 61:1–3). It is in the poor that his contemporary followers see and minister to their Lord (Matt 25:31–46); the poor are blessed, and the rich are damned (Luke 1:46–56; Luke 6:20–26; Matt 8:2, 18–20; Luke 14:12–14; Luke 16:19–31).

Christ's followers are to identify with the poor in practical, costly ways. Identification with the needy was a matter of paramount importance for Christ himself and has been a mark of all authentic followers since. Active practical involvement in ameliorating the plight of the poor is a sure indication of spiritual infidelity, or worse (Matt 25:31–46).

Early believers exemplified their risen Lord's concern for the poor in such remarkably practical ways that they "had everything in common," and "there were no needy persons among them." Sharing of resources is a sacrifice with which God is pleased (Heb 13:16). It is no wonder that early believers were not called Christians, but followers of "the Way" (Acts 2:42–47; 4:32–37; see also Acts 9:2; 19:9, 23; 22:4; 24:14, 22).

The New Testament record is replete with this theme. Paul worked hard to help the weak and in his farewell to the sorrowing Ephesian elders admonished them to do the same (Acts 20:17–38). The impoverished congregations of Macedonia pleaded for the privilege of sharing with the needy (2 Cor 8:1–15), and the church in Philippi contributed to the needs of Paul (Phil 4:14–19). Significantly, assurance of salvation for John rests in part on one's generosity to the needy (1 John 3:7–20; James 1:26–27; 2:14–26; see also Luke 14:12–14; Acts 11:27–42; 2 Cor 9:1–15; Gal 2:10/Acts 21:17ff; Gal 6:7–10; Heb 13:16).

God chooses to work through the poor and the weak rather than through the rich and the strong. Mary, humble fiancée of Joseph the carpenter, was chosen to bear, nurture, and train the incarnate Son of God. The cost to her was, not only her reputation and the life-long stigma of conceiving a child out of wedlock in a shame and guilt culture, but a life of distress and misunderstanding as the earthly mother of a man who so irritated the respectable guardians of Jewish orthodoxy that he drove them to murder him. This is the human cost of obedience and divine favor (Matt 1:18–21; cf. Luke 1:26–38; 1 Cor 1:16–31; 2 Cor 12:7–10; James 2:5).

Some religious leaders loved money, "peddling the word of God for profit" (2 Cor 2:17). "Godliness" could be lucrative (1 Tim 6:3–5). Jesus exposed the ugly reality behind the pious façade of self-justification and professional religiosity of some of his contemporaries, describing them as "full of greed and self-indulgence" (Matt 23:25). The failure of Christian teachers to practice what they preach so compromises their credibility as spokespersons for the one whose teachings and way of life they represent (James 3:1; cf. Matt 7:1–5; Rom 2:21–24). "My mother and my brothers are those who hear God's word and put it into practice," Jesus said (Luke 8:21; cf. Matt 7:21–27; Luke 6:46; 11:28; James 1:22–27). Paul is emphatic that the one who loves money is disqualified from spiritual leadership positions in the church (1 Tim 3:3). Those whose lives and preoccupations revolve around personal security are living as "enemies of the cross" (Phil 3:17–21).

Genuine repentance is inevitably marked by sacrificial generosity. True worship involves parting with what is most cherished (Rom 12:1–21). The poor widow's two copper coins—worth only a fraction of a penny—were of much greater significance than the large donations of the rich. It is interesting to note that Jesus does not appear to have been unduly concerned with whether the recipient of the gift was worthy or not. In this case the widow gave all that she had to a corrupt temple regime. Jesus did not regard this as waste since he was more concerned with the widow's motives than with the relative merits of the recipient. Jesus commended Mary, who "wasted" the expensive perfume on his feet (Mark 12:41–44; see also Mark 14:1–9; John 12:1–8).

Christ's followers are not called to self-fulfillment, but to self-denial. As an ultimate goal, self-fulfillment is an elusive, ever receding horizon. For the Christian self-fulfillment is a byproduct of serving others. To live a self-indulgent life is to fritter away eternal opportunity. Peter, rebuking Jesus for his determination to suffer, was disconcerted to hear that his understandable concern for his Lord's well-being was not merely inappropriate but positively satanic. "Out of my sight, Satan!" Jesus said. "You do not have in mind the things of God, but the things of men" (Mark 8:31–38).

As they encouraged fellow believers in Lystra, Iconium, and Antioch, Paul and Barnabas explained that the path of obedience would lead through extraordinary hardships. Indeed, "God has put us apostles [missionaries] on display at the end of the procession, like men condemned to die in the arena," Paul declared, invoking an image that would have been familiar throughout the brutal Roman empire, with its insatiable lust for bloody gladiatorial spectacles (1 Cor 4:1–16; see Acts 14:19–22). Christ's followers are not called to be first but last, not masters but servants. This is a constant refrain of both Jesus and Paul, borne out in their lives and held out as an example to follow (Rom 8:18–39; 1 Cor 4:9–16; 2 Cor 4:1–18; 6:3–10; 11:16–12:10; Mark 9:33–37; Luke 13:22–29).

Genuine repentance always contains a practical, economic dimension. It is important to note that the "fruit in keeping with repentance" to which John the Baptist called his listeners involved economic relationships. Further, Luke makes the point that when Zacchaeus repented he not only paid back four times as much as he had extorted but gave half of his possessions to the poor. "Today," Jesus said, "salvation has come to this house" (Luke 19:1–9; see also Luke 3:7–14; Acts 2:42–47; 4:32–5:1; and 10:2 where Cornelius is deemed to be a righteous man because he "gave generously to those in need"). Not religious orthodoxy but one's relationship with the needy is the true indicator of a person's standing with God (Matt 25:3–46; Luke 10:25–37).

Repentance by the rich is rare because of the economic cost involved (Acts 19:23–28). Jesus had many dealings with the rich. His message to them was that they too could be converted. This conversion would result in radically new relationships to their wealth and to the poor. Although the rich young ruler did not repent (Luke 18:18–30) and only a few Pharisees—such as the apostle Paul—became followers, the joyful repentance of Zacchaeus holds out hope for the rich (Luke 19:1–9). Timothy is urged to "command" rich believers "not to be arrogant nor to put their hope in wealth . . . to do good, to be rich in good deeds, and to be generous and willing to share" (1 Tim 6:17–19).

Not mental assent to a series of theologically correct propositions but obedience distinguishes the true followers of Jesus from frauds. Echoing Habakkuk and Paul, the author of the letter to the Hebrews reminds readers that the righteous person *lives* by faith. The NT understanding of faith is emphatically on practice, not mere theory (Heb 10:19–12:12). The faith for which the ancients were commended was deemed authentic because it issued in correspondingly appropriate conduct, no matter how odd or counter-intuitive such behavior must have seemed at the time (James 2:14–26; compare Hab 2:3–4; Rom 1:16–17; Acts 6:7; 7:53).

Implications of the Biblical Teaching

When within a given social context we are rich, it follows that what the Bible says *to* and *about* the rich, it says *to* and *about* us. Missionaries are not an exception to this rule. *Wealth* and *poverty* are among the most frequently recurring themes in our Christian Scriptures. While gross material inequity in close social proximity poses profound relational, communicatory, and strategic challenges for missionaries, more fundamental are the complex questions of ethical integrity that challenge any wealthy follower of Jesus moving in contexts of profound poverty. Among those of us who make our living by speaking *for* God and *about* God, Christian missionaries—perhaps more than any other professional religious group—are acutely aware of the need for consistency between what they say they believe and how they actually live.

I recall the story told to me by missionary-linguist Paul Thiessen, who with his wife and children lived and has been working for several decades among the Siamou in Burkina Faso.[14] As one of eight children born to a poor cobbler in a small Mennonite community in Southern Manitoba, he recalled the shame of having to go to school wearing worn, hand-me-down clothes and shoes and carrying a lunch of simple lard and bread sandwiches. Among some of his better memories was listening to his minister preaching on biblical themes that stressed God's concern for the poor and the prospect of frightful judgment for the rich. As missionaries he and his family settled in the largest village of Siamou-speaking people—a community of an estimated eight hundred. The most powerful man in the region was the chief, whose prestige was enhanced by his possession of an old broken bicycle. As Paul began the work of Bible translation, the numerous passages from which he had once derived

---

14. See the Ethnologue website for information on Siamou. http://www.ethnologue.com/show_language.asp?code=sif

consolation now made him uncomfortable. The tables had been turned. Caught in the glare of God's word as interpreted by his neighbors, the status he now occupied left him and his family embarrassingly exposed, raising deep questions about their integrity.

This, then, is the substance of my argument, here reiterated: (1) Western missionaries frequently discover themselves to be relatively wealthy within their ministry contexts; (2) when this is so, what the Bible says *to* and *about* the wealthy it says to and about the missionaries themselves; (3) since the Christian faith is above all a relational faith, lived out in actual social and cultural contexts, the whole gospel is potentially contradicted, obscured, or subverted by the good news of plenty, of which the missionary himself or herself constitutes "exhibit A"; and (4) in addition to the multifaceted communicatory, strategic, and relational consequences issuing from a missionary's relative affluence, fundamental ethical questions must be addressed because of scriptural teaching on the relationship between rich and poor and between God's people and their possessions.

Conscientious missionaries have tended to respond to this state of affairs in one of four ways: (1) they might associate primarily with those of approximately equal social and economic privilege and carry out ministry among the poor on a strictly "personage–to–personage" basis;[15] (2) they might assume a simple lifestyle that they hope belies the extent of their privilege, whilst surreptitiously maintaining the benefits of Western entitlement in critical areas such as medical care, transportation, education of children, and retirement; (3) they might shift the debate from the *moral/ethical* dimensions of gross economic inequity among Christians living in close social proximity to the realm of *mission strategy* and the merits of church independence vis-à-vis interdependence; and (4) they might adopt a radically incarnational lifestyle, giving up privilege and living as those among whom they minister.

While each of these approaches can be defended on practical grounds, I have proposed a fifth approach: the appropriation of a biblically informed and contextually appropriate status of "righteous rich."

---

15. Christian psychiatrist Paul Tournier was a leading pioneer in the field of "medicine of the person," i.e., understanding and treating people holistically. A prolific author, his first book, *The Healing of Persons,* was published in 1940. See http://en.wikipedia.org/wiki/Paul_Tournier for a list of his publications.

Toward a Missiology of the "Righteous Rich"

When I wrote the first edition of my book *Missions and Money*, my concluding chapter, bravely titled "Grappling with Affluence," made vague calls to bring missionary lifestyles and strategies into conformity with NT teaching on the *incarnation* as both theologically descriptive and strategically prescriptive, on the *cross* as both symbol of the atonement and prescription for the only way of life promised to the followers of Jesus, and on *weakness* as the channel of God's transforming power. However, I was unable to specify just what this change might entail. I invited readers to become part of an ill-defined, inchoate "Fellowship of Venturers in Simpler Living,"[16] and to this day I still receive a trickle of letters from idealistic, conscience-stricken Western missionaries wrestling with complex personal questions regarding lifestyle, sharing, tithing, children's education, health care, and retirement.

If the second edition of my book is more constructive in its conclusions, this is due in large part to the contributions of Christopher J. H. Wright, who wrote a chapter entitled "The Righteous Rich in the Old Testament,"[17] and to Justo L. Gonzalez, who wrote two chapters: "New Testament Koinonía and Wealth" and "Wealth in the Subapostolic Church."[18] To the extent that my thinking on these matters has moved toward a more helpfully constructive conclusion, I am indebted to both the writings and the example of Jacob A. Loewen (1922–2008) and his wife Anne, venerable Christian pilgrims, missionaries, linguists, and anthropologists.[19]

Each individual in any society is defined by a series of statuses that are acknowledged and recognized by other members of that society. It is understood that each status carries with it certain roles and their associated behavioral expectations, which vary with the social context. Human identities and relationships are shaped by the complex interplay of recognized statuses, roles, and self-images that comprise the society. In the words of Loewen:

16. Jonathan J. Bonk, *Missions and Money*, 111–32, passim.

17. Jonathan J. Bonk, *Missions and Money: Affluence as a Missionary Problem . . . Revisited*, 191–201.

18. Ibid., 203–21, and 223–35.

19. Jacob A. Loewen, one of the most self-transparent missionaries it was ever my privilege to meet, wrestled in deeply insightful ways about missionary roles. Particularly helpful is his essay, "Missions and the Problems of Cultural Background," in *The Church in Mission: A Sixtieth Anniversary Tribute to J. B. Toews* (ed. A. J. Klassen; Fresno, CA: Mennonite Brethren Church, 1967) 286–318. See also two articles co-authored with his wife, Anne Loewen, "Role, Self-Image and Missionary Communication," and "The 'Missionary' Role," appearing in *Culture and Human Values: Christian Intervention in Anthropological Perspective. Selections from the Writings of Jacob A. Loewen* (Pasadena: William Carey Library, 1975) 412–27; 428–43.

> Roles are the traditional ways people act in given situations. They are learned within the cultural setting. Very frequently the missionary is quite unconscious of this inventory of roles which he brings with him, and so never questions their legitimacy. But we must point out that even the very role of a missionary—a person paid by a foreign source to live in a strange country and to preach a new religion—is quite difficult for most people to understand.[20]

For a missionary's communication of the gospel to be effective, teaching must be accompanied by personal behavioral and character traits that are consistent with what is being taught. Role sincerity is absolutely crucial to missionary integrity. Those who make a living by being religious are often tempted to act and speak as if all the points they make are personal convictions. When this happens, *role insincerity* functions as a contradicting "paramessage."[21] As the old adage notes, "What you are speaks so loud that the world can't hear what you say."

Loewen points out that until a newcomer has been duly incorporated into the established network of relationships, members of a society will not know how to act toward him or her. This is why early explorers and traders in North America often found it necessary to become blood brothers to individual tribesmen. Once such a link had been established, the whole group knew how to behave toward the newcomer, even though the newcomer might not yet know what was expected of him. While most societies allow for a period of trial and error for newcomers to learn to play their roles appropriately, if a newcomer persists in unpredictable or inappropriate behavior beyond the allowed limit, he or she will be judged to be unreliable at best, perhaps even false.

A related problem arises from "roles" appropriated by a new missionary. He or she behaves in ways which, in that society—unbeknownst to the missionary—mark him or her as belonging to a given status. When the missionary fulfills only a part of expected behavior associated with the status and its accompanying roles, there are problems, and people may feel deeply betrayed or angry. For example, many

---

20. Jacob A. Loewen, "Missions and the Problems of Cultural Background," 291.

21. Loewen relates the story of the healing of Pastor Aureliano's wife, who was ill with malaria. The missionaries "pretended" to believe James 5:14–15 ("Is any one of you sick? He should call the elders of the church to pray over him and anoint him with oil in the name of the Lord. And the prayer offered in faith will make the sick person well . . ."), but their prayer for her was not effectual. Later, the Indian pastors prayed for her healing, this time with the desired result. When the missionaries asked why they had not been invited to participate in the prayer, Pastor Aureliano explained that it had been evident that they did not really believe, and that according to the text itself, their prayers would be ineffective. (Jacob A. Loewen, "Missions and the Problems of Cultural Background," 289–92.)

missionaries, in an effort to help people economically, have unwittingly assumed the role of patron or feudal master. When they then refuse to fulfill the obligations associated with that role, people are confused, frustrated, and even angry. They question the sincerity and honesty of that missionary.[22]

Should, or could, missionaries embrace the status of "righteous rich" and learn to play its associated roles in ways that are both culturally appropriate and biblically informed? The Christian Scriptures seem to draw a sharp distinction between the righteous who are prosperous and the rich who are unrighteous, and the distinction between the two is determined chiefly on the basis of their respective dealings with the poor. It would seem absolutely vital for missionaries to make the biblical study of this subject an essential part of both their preparation and their ongoing spiritual journey.

Representative of this genre of scriptural teaching are six representative texts—four from the OT and two from the NT: Job 29:11–17; 31:16–28; Deut 15:1–11; Neh 5:1–12; 1 John 3:16–20; and 1 Tim 6:6–10, 17–19. The translations that follow are from the NIV.

> Job 29:11–17: [11]Whoever heard me spoke well of me, and those who saw me commended me, [12] because I rescued the poor who cried for help, and the fatherless who had none to assist him. [13] The man who was dying blessed me; I made the widow's heart sing. [14] I put on righteousness as my clothing; justice was my robe and my turban. [15] I was eyes to the blind and feet to the lame. [16] I was a father to the needy; I took up the case of the stranger. [17] I broke the fangs of the wicked and snatched the victims from their teeth.
>
> Job 31:16–28: [16] If I have denied the desires of the poor or let the eyes of the widow grow weary, [17] if I have kept my bread to myself, not sharing it with the fatherless--[18] but from my youth I reared him as would a father, and from my birth I guided the widow--[19] if I have seen anyone perishing for lack of clothing, or a needy man without a garment, [20] and his heart did not bless me for warming him with the fleece from my sheep, [21] if I have raised my hand against the fatherless, knowing that I had influence in court, [22] then let my arm fall from the shoulder, let it be broken off at the joint. [23] For I dreaded destruction from God, and for fear of his splendor I could not do such things. [24] If I have put my trust in gold or said to pure gold, "You are my security," [25]if I have rejoiced over my great wealth, the

---

22. Jacob A. Loewen and Anne Loewen, "Role, Self-Image and Missionary Communication," 426–27, passim.

fortune my hands had gained, **26** if I have regarded the sun in its radiance or the moon moving in splendor, **27** so that my heart was secretly enticed and my hand offered them a kiss of homage, **28** then these also would be sins to be judged, for I would have been unfaithful to God on high.

Whether we subscribe to the "hidden hand of the market" as the source of all good things, or whether we detect in the regional, national, and global marketplace the not-so-hidden hand of the economically and politically powerful, it is clear that Job understood himself to be personally responsible for playing a proactive role in the material well-being of poor people in his orbit, and that this is the way God wanted him to be. At the very least, a wealthy missionary will need to be prepared to explain why God-fearing Western missionaries should be considered exempt from this ancient standard and whether God has changed His mind since Adam Smith in the eighteenth century so kindly rectified the muddled idealism of apparently unworkable Mosaic economics.

> Deuteronomy 15:1–11: **1**At the end of every seven years you must cancel debts. **2**This is how it is to be done: Every creditor shall cancel the loan he has made to his fellow Israelite. He shall not require payment from his fellow Israelite or brother, because the LORD's time for canceling debts has been proclaimed. **3**You may require payment from a foreigner, but you must cancel any debt your brother owes you. **4**However, there should be no poor among you, for in the land the Lord your God is giving you to possess as your inheritance, he will richly bless you, **5**if only you fully obey the Lord your God and are careful to follow all these commands I am giving you today. **6**For the Lord your God will bless you as he has promised, and you will lend to many nations but will borrow from none. You will rule over many nations but none will rule over you. **7**If there is a poor man among your brothers in any of the towns of the land that the Lord your God is giving you, do not be hardhearted or tightfisted toward your poor brother. **8**Rather be openhanded and freely lend him whatever he needs. **9**Be careful not to harbor this wicked thought: "The seventh year, the year for canceling debts, is near," so that you do not show ill will toward your needy brother and give him nothing. He may then appeal to the Lord against you, and you will be found guilty of sin. **10**Give generously to him and do so without a grudging heart; then because of this the Lord your God will bless you in all your work and in everything you put your hand to. **11**There will always be poor people in the land. Therefore I command you to be openhanded toward your brothers and toward the poor and needy in your land.

If the principles, ideals and objectives outlined in Deut 15:1-11 (cf. Lev 25:8-17) have any kind of legitimacy across time and cultures, one may well ask whether any nations today could be deemed righteous. Whether or not such practical concerns should be expected to characterize Western nations—descended from a Christendom that was and is far from *Christian*—the people of God, especially missionaries, must explain how the relationship between rich and poor is to be addressed in similarly appropriate and practical ways today.

> Nehemiah 5:1-12: **1**Now the men and their wives raised a great outcry against their Jewish brothers. **2**Some were saying, "We and our sons and daughters are numerous; in order for us to eat and stay alive, we must get grain." **3**Others were saying, "We are mortgaging our fields, our vineyards and our homes to get grain during the famine." **4**Still others were saying, "We have had to borrow money to pay the king's tax on our fields and vineyards. **5**Although we are of the same flesh and blood as our countrymen and though our sons are as good as theirs, yet we have to subject our sons and daughters to slavery. Some of our daughters have already been enslaved, but we are powerless, because our fields and our vineyards belong to others." **6**When I heard their outcry and these charges, I was very angry. **7**I pondered them in my mind and then accused the nobles and officials. I told them, "You are exacting usury from your own countrymen!" So I called together a large meeting to deal with them **8**and said: "As far as possible, we have bought back our Jewish brothers who were sold to the Gentiles. Now you are selling your brothers, only for them to be sold back to us!" They kept quiet, because they could find nothing to say. **9**So I continued, "What you are doing is not right. Shouldn't you walk in the fear of our God to avoid the reproach of our Gentile enemies? **10**I and my brothers and my men are also lending the people money and grain. But let the exacting of usury stop! **11**Give back to them immediately their fields, vineyards, olive groves and houses, and also the usury you are charging them—the hundredth part of the money, grain, new wine and oil." **12**"We will give it back," they said. "And we will not demand anything more from them. We will do as you say." Then I summoned the priests and made the nobles and officials take an oath to do what they had promised.

For those of us who are wealthy, it is sobering to find in the Scriptures scarcely any record of repentance on the part of the rich. Here in Nehemiah is one heartening instance, a reminder that no matter how complicated the issues or how deeply entrenched and personally vested the self-interests, it is possible to repent. What would repentance look like from the vantage point of powerful mission organizations in contexts of poverty? That is difficult to say, since the righteous rich missionary or mission agency, while informed biblically, must be defined contextually.

> 1 John 3:16–20: **16**This is how we know what love is: Jesus Christ laid down his life for us. And we ought to lay down our lives for our brothers. **17**If anyone has material possessions and sees his brother in need but has no pity on him, how can the love of God be in him? **18**Dear children, let us not love with words or tongue but with actions and in truth. **19**This then is how we know that we belong to the truth, and how we set our hearts at rest in his presence **20**whenever our hearts condemn us. For God is greater than our hearts, and he knows everything.

This passage, and many others like it, makes acutely uncomfortable public reading when wealthy missionaries serve in contexts of dire poverty.

> 1 Timothy 6:6–10, 17–19: **6**But godliness with contentment is great gain. **7**For we brought nothing into the world, and we can take nothing out of it. **8**But if we have food and clothing, we will be content with that. **9**People who want to get rich fall into temptation and a trap and into many foolish and harmful desires that plunge men into ruin and destruction. **10**For the love of money is a root of all kinds of evil. Some people, eager for money, have wandered from the faith and pierced themselves with many griefs. . . . **17**Command those who are rich in this present world not to be arrogant nor to put their hope in wealth, which is so uncertain, but to put their hope in God, who richly provides us with everything for our enjoyment. **18**Command them to do good, to be rich in good deeds, and to be generous and willing to share. **19**In this way they will lay up treasure for themselves as a firm foundation for the coming age, so that they may take hold of the life that is truly life.

Contained in these texts are the minimal guidelines—"righteous rich templates" in a manner of speaking—that should guide the righteous rich whatever their time or place. That such standards will be applied to wealthy missionaries by the poor among whom they live and work is a certainty, and they should be. The challenge for any wealthy missionary will be to make sure that he or she is seen as righteous, according to the standards of the group in which he or she lives and works, and above all, in ways that consistently reflect the mind of Christ whom he or she represents.

I have been involved in the training and nurturing of missionaries for much of my adult life. For the past eight years I have had the extraordinary privilege of serving Christian leaders and missionaries from around the world at Overseas Ministries Study Center and of assisting them through our community and programs in their quest for spiritual, professional, and intellectual renewal. It is natural that I should bring my paper to a conclusion by proposing that our training and retraining curricula and on-field orientations should include courses and forums for serious, sustained discussion of this troublesome issue. To my knowledge, systematic exploration of the dynamics and missiological implications of economic inequity in close social proximity is not usually a part of missionary training, on-field orientation, or postgraduate mission studies. Included in every mission studies curriculum should be at least one seminar exploring biblical teaching on wealth and poverty, the rich and the poor, with implications drawn and applications made for Christian missions and missionaries.[23]

---

23. Most Western seminaries offering graduate training for missionaries do not address this issue to any significant degree, and those that do tend to use my book. Sometimes I am called upon to come and engage in dialogue with students who have read my book. Other seminaries have invited me to conduct a seminar in their Doctor of Missiology programs. While I welcome such opportunities, teaching on the subject should begin much earlier at the undergraduate level. It is opportunities such as these that have embarrassed me into thinking beyond the book that I researched and wrote in 1987–1988 and published in 1991.

RESPONSE TO BONK

Liz Mosbo VerHage

Jonathan Bonk's paper reflects decades of thought and practice from an experienced and self-aware leader in the field of international missions. His landmark work on this topic, *Missions and Money: Affluence as a Western Missionary Problem,* and his subsequent work with diverse ministry partners around the globe reveals a practitioner able humbly to shine light on how theological ethics and historical narratives shape faithful witness and mission in various contexts. I am grateful for the opportunity to interact with Bonk's thoughtful analysis of the ways in which affluence, context, and witness affect each other around the world.

While Bonk's writings lead the church to consider the realities of economic inequities in the international missions context, from my perspective as a teacher/pastor/activist in urban and diverse settings within the United States, there is also much wisdom within Bonk's argument that informs theological and missional thinking stateside. This response will look briefly at Bonk's thought in dialogue with three assertions rising from and in response to his work: that *context* informs how we discern (as well as witness) Scripture, that economics are *ecclesial*, and that *reciprocal solutions to affluence* free both the rich and the poor.

Context Shapes Scripture

Bonk opens his paper by rooting his theological sensitivities in *context.* He names as formational to his thesis his personal experiences, particular relationships he formed and struggled with overseas, and various world cultures where he was educated and did ministry. He points out that hermeneutics for missionaries must be carefully dependent on the context of those hearing the Word. Bonk argues that a missionary *lifestyle* may communicate "a gospel of plenty" and get in the way of the missionary *verbally* communicating with integrity the gospel of Christ. If we reflect on the missionary experience formed in this "context crucible," marked by Bonk's often repeated reality of "gross economic and social inequity in close social proximity," the wider church is given a case study. Bonk says that for the missionary it is obvious why the rich do not want to live near the poor—and if they do, "[T]he rich must protect themselves and their possessions with walls, bars, dogs, armed guards, the society of the similarly privileged, and, if necessary, lethal violence or even war." The tension between the economic realities of the West and the two-thirds world is on stark, disturbing display in the missionary context, but these dynamics also shape the church in more affluent contexts in North America and in an urban center like Chicago. It may be easier to ignore the bars of gated mansion communities when they are in the suburbs, or to live and worship in contexts that do not bring the relative rich and poor into contact with each other here in Chicago, but the truth remains that gross economic disparity exists throughout our world and in stateside churches. The missionary may only have to look at it more often.

Whether we are seminarians, pastors, academics, or missionaries, grappling with context is a critical component of discipleship, particularly as it relates to discerning Scripture. Bonk nods to this concept when he discusses Newbigin and current conflicts within the global church, where "American and African churches appear to be using the *same book*, [but] they are in fact reading quite *different Bibles.*" For evangelical Christians few areas are as sacred as discussing how we discern truth in Scripture. While this is not the place for a full treatment of the question of contextual and missional hermeneutics and evangelical temptations toward biblicism, Bonk's insistence on doing contextual ministry requires the church to discern Scripture with more careful attention to context. John Howard Yoder, a theologian, churchman, and fellow Anabaptist missiologist alongside Bonk, helps us root the hermeneutic question in the practices and worship of concrete, specific congregations.

Yoder famously argued that the *church is* a social ethic, it does not have an ethic. In other words, simply by being the "people of God in the world [it] is a public witness, or is 'good news' for the world."[1] Yoder argues that the church exists in a *diaspora* setting, being the faithful minority sent into a foreign majority land to witness and prefigure the coming kingdom of God. A gift from the Anabaptist tradition is this invitation to see everything outside of the church as a foreign land, ripe for missionary activity of all kinds, because the church is so counter-cultural and so radically "other" in its position as resident aliens among the powers that be. This "otherness" of the church is why Yoder goes on to argue that, "What we do about social justice or about education should then be no less 'missionary' than what we do about crossing linguistic or political borders and communicating our convictions

---

1. John Howard Yoder, *For the Nations: Essays Evangelical and Public* (Grand Rapids: Eerdmans, 1997) 6.

to unbelievers."[2] Yoder's thoughts also deeply influenced the missional thinking of Lesslie Newbigin who charged western conservative evangelicals of the twentieth century with being especially guilty of overlooking how their zeal for foreign missions was "confusing the Gospel with the values of the American way of life without realizing what they were doing."[3] The historic evangelical temptation of appealing to a notion of "pure gospel," which may remind us of Fundamentalist and Modernist debates and the neoevangelical movement, is rooted in this misunderstanding of how context affects discernment of Scripture.

Since the early church began, disciples disagreed over whether Gentiles had to first become Jewish in order to follow Jesus, and the church continues to struggle with what it looks like to discern Scripture in context. As Newbigin explains:

> Neither at the beginning, nor at any subsequent time, is there or can there be a gospel that is not embodied in a culturally conditioned form of words. The idea that one can or could at any time separate out by some process of distillation a pure gospel unadulterated by any cultural accretions is an illusion.[4]

Neither I nor Newbigin nor Bonk is arguing some reductionist form of hermeneutic such as anything goes in terms of translating or understanding the Scriptures. These thinkers are not arguing some form of weakening the truth of the pure gospel but are instead trying to acknowledge the reality of context already at work. This is why Yoder insists that we discern Scripture together, within the church, as a community that is at once shaped separately from the foreign land outside our doors and also actively participates in mission work oriented toward and for the world. The point here is that if we do not withdraw to the church as the place truthfully to discern Scripture, another narrative and set of priorities is already working to shape us, whether we acknowledge it or not. That context may be the influence of pervasive assumptions that prop up commitments like consumerism, advertising, or greed, as Bonk mentions. Perhaps it is the conviction that we are in control and so deserve, demand, or can determine our own economic status. Perhaps it is assumptions we bring to the text from our social location, experiences, gender, race, or education. Yoder wants to tell the truth about those influences on our lives so that

---

2. Ibid., 7

3. Lesslie Newbigin, *Foolishness to the Greeks: The Gospel and Western Culture* (Grand Rapids: Eerdmans, 1986) 2.

4. Ibid., 4

we can be counter-cultural to the world and intentionally reorder our desires within the church. Then the church as a fellowship of believers is equipped to go back into the world, secure in an alternate set of priorities shaped by a communal, ecclesial reading of Scripture. Such a reading considers such issues as language, culture, economics, and race and also considers how to witness good news in the present context. I am reminded of the ways that doing cross-cultural ministry in the United States—whether in urban, suburban, or rural contexts—may mean encountering similar realities as those met in cross-cultural ministry overseas. Issues of translation, roles, and inequity deeply shape the message and the messenger. With Bonk, I would argue that without intentionally unmasking the economic assumptions by which missionaries have been shaped we risk battering the integrity of the gospel message and reforming it into our own image.

Economics are Ecclesial

Given that the church must discern communally what the good news is and how faithfully to reorder life around a gospel ethic, it matters a great deal who comprises the church. As Bonk testifies, economic disparities often separate us from each other, including missionary from disciple, and notably—Christian from Christian—due to discomfort, greed, guilt, or lack of access. Churches too often gather into local congregations that are based along lines drawn by the world, instead of doing the work to acknowledge what is already separating us, brother from sister, within the body of Christ. We must intentionally practice reading and discerning Scripture in community with those from diverse economic realities in order to be able to "re-member" the multi-faceted body of Christ.

For example, western readers of Scripture are often indebted to enlightenment and individualized thinking when it comes to economic decisions. Justo Gonzalez, who contributed two new chapters to Bonk's second edition *Missions and Money: Affluence as a Missionary Problem . . . Revisited*, draws on the NT concept of *koininia*, fellowship where all was in common, to describe the preferred vision of ecclesial relationships in relation to wealth. In another text, Gonzalez (along with Catherine Gonzalez) argues that it is through preaching and the sacramental acts of the church that local context is exhibited and also extended. A particular local congregation is "linked across political and social boundaries *spatially*, and across the generations and centuries *temporally*. To preach to the community of the baptized is to speak to those who are born again to see the world from a new, theological perspective."[5] So the acts of the church—proclaiming good news, formation, baptizing and celebrating the Lord's Supper, even having council meetings on Monday nights—do not happen separate from a context shaped by economic status, racial and cultural differences, etc. Community in the church can bridge economic divides by inviting us to listen to neighbors and friends whose context of having more or less, or needing more or less, now shape us. We reread the biblical imperatives to care for the poor differently when ideals become people with names and faces and children, when guilt becomes freedom to act as a disciple alongside the help of others, and when financial choices become one of the many areas of life where we repent and ask our friends to help us discern faithfully.

Reciprocal Solutions to Affluence

Bonk also confesses that affluence is a problem for the wealthy in the missionary context. He stresses that there is a narrow stream of biblical evidence that comforts the rich and distresses the poor, and a wide stream of evidence distressing the rich and comforting the poor. He concludes with offering a paradigm for missionaries to operate as the "righteous rich," a concept derived from OT and NT models. Bonk seems to be affirming the life-giving ways of using affluence for others, neither eschewing its benefits nor upholding an unspoken code meant to enshrine missionary wealth. Bonk's concept of the righteous rich may be strengthened by a more strongly articulated consideration of two concepts: the structural/systemic realities of *power and privilege*, and the corresponding need to practice righteousness/justice in *reciprocal* ways. Poverty and wealth carry with them dimensions of power and privilege within the missionary and ministry context, such as whose opinions on ministry are heard, whose job is in jeopardy, or who is able to afford attending seminary. This is why Yoder calls the work of Christ on the cross a primarily *political* act because it challenges all social and communal interactions that involve power to be submitted to Christ, whether from the sword or from access to a wealthy social network. Both the idolatry of affluence and the suffering of poverty harm our theological conceptions of ourselves and of others. The idol of affluence allows the rich falsely to believe that they are in control of their lives and their futures instead of dependent on God

---

5. Arthur Van Seters, "The Local Context," in *Preaching as a Social Act: Theology and Practice* (ed. Arthur Van Seters; Nashville: Abingdon, 1988) 22, summarizing the argument from Gonzalez. This collection of essays provides several engaging reflections, including thought on how social location of both preacher and listener affects interpretation of the Word.

as stewards of their possessions and all of life given by the Creator. The suffering of poverty pushes the poor to believe that they are intrinsically worth less in God's eyes, or in the church's eyes, and often throws life-threatening roadblocks onto the journey of discipleship.

Practicing what it means to be the "righteous rich" also demands that the rich repair their relationships with the poor with an eye toward reciprocity. The rich may be benefitting from systemic realities that keep or make the poor poor. They may not be aware of all that they receive or are given from the poor. The rich may also need intentionally to share resources and education with indigenous leaders in order to listen to voices from contexts and countries that do not traditionally have access to the trappings of wealth. (This is part of Bonk's ongoing work.) We deeply need each other across these contextual divides, and I am convinced that our witness to the world is dramatically improved when we do the hard, intentional work of reciprocal sharing and learning within the church.

If we take seriously Bonk's call to repentance in the church, this practice may pave the way for us to start realizing these contexts and truths that shape our ministry and scriptural discernment. If the church works effectively to repair the violence that economic disparities exacts on us and our neighbors, it might result in freeing us to rearrange our commitments, our time, or even the questions that we ask about our reality regarding wealth. Together we might then continue to care for the poor, the powerless, and the vulnerable widow, orphan, and alien, maybe even while we sit next to them on Sunday morning.

DECORUM AND DEEDS IN 1 TIMOTHY 2:9-10 IN LIGHT OF *EPHESIACA* BY XENOPHON OF EPHESUS

Gary G. Hoag

My aim with this article is to present a fresh reading of 1 Tim 2:9–10 with the aid of a scantly referenced ancient source, *Ephesiaca*, by Xenophon of Ephesus. This reading results from my doctoral research and forthcoming PhD dissertation.[1] It pertains to the symposium theme because an understanding of the instructions regarding decorum and deeds serves as a basis for discussion of and formation of a Christian view of wealth and possessions.[2]

To accomplish this aim I will introduce *Ephesiaca*, follow Vernon Robbins's five-step socio-rhetorical methodology, and offer conclusions.[3] In all, my argument has seven parts. First, I will broadly sketch the reception and dating of *Ephesiaca* in scholarship. Second, in analyzing the social and cultural texture I will explore the *Sitz im Leben* of the rich in Ephesus in the first century CE by using ancient sources that precede 1 Timothy and *Ephesiaca*. Third, in dealing with the inner texture of 1 Tim 2:9–10, I will present the text, a translation, and review scholarship and interpretive issues. Fourth, with intertexture I will present the lexical overlap between 1 Timothy and *Ephesiaca* and the findings that emerge. Fifth, with regard to ideological texture, I will examine the implications of the findings for understanding rich women in Ephesus in the first century CE. Sixth, in dealing with sacred texture, I will compare insights that have surfaced in 1 Tim 2:9–10 to related NT texts. Seventh, in conclud-

---

1. Gary Hoag, "The Teachings on Riches in 1 Timothy in light of *Ephesiaca* by Xenophon of Ephesus" (forthcoming PhD diss., Trinity College: Bristol, U.K., 2012). The dissertation has a more lengthy examination of 1 Tim 2:9–10 and other teachings on riches in 1 Timothy.

2. I want to thank my symposium respondent, Lyn Nixon, for her thoughtful interaction with my paper and for her subsequent recommendations to strengthen or clarify my argument. Some of the following footnotes respond to her input.

3. Vernon Robbins, *Exploring the Texture of Texts: A Guide to Socio-Rhetorical Interpretation* (Valley Forge, PA: Trinity, 1996) 1–5. Robbins's model has five steps: *inner texture, intertexture, social and cultural texture, ideological texture,* and *sacred texture*. In applying the model, I have chosen to adapt the order of the steps believing that context precedes texts.

ing I will offer a fresh reading of 1 Tim 2:9-10 in light of *Ephesiaca* as a basis for biblical interpretation and modern application.

Ephesiaca by Xenophon of Ephesus

Ephesiaca is a story about a young Ephesian couple, Anthia and Habrocomes, who fall in love in Ephesus and endure wild adventures that test their character and commitment to each other.[4] Hesychius of Miletus, a historian from the fifth or sixth century CE, provides the lone testimony ascribing authorship to a person named Xenophon with a provenance of Ephesus. This is recorded in *Suda*, the tenth century Byzantine Greek historical encyclopedia: "Xenophon of Ephesus, historiographer. *Ephesiaca*. It is a love story in ten books about Habrocomes and Anthia; and *The City of the Ephesians*, and other works."[5]

As *Suda* says the love story has ten books and the only extant copy of *Ephesiaca* has only five, Bürger[6] and Rohde[7] have argued that *Ephesiaca* is a second or third century CE epitome of a longer work. This was the majority opinion on *Ephesiaca* for much of the last century, which may be the reason many biblical scholars have not paid much attention to it.

Thinking the text to be intact and discontented with the epitome theory, Hägg[8] and O'Sullivan[9] have explained the *Suda* discrepancy between five and ten books as either a scribal error in the transmission of Hesychius or the *Suda* (the difference being between *i v* and *e v*) or by stating that the book divisions in the copy available

---

4. My initial research on *Ephesiaca* began in Greek with the text in *TLG* and in English with the translation in B. P. Reardon, ed., *Collected Ancient Greek Novels* (Berkeley: University of California Press, 1989) 125-69. While working on my dissertation, *Ephesiaca* was published. See Jeffrey Henderson, ed., *Anthia and Habrocomes by Xenophon of Ephesus* (Loeb Classical Library; Cambridge: Harvard University Press, 2009) 199-365. All *Ephesiaca* citations follow this translation.

5. For the Greek text see *TLG*: Xenophon Scr. Erot., *Testimonion*, 0641.002; or F. Jacoby, *Die Fragmente der Griechischen Historiker (FGrH) #419*. Leiden: Brill, 1969; and for English see Henderson, *Anthia and Habrocomes*, 208.

6. Bürger, Gottfried. "Zu Xenophon von Ephesus," *Hermes* 27 (1892) 36-67.

7. Erwin Rohde, *Der Griechische Roman und Seine Vorläufer* (Leipzig: Breitkopf & Härtel, 1876) 38-54.

8. Tomas Hägg, "Die Ephesiaka des Xenophon of Ephesus: Original or Epitome?" *Classica et Mediaevalia* 27 (1966) 118-61; and *The Novel in Antiquity* (Berkeley: University of California Press, 1983) 21.

9. James O'Sullivan, *Xenophon of Ephesus: His Compositional Technique and the Birth of the Novel* (Berlin: Walter de Gruyter, 1995) 134.

to Hesychius were different. The divergent views on transmission have also affected the dating of the text.

Proponents of the epitome theory have tended to date *Ephesiaca* as the work of a second or third century CE epitomist. Those who argue that the text is intact and authored either by Xenophon or pseudonymously have tended to argue for a mid-second century CE date. Adherents to the latter view, such as Reardon, have based their thinking on how scholars have classified the five early Greek novelists into two groups: the *Presophistic* (Chariton and Xenophon) and the *Sophistic* (Achilles Tatius, Longus and Heliodorus).[10] As there is overlap in language and style between the two *Presophistic* works, *Chaereas and Callirhoe* by Chariton and *Ephesiaca* by Xenophon of Ephesus, scholars agree that either one borrowed from the other or both relied on the same source material. For decades the prevailing and somewhat subjective opinion of Gärtner, Reardon, Papanikolaou, and others has been that Chariton predates Xenophon of Ephesus.

In 1995 O'Sullivan analyzed Xenophon's composition technique and concluded that he used formulaic phrases and repeating themes coupled with the influence of oral storytelling to create a new genre, the novel, which others such as Chariton would refine. In so doing O'Sullivan reversed the chronology of the *Presophistic* works and estimated new dates: 50 CE for *Ephesiaca* and 55 CE for *Chaereas and Callirhoe*.[11] This would place Xenophon of Ephesus, or the pseudonymous author, in the same general timeframe as the Apostle Paul, and with a provenance of Ephesus, it also locates *Ephesiaca* in the geographic area where the Pauline mission was centered from about 52–54 CE.[12]

While more evidence would be required to choose a date conclusively, it appears the majority opinion may have shifted to Xenophon of Ephesus predating Chariton. Henderson in the introduction to *Anthia and Habrocomes* says:

> If the narrative elements that both novels share is the result of borrowing, it is impossible to tell who borrowed from the other: is what we find in

---

10. Reardon, *Collected Ancient Greek Novels*, 5–9.

11. O'Sullivan, *Xenophon of Ephesus*, 30–98, 145–70. As *Charaeas and Callirhoe* is referenced in *Persius* 1.134, it is probable that the story was well known by 60 CE. Cf. T. Whitmarsh, "The Greek Novel: Titles and Genre," *American Journal of Philology* 126 (2005) 587–611; Bridget Gilfillan Upton, *Hearing Mark's Endings: Listening to Ancient Popular Texts through Speech Act Theory* (Leiden: Brill, 2006) p. xv. Gilfillan Upton dates *Ephesiaca* "roughly contemporary to Mark's gospel."

12. My intent in mentioning these dates is not to cause this article to digress to discussions on the authorship and date of 1 Timothy but to show that recent scholarship has located *Ephesiaca* in broadly the same timeframe as the ministry of Paul in Ephesus.

X. [Xenophon of Ephesus] a clumsy borrowing from Chariton or something clumsy that Chariton found in X. and improved? Or did both draw independently from an existing stock of novelistic elements. In any event, it is clear that X. and Chariton treat their material, whatever its sources, differently, and if overall sophistication is a sign of progress in genre, then X. should be dated earlier than Chariton.[13]

Based on composition analysis of *Ephesiaca*, there appears to be a growing consensus that it is plausible to read *Ephesiaca* as a first century CE document with a provenance of Ephesus. This opens the door for using *Ephesiaca* as a lens for reading texts such as 1 Timothy and passages like 2:9–10, which have heretofore been hard to interpret.

As the wealthy are in view in both texts, this exercise may prove helpful in offering a fresh reading of 1 Tim 2:9–10 where the function of some terms has been unclear.

Social and Cultural Texture[14]

The public record of inscriptions presents Ephesus as "the first and greatest metropolis in Asia" in the first century CE.[15] The city held this distinction in the Greco-Roman world for three primary reasons: Ephesus was the sacred home of Artemis and the Artemisium, it was the Roman Imperial Capital of the province of Asia, and it was a multicultural Mediterranean hub for transport, trade, and traditions. The significance of these three characteristics of Ephesus for locating the *Sitz im Leben* of the rich in Ephesus in the first century CE will be explored below.

Artemis, the Artemisium and the Rich

"Great is Artemis of the Ephesians!"[16] The outcry incited by Demetrius and the silversmiths was about more than their troubled trade. They judged that Paul's ministry had tarnished the fame of Artemis, whom "all Asia and the world worship," and

---

13. Henderson, *Anthia and Habrocomes*, 209–10.

14. Robbins, *Exploring the Texture of Texts*, 71: "Investigation of the social and cultural texture of a text includes exploring the social and cultural 'location' of the language and the type of social and cultural world the language evokes or creates."

15. *Die Inschriften von Ephesos* (*IvE*) 647, 1541, 1543, 1551, 1555.

16. Acts 19:28 and 34.

that her temple, the Artemisium, "may count for nothing."[17] Though the impact of Paul's ministry was widespread in Asia, he would be forced to leave Ephesus due to this uproar started by a merchant worried about the international standing of their city, its sacred reputation tied to Artemis, *and* money. Ancient sources confirm the centrality of Artemis in life for the rich in Ephesus.

Strabo identifies Ephesus as the birthplace of Artemis.[18] Himerios reveals the divine ties between the goddess and the city in ancient thinking: "When the leader of the Muses divided all the earth beneath the sun with his sister, although he himself dwells among the Greeks, he appointed that the inheritance of Artemis would be Ephesus."[19] Ephesus was her city.[20]

Antipater of Sidon called Artemis the "Queen of the Ionians" and named her temple one of the "Seven Wonders of the World."[21] It was widely known as a safe place of asylum.[22] Dio Chrysostom adds that it was a secure storehouse for the riches of Ephesus *and* the world.

> You know about the Ephesians, of course, and that large sums of money are in their hands, some of them belonging to private citizens and deposited in the temple of Artemis, not alone money of the Ephesians, but also of aliens and of persons from all parts of the world, and in some cases of commonwealths of kings, money which all deposit there in order that it may be safe...[23]

People visited Ephesus to see the Artemisium, honor the goddess, make offerings and deposit their riches in her precincts. Strabo recounts an occasion in which, Aristarcha, almost certainly wealthy as she was "held in very high honor," received an oracle from the goddess.

---

17. Acts 19:27.

18. *Geography* 14.1.20; 11.5.1–4.

19. *Oration* 60.3; Christine M. Thomas, "At Home in the City of Artemis: Religion in Ephesos in the Literary Imagination of the Roman Period," in *Ephesos Metropolis of Asia: An Interdisciplinary Approach to its Archaeology, Religion, and Culture* (ed. Helmut Koester; Valley Forge, PA: Trinity, 1995) 97.

20. Plato, *Cratylus* 406B; Richard Oster, "The Ephesian Artemis as an Opponent of Early Christianity," *Jahrbuch für Antike und Christentum* 19 (1976) 39. Cf. Strabo, *Geography* 14.1.6; Pausanias, *Guide to Greece* 4.31.8; 9.2.3.

21. *Greek Anthology* 9.970; 9.58.

22. Apollonius of Tyana, *Letter* 65. Cf. Strabo, *Geography* 14.1.23; Suetonius, *Tiberius* 37; Tacitus, *Annals* 3.60–63.

23. *Oration* 31.54. This testimony is dated ca. 97–112 CE.

> When the Phocaeans where setting sail from their homeland an oracle was delivered to them, it is said, to use for their voyage a guide received from the Ephesian Artemis. Accordingly, some of them put in at Ephesus and inquired in what way they might procure from the goddess what had been enjoined upon them. Now the goddess in a dream, it is said, had stood beside Aristarcha, one of the women held in very high honor, and commanded her to sail away with the Phocaeans taking with her a certain reproduction [of Artemis] which was among the sacred images. This done, and the colony finally settled, they not only established the temple, but also did Aristarcha the exceptional honor of appointing her priestess. Further, in the colonial cities [of Marseilles] the people everywhere do this goddess honors of the first rank.[24]

By recruiting the rich in this way, the glory of the goddess spread, additional offerings were given, more temples erected, and the profits for the silversmiths grew. Aristarcha was not alone in this. Inscriptions testify that rich Ephesians who funded the priesthood of Artemis would in return receive honor and positions of status. One inscription illustrates this in recording the name of a high priestess, Claudia Ammion, the wife of P. Gavius Capito, the high priest of Asia.[25]

Artemis expected the support of rich people *and* civic leaders. Vitruvius records that a magistrate was fined for failing to perform an annual sacrifice where a shepherd found the marble used in the Artemisium.[26] Artemis *owned* the rich, and the rich *owned* Artemis, *literally*. The rich of the slope houses did not have to go to the temple to see the goddess; they had statues of her at home.[27] She watched over them and their riches and secured their future. Those who served her were lauded for their *eusebeia*, "piety," to the goddess *and* to Rome.[28]

---

24. *Geography* 4.1.4–5. Strabo speaks of other temples of Artemis. Cf. J. Murphy-O'Connor, *St. Paul's Ephesus: Texts and Archaeology* (Collegeville, MN: Liturgical, 2008) 6.

25. *IvE* 681; E. A. Judge and James R. Harrison, "Ethical Terms in St. Paul and the Inscriptions of Ephesus," in *The First Christians in the Roman World: Augustan and New Testament Essays* (WUNT 229; Tübingen: Mohr Siebeck, 2008) 377. For further examples of rich supporters of Artemis see *IvE* 430, 492, 989; cf. the first century CE *kourētes* lists in *IvE* 1001–1020.

26. *On Architecture* 10.2.11–15.

27. Maria Aurenhammer, "Sculptures of Gods and Heroes from Ephesos," in *Ephesos Metropolis of Asia: An Interdisciplinary Approach to its Archaeology, Religion and Culture* (ed. Helmut Koester; Valley Forge, PA: Trinity, 1995) 276, figures 2–3.

28. BAGD, 326. *IvE* 27 provides a lengthy Ephesian example of the *eusebeia* of G. Vibius Salutaris in 104 .CE

The Rich in the Roman Imperial Capital of Asia

The Romanization of Ephesus was a key factor that ensconced the rich in leadership roles for generations. In 133 BCE Ephesus became part of the Roman Republic. In 126 BCE Manius Aquilius restructured its government. He implemented a two-house system with a *boulē*, "council," fixed at 450 members, and an *ekklēsia tou dēmou*, an "assembly of the people," led by a *grammateus*, "secretary."[29] Jerome Murphy-O'Connor reveals Rome's motives.

> Rome was too clever to modify the traditional institutions of the Greek cities, because that would have been deeply resented. Instead it preserved the form while radically changing the content. It introduced a property qualification for membership in the *ekklesia* and tended to grant its members life tenure. Thus Rome ensures that whatever power the city retained was wielded by those with an aversion to change and a strong personal interest in preserving the *status quo*.[30]

In this action, Rome intentionally shifted the role of the council from serving as executive committee of a rotating assembly to becoming a powerful perch where rich property owners could sit for life. Though the people ran Ephesus during the Republic, the rich ran it in the Empire and would be rewarded for showing respect to Rome.

In 29 BCE Augustus named Ephesus the capital of the province of Asia and set up sacred precincts to Dea Roma and Divus Iulius. Oversight of the imperial cult was assigned to the *koinon*, "the new provincial nobility," wealthy people who served as the interface between Rome and Asia, and in reciprocity could be admitted into the equestrian order.[31] Augustus also answered the zeal of Ephesian leaders to support Rome with building projects. These contributed to the prosperity of the city that continued through the Julio-Claudian era (27 BCE–68 CE).[32]

As Paul's ministry in Ephesus flourished, it threatened not only the name of Artemis throughout Asia but also the standing of the city with Rome. This may explain why the riot in Acts 19:23–41 was able to be controlled so quickly by the

---

29. T. Robert S. Broughton, "Roman Asia," in *An Economic Survey of Ancient Rome* (ed. Tenney Frank; Baltimore: Johns Hopkins University Press, 1938) 814.

30. Murphy-O'Connor, *St. Paul's Ephesus*, 34.

31. Guy M. Rogers, *The Sacred Identity of Ephesos: Foundation Myths of a Roman City* (London: Routledge, 1991) 9 on IvE 27. Cf. Paul R. Trebilco, *The Early Christians in Ephesus from Paul to Ignatius* (Grand Rapids: Eerdmans, 2007) 14.

32. *IvE* VIII, 2, pp. 88–99, 104–11 for inscriptions that feature *Iulios* or *Klaudios* in this era.

grammateus, no doubt a rich, influential leader. Neither this leader nor the people wanted word of a riot to reach Rome. The rich in Ephesus were *respectfully* Roman, which secured their place locally, their status provincially, and their prominence internationally. Simultaneously, they were *richly* Greek.

The Rich in the Multicultural Mediterranean Hub of Transport, Trade, and Traditions

Ephesus was located at the intersection of two main roads, and its harbor was the gateway to the world. Strabo and Pliny cite Artemidorus, an Ephesian geographer, who tells of the two key roads in antiquity: the "common highway" which connected East and West, India to Ephesus, and the North-South road in western Asia Minor.[33] To and from this port Ephesians could travel the world and welcome visitors. At the confluence of the roads and the harbor was the emporium, which Strabo described: "And the city, because of its advantageous situation in other respects, grows daily more prosperous, and is the largest emporium in Asia this side of the Taurus."[34] Here rich Ephesians and visitors could buy, sell, and trade the luxuries of the world.[35]

People with varying levels of wealth and from different social stations mixed in this multicultural city. To illustrate this Murphy-O'Conner cites a stele of fishermen and fishmongers who contributed toward the building of a customs house (c. 54–59 CE).[36] Horsley concurs that the stele reflects a wide range of ethnic diversity and social status.[37] Harland found this stele shows that Ephesians both worked *and* worshipped together. It had dual altars with a shrine to the gods of Samothrace deemed the "divine protectors of those at sea" and the "patron deities of the fisherman and fish dealers."[38] In association meetings it would have been common to have meals

---

33. Pliny 2.242-3; cf. Strabo, *Geography* 14.2.29; also Diodorus Siculus 3.11.2 attests to the accuracy of Artemidorus.

34. *Geography* 14.1.24.

35. Ephesians enjoyed wares from Persia to Italy. Cf. Athenaeus 525c, 689a; Susanne Zabehlicky-Scheffenegger, "Subsidiary Factories of Italian Sigillata Potters," in *Ephesos Metropolis of Asia: An Interdisciplinary Approach to its Archaeology, Religion and Culture* (ed. Helmut Koester; Valley Forge, PA: Trinity, 1995) 217-28; Philip A. Harland, *Associations, Synagogues, and Congregations: Claiming a Place in Ancient Mediterranean Society* (Minneapolis: Fortress, 2003) 38-44.

36. Murphy-O'Connor, *St. Paul's Ephesus*, 28.

37. S. R. Llewelyn and G. H. R. Horsley, eds., *New Documents Illustrating Early Christianity* (North Ryde, NSW: Ancient History Documentary Research Centre, Macquarie University, 1981-2002) 108-9.

38. *IvE* 20.70-71.

and make sacrifices to these gods, and the rich are immortalized for paying for these activities.[39]

The rich also paid for community entertainment and events that celebrated their Greek traditions.[40] Strabo adds: "A general festival is held there annually. And by certain custom the youths vie for honor, particularly in the splendor of their banquets."[41]

As part of their Greek culture, philosophical schools would have been active in Ephesus: Stoics, Cynics, Epicureans, and others. In relation to the rich Malherbe has shown that their teaching on handling riches ranged from being money-grubbers to rejecting all wealth.[42] No doubt, these groups influenced popular thinking and the rich who listened to them.

A guiding Greek influence on rich Ephesian men came from their training as *ephebes*. Adolescent males considered to be future leading citizens would receive civil leadership and military training. The instruction included the liturgies expected of them: to confer benefits on those who can make a return and from whom they could expect a return.[43] In this light *Ephebes* were taught the social and cultural rules for handling riches as benefactors for the city.

The lifestyle expectations of rich Ephesian women were shaped by Roman sumptuary laws such as *lex Fannia* (161 BCE) and *lex Licinia sumptuaria* (143 BCE). Additionally, with Roman building projects came statues of the Emperors *and* their

---

39. *IvE* 2061, 3066. Cf. Harland, *Associations*, 40, and Heinrich Zabehlicky, "Preliminary Views of the Ephesian Harbor," in *Ephesos Metropolis of Asia: An Interdisciplinary Approach to its Archaeology, Religion and Culture* (ed. Helmut Koester; Valley Forge, PA: Trinity, 1995) 201–15.

40. Inscription evidence shows rich benefactors paid for Dionysian performers: *IvE* 22; athletes of Heracles in *IvE* 1084, 1087, 1088, 1089, 1909, 1122; and gladiators in *IvE* 225, 240, 241; and *IGladiateurs* 200, 201, 202, 204, 205, 206, 207, 208.

41. *Geography* 14.1.20. *Ephesiaca*, the ancient testimony to be explored further in this article, offers perhaps the best illustration of this annual festival in 1.1–2. See also *IvE* 27.

42. For recent exploration of riches in a related passage, 1 Tim 6:17–19, see Abraham J. Malherbe, "Godliness, Self-Sufficiency, Greed, and the Enjoyment of Wealth: 1 Timothy 6:3–19, Part 1," *NovT* 52 (2010) 376–405; and "Godliness, Self-Sufficiency, Greed, and the Enjoyment of Wealth: 1 Timothy 6:3–19, Part 2," *NovT* 53 (2011) 73–96. Malherbe has been profoundly helpful in locating the polemic and paraenetic passages on riches in 1 Timothy within the greater realm of Greco-Roman moral philosophy and popular maxims in the ancient Mediterranean world. To complement his work I explored Ephesian evidence for this article and even more deeply in my forthcoming dissertation.

43. On the cycle of reciprocity see A. R. Hands, *Charities and Social Aid in Greece and Rome* (Ithaca, NY: Cornell University Press, 1968) 30–31, 118–20; and J. Bassler, *God & Mammon: Asking for Money in the New Testament* (Nashville: Abingdon, 1991) 17–33.

wives. The way these ladies were depicted in statuary also undoubtedly affected the deportment of rich women in Ephesus.[44]

Summary: Sitz im Leben of the Rich in Ephesus in the first century CE

For the rich in Ephesus life consisted of enjoying the amenities of living in a multicultural Mediterranean hub, while also maintaining their place in relationship to the gods and the people with whom they lived, worked, and worshipped. By being *respectfully* Roman rich Ephesians *owned* the city. In also being *richly* Greek they *owned* Artemis, and because she watched over them and guarded their wealth in the Artemisium, it appears that Artemis *owned* them.

Inner Texture of 1 Timothy 2:9–10

> **9** Likewise, also [I desire] women to adorn themselves in respectable apparel with modesty and discretion, not in plaits with gold or pearls or costly clothing, **10** but with good deeds, as fitting women who profess piety to God.

This text appears in the literary context of 1 Timothy.[45] It is directed toward *gynaikas*, "wives" or "women," in the household of God, and the handling of riches is broadly in view.

In antiquity *gynē* is used broadly to encompass any female, from an unmarried virgin to an elderly married woman.[46] They are in "respectable apparel with modesty and discretion to adorn themselves" (*en katastolē kosmiō meta aidous kai sōphrosynēs kosmein heautas*). The instructions are clarified first with a negative list: "not in plaits with gold or pearls or costly clothing" (*mē en plegmasin kai chrysiō*

---

44. Peter Scherrer, "The City of Ephesos: From the Roman Period to Late Antiquity," in *Ephesos Metropolis of Asia: An Interdisciplinary Approach to its Archaeology, Religion and Culture* (ed. Helmut Koester; Valley Forge, PA: Trinity, 1995) 104. Scherrer cites the example of a statue of Livia, the wife of Augustus, unearthed in one of the slope houses of the rich.

45. As 1 Tim 2:9–10 falls within the greater context of 2:9–15, some at the symposium inquired as to why my paper covers only two verses. As the handling of riches is in view in my dissertation and this paper, my focus is on 2:9–10. For more on how my findings from 2:9–10 can be read alongside 2:11–15, see n. 95.

46. This definition dates to the fifth century BCE in Euripides, *Orestes* 309, of Electra; cf. BAGD, 168. Contra: Sharon Hodgin Gritz, *Paul, Women Teachers, and the Mother Goddess at Ephesus: A Study of 1 Timothy 2:9–15 in Light of the Religious and Cultural Milieu of the First Century* (Lanham, MD: University Press of America, 1991) 158, who argues that *gynaikes* should only be translated as "wives."

ē margaritais ē himatismō polytelei), then a positive one: "but with good works, as fitting women who profess piety to God" (*all' ho prepei gynaixin epangellomenais theosebeian, di' ergōn agathōn*). Inner textual analysis requires these words to be examined in three areas: adornment in the ancient Mediterranean world, prohibitions, and expectations.[47]

Adornment in the Ancient Mediterranean World

The term *kosmeō*, meaning "decorate" or "adorn," was used in antiquity to describe any female using *kosmos* ("finery") for beautification, dating back as early as Hesiod (eighth century BCE).[48] In addition to celebrating the female form, Hesiod reveals that adornment with precious items such as gold, silver, flowers, and other rich apparel also had another purpose.

> And the goddess bright-eyed Athene girded and *clothed* [*kosmēse*] her with silvery raiment, and down from her head she spread with her hands a broidered veil, a wonder to see; and she, Pallas Athene, put about her head lovely garlands, flowers of new-grown herbs . . . he brought her out, delighting in the *finery* [*kosmō*] which the bright-eyed daughter of a mighty father had given her, to the place where the other gods and men were. And wonder took hold of the deathless gods and mortal men when they saw that which was sheer guile, not to be withstood by men.[49]

Adornment captivated the gods *and* men; neither could withstand it. It would become an avenue for women to gain power in the patriarchal ancient world. Collins uncovers a similar sentiment in Hellenistic Judaism: spurious motives were suspected of adorned women (137–107 BCE).

> By reason of their lacking authority or power over man, they scheme treacherously how they might entice him to themselves by means of their looks. . . . Accordingly, order your wives and your daughters not to adorn their heads and their appearances so as to deceive men's sound minds.[50]

---

47. Robbins, *Exploring the Texture of Texts*, 7: "Inner textual analysis focuses on words as tools of communication. . . . This analysis works only with a basic sense of the words. The analyst looks at and listens to the ways in which the text uses these words." In response to Nixon's call for clarity here: the inner texture of this text reveals a three-part "argumentative" texture, thus the terms within the three parts of the argument (adornment, prohibitions, expectations) must be read in light of ancient sources.

48. *Works and Days* 69–76.

49. Hesiod, *The Theogony of Hesiod* 573, 587. Italics and brackets mine.

50. *The Testament of Reuben*, 5:1, 5. Cf. Raymond Collins, *1 and 2 Timothy and Titus* (New

As external adornment was often connected to enticement or deceit, women were to avoid this activity. Marshall believes this was the case in the first century CE, citing Philo:

> When they [women] heard this, they ceased to think of or to pay the very slightest regard to their character for purity of life, being quite devoid of all proper education, and accordingly they consented, though during all the rest of their lives they had put on a hypocritical appearance of modesty, and so now they adorned themselves with costly garments, and necklaces, and all those other appendages with which women are accustomed to set themselves off, and they devoted all their attention to enhancing their natural beauty, and making it more brilliant (for the object of their pursuit was not an unimportant one, being the alluring of the young men who were well inclined to be seduced), and so they went forth into public.[51]

Winter describes this trend as the appearance of "new" women, identifiable with dress codes in Roman law and society.[52] The "new" women were breaking the rules. An ancient perspective of this alternative behavior can be found in a letter from Seneca to his mother (c. 41–49 CE).

> Unchastity, the greatest evil of our time, has never classed you with the great majority of women. Jewels have not moved you, nor pearls . . . you have not been perverted by the imitation of worse kind of women that leads even the virtuous into pitfalls . . . You have never blushed for the number of children, as if it mocked your age . . . You never tried to conceal your pregnancy as though it was indecent, nor have you crushed the hope of children that were being nurtured in your body. You have never defiled your face with paints and cosmetics. Never have you fancied the kind of dress that exposed no greater nakedness by being removed. Your only ornament, the kind of beauty that time does not tarnish, is the great honor of modesty.[53]

Honorable Roman women were to adorn themselves with modesty and chastity in the first century CE. The term in 1 Tim 2:9, *aidōs* ("modesty") connotes avoiding

---

Testament Library; Louisville: Westminster John Knox, 2002) 68.

51. *On the Virtues* 39. Cf. Seneca *On Benefits*, 7.9; I. Howard Marshall, *The Pastoral Epistles* (New International Critical Commentary; Edinburgh: T. & T. Clark, 1999) 450. Brackets mine.

52. Bruce Winter, *Roman Wives, Roman Widows: The Appearance of New Women and the Pauline Communities.* (Grand Rapids: Eerdmans, 2003) 97–109; cf. Plutarch, *Advice to the Bride and Groom* 139C.

53. *Ad Helviam*, 16.3–5; Cf. Winter, *Roman Wives*, 98.

clothing that would be sexually enticing.⁵⁴ The modest Roman woman was to wear a *stolē* as a symbol of chastity and to differentiate herself from the *hetairai*, prostitutes or courtesans, who wore the *toga* in public.⁵⁵ Thus, the word *katastolē* coupled with the adjective *kosmiō* and *meta aidous* appears to agree with the Roman expectation of sexually modest versus seductive apparel.

Based on Ando's work on provincial loyalty and imperial ideology, Winter thinks the situation would have been the same in Ephesus as in Rome. Thus, the consensus reads 1 Tim 2:9 as consistent with Jewish moralists and respecting Roman codes for female decorum.⁵⁶

Prohibitions

The text calls women to avoid "braids or plaits," "gold," "pearls" and "costly clothing." The common explanation for this is that such ornamentation was associated with *hetairai*.⁵⁷

A closer look at ornamentation in the first century CE Greco-Roman world reveals that it was actually widely accepted for modest women to wear gold, purple, and to dye their hair or wear it elaborately, but the line between what was appropriate and inappropriate was becoming unclear.⁵⁸ Valerius Maximus (14–37 CE) attests that liberty had turned to license: sumptuous adornment had become the primary joy and focus of women.⁵⁹

The first prohibition regarding *plegmasin* ("braids" or "plaits") points to a hairstyle. The term, only here in the NT, comes from the root, *plekō*, referring to

---

54. Marshall, *The Pastoral Epistles*, 449. Cf. Ezek 23:20 and 3 Macc 1:19, 4:5. See also: Spicq, *TLNT* 1:41–44; Bultmann, *TDNT* 1:169–71; and Llewelyn and Horseley, eds., *New Documents* III, § 8, 11, 13.

55. P. Zanker, *The Power of Images in the Age of Augustus* (Ann Arbor: University of Michigan Press, 1988) 165. Cf. Horace, *Satires* 1.1.62–63.

56. Winter, *Roman Wives*, 97. Cf. Clifford Ando, *Imperial Ideology and Provincial Loyalty in the Roman Empire* (Classics and Contemporary Thought 6; Berkeley: University of California Press, 2000) 233. See also *IvE* 6, line 14. The inscription honors the *katastolēs kai sōphrosynēs*, "modesty and decency," of a gymnasiarch; see Luke Timothy Johnson, *The First and Second Letters to Timothy: A New Translation and Introduction* (Anchor Bible 36; New York: Doubleday, 2001) 199–200.

57. T. McGinn, *Prostitution, Sexuality and the Law in Ancient Rome* (Oxford: Oxford University Press, 1998) 154–70. Cf. Winter, *Roman Wives*, 97–122.

58. Winter, *Roman Wives*, 103.

59. *Memorable Doings and Sayings* 2.1.5: "A woman's only joy and glory was in her dress and ornaments that were called *mundus muliebris*." Cf. Winter, *Roman Wives*, 103–4.

something "twisted."⁶⁰ In reading this prohibition most scholars point to the parallel thought in *1 Pet 3:3–4* (though different words are used: *emplokēs trichōn*) and posit that rich women should avoid ostentatious hairstyles.⁶¹

Quinn and Wacker prefer the word "coiffure" for *plegmasin* based upon its absence in the NT and LXX and its use in antiquity (Euripides, Plato, Philo and Josephus) pointing to items woven elaborately or with intertwined ornamentation.⁶² In the coiffure the hair may have been braided or woven with valuables. A reading suggested by Mounce may support this view.

Mounce sees the structure of the prohibition phrase as speaking of only two negative traits rather than multiple prohibitions because of the placement of *ē*, which is repeated twice: "braided hair that is adorned with gold or pearls" (*plegmasin kai chrysiō ē margaritais*) "or costly clothing" (*ē himatismō polytelei*).⁶³ The language seems to be prohibiting some type of coiffure as suggested by Quinn and Wacker, though the function of *plegmasin* has eluded scholars.

The first form of ornamentation "gold," most commonly refers to coins in the NT. It is among the decorum to be avoided in 1 Pet 3:3, another reason scholars consider 1 Tim 2:9–10 as mirroring the message of that text, though "pearls" are not mentioned there. Adornment with pearls in antiquity was tied to shameful sumptuousness: "There is nothing that a woman will not permit herself to do, nothing that she deems shameful, when she encircles her neck with green emeralds, and fastens huge pearls to her elongated ears."⁶⁴

The prohibition of costly clothing connotes imprudent or promiscuous apparel. Towner supports this with testimony from Philo:

> For two women live with each individual among us, both unfriendly and hostile to one another, filling the whole abode of the soul with envy, and jealousy, and contention; of these we love the one looking upon her as

---

60. BAGD, 667; *plekō* appears in Matt 27:29; Mark 15:17; and John 19:2 referring to the "twisted" crown of thorns.

61. Juvenal, *Satires* 6; S. Baugh, "A Foreign World: Ephesus in the First Century," in *Women in the Church: A Fresh Analysis of 1 Timothy 2:9–15* (ed. Andreas Köstenberger, Thomas Schreiner, and H. Scott Baldwin; Grand Rapids: Baker, 2005) 47–48.

62. Jerome D. Quinn, and William C. Wacker, *The First and Second Letters to Timothy: A New Translation with Notes and Commentary* (Eerdmans Critical Commentary; Grand Rapids: Eerdmans, 2000) 196. Cf. Euripides, *Ion* 1393; Plato, *Laws* 734E, *Timaeus* 79D; Philo, *Ebr.* 101, *Som.* 1.204, 206, *Mos.* 2.111; Josephus, *Ant* 2.220, 221, 224, 246; 12.72, 79.

63. W. D. Mounce, *The Pastoral Epistles* (WBC 46; Nashville: Thomas Nelson, 2000) 114.

64. Juvenal, *Satires* 6.458–9. Cf. Winter, *Roman Wives*, 104–5.

being mild and tractable, and very dear to and very closely connected with ourselves, and she is called pleasure; but the other we detest, deeming her unmanageable, savage, fierce, and most completely hostile, and her name is virtue. Accordingly, the one comes to us luxuriously dressed in the guise of a harlot and prostitute, with mincing steps, rolling her eyes about with excessive licentiousness and desire, by which baits she entraps the souls of the young, looking about with a mixture of boldness and impudence, holding up her head, and raising herself above her natural height, fawning and giggling, having the hair of her head dressed with most superfluous elaborateness, having her eyes penciled, her eyebrows covered over, using incessant warm baths, painted with a fictitious colour, exquisitely dressed with costly garments, richly embroidered, adorned with armlets, and bracelets, and necklaces, and all other ornaments which can be made of gold, and precious stones, and all kinds of female decorations; loosely girdled, breathing of most fragrant perfumes, thinking the whole market her home; a marvel to be seen in the public roads, out of the scarcity of any genuine beauty, pursuing a bastard elegance.[65]

This ancient description of contrasting women captures the scholarly consensus on 1 Tim 2:9–10. The prohibitions to women regarding adornment appear to reflect the call to be a woman of virtue versus a woman of pleasure, a notion to be tested in light of *Ephesiaca*.

Expectations

The text offers a twist on the kind of decorum expected of modest women. They are to be adorned "with good deeds, as fitting women who profess piety to God."

We see an expanded usage of the term *kosmeō* beyond decorum to deeds by the Jewish scribe Ben Sirach (second century BCE), who refers to the "wondrous deeds" of Elijah.[66] In like manner Diodorus Siculus (first century BCE) also points past external array:

> The Corinthians, concluding that it was only right to assist people who were offshoots of themselves, voted to send as general Timoleon, son of Timaenetus, a man of highest prestige amongst his fellow citizens for

---

65. *The Sacrifices of Abel and Cain* 21. Cf. Phillip H. Towner, *The Letters to Timothy and Titus* (New International Commentary on the New Testament; Grand Rapids: Eerdmans, 2006) 209.

66. *Sir* 48:4–11 (NRSV).

bravery and sagacity as a general and, in a word, splendidly *equipped* with every virtue.[67]

To be "splendidly equipped" was to be adorned with qualities esteemed as virtuous. This echoes the Stoic philosophers who urged people to adorn themselves with four cardinal virtues: *sophia, andreia, dikaiosunē,* and *sōphrosunē,* "wisdom, courage, uprightness, and chastity."[68] Sadly, in actuality, the focus of men was often on titles and positions, and the focus of women was on ornamentation, which led Stoics such as Epictetus to ask, "Can it be that the human is the only creature without a special virtue but must resort to his hair, clothes, and ancestors?"[69] Rather than inward adornment with virtues, the rich wore it in their hair, flaunted it in costly garb, and also paid for it in inscriptions that celebrated their *eusebeia,* "piety."

The idea of service or piety to God, *theosebeia*, must be understood in light of *eusebeia*, which in Ephesus pointed to deeds expected of those in priestly service to Artemis.[70] Female priestesses had at least four different titles. Duties included: underwriting cult activities at the Artemisium, decorating for cult festivals, serving in the temple, and insuring that imperial cultic duties were also handled.[71] Interestingly, one inscription from the *kourētes*, ("priests") list dated 97–100 CE, celebrates the *eusebeia* of Vedia Marcia, who held three of the four female roles.[72] Rich Ephesians were lauded for their *eusebeia* to Artemis and/or the imperial cult.[73]

Summary of Inner Texture: 1 Timothy 2:9–10

This review of scholarship has surfaced three interpretive issues that remain unclear. Regarding adornment, should 1 Tim 2:9–10 be read as calling women to comply

---

67. Diodorus Siculus 16.65.2. Italics mine.

68. Towner, *The Letters to Timothy and Titus*, 207.

69. *Fragment* 18. Cf. Collins, *1 and 2 Timothy and Titus*, 68.

70. Towner, *The Letters to Timothy and Titus*, 171–75. See the excursus on *eusebeia*; cf. IvE 27, ll. 344–45.

71. Baugh, "A Foreign World," 35–36; cf. Rogers, *The Sacred Identity of Ephesos*, and IvE 27 for details regarding cultic practices.

72. *IvE* 1017.

73. *Eusebeia,* ("piety") to Artemis and/or the Iimperial cult is celebrated in public record in: IvE 11, 17, 21, 24, 26, 27, 203, 217, 233, 236, 237, 296, 302–4a, 314/5, 666a, 680, 683a, 690, 702, 824, 853, 886, 892, 941/2, 957, 989a, 1001–6, 1008–10, 1012–24, 1028–30, 1032–38, 1040–44, 1047–51/3, 1065–67/8, 1084, 1352, 1380, 1480, 1538, 1565, 1578b, 1579, 1588, 1598, 1859, 2090, 2426, 3041, 3059, 3118, 3263, 3408, 3419, and 4336.

with Jewish norms and Roman codes for modesty, or may it refer to other social realities? On prohibitions, should they be read as referring to the "new" women, or could there be something else in view? Pertaining to expectations, is the text calling Christian women to continue to serve as pious citizens, or might it be calling them to a different lifestyle in this social and cultural setting? To attempt to clarify these issues, I will offer what Xenophon of Ephesus may add to the mix.

Intertexture[74]

The language of 1 Tim 2:9–10 is present in *Ephesiaca*. These terms, common to both texts, will be reviewed below as used by Xenophon of Ephesus: *gynaikes, kosmeō/ kosmos, plegma, chrysion, sōphrosunē, polytelēs prepei, ergai agathai,* and *theosebeia*.

First, *gynaikes* is the most common overlapping term between 1 Tim 2:9–10 and *Ephesiaca*, occurring thirty-one times. Its use in *Ephesiaca* is consistent with our understanding of the term in antiquity. It primarily refers to a wife or a married woman but its broader usage includes any female from an unmarried girl of marriageable age to an elderly woman.[75]

The second term, *kosmeō* ("adorn"), appears eight times as a verb and eight times as the noun "adornment." It is used in four settings: three times referring to adorning a corpse for burial, once as wearing the apparel of a prostitute, three times as being adorned for a lover, and once (in the following quotation) related to dressing to imitate Artemis in the annual procession to the Artemisium.

> A local festival for Artemis was underway, and from the city to her shrine, a distance of seven stades, all the girls had to march sumptuously adorned [*kosmēmenas*], as did all the ephebes. . . . The procession marched along in file, first the sacred objects, torches, baskets, and incense, followed by horses, dogs, and hunting equipment, some of it martial, most of it peaceful <. . .> each of the girls was adorned [*ekekosmēto*] as for a lover. Heading the line of girls was Anthia, daughter of Megamedes and Euippe, locals.

---

74. Robbins, *Exploring the Texture of Texts*, 40: "Intertexture is a text's representation of, reference to, and use of phenomena in the 'world' outside the text being interpreted. In other words, the intertexture of a text is the interaction of the language in the text with 'outside' material and physical 'objects,' historical events, texts, customs, values, roles, institutions, and systems."

75. In *Ephesiaca* Anthia leads the procession described not as a *gynē* but with the related term *parthenos*, an unmarried girl of marriageable age seeking to become a wife. The purpose of the procession appears, in part, to be for girls of marriageable age to find a mate. In antiquity (cf. n. 46) unmarried girls of marriageable age can also be referred to with the term *gunaikes,* and this is the case with Anthia, as *gynē* is used of her in *Ephesiaca* 1.6.3, before her marriage.

> Anthia's beauty was marvelous and far surpassed the other girls. She was fourteen, her body was blossoming with shapeliness, and the adornment [*kosmos*] of her dress enhanced her grace.... Often when seeing her at the shrine, the Ephesians worshiped her as Artemis, so also at the sight of her on this occasion the crowd cheered.[76]

In the festival for Artemis it was customary to wear specific attire to honor the goddess who *owned* Ephesus. Because of her exceptional beauty and prominent parents, Anthia was privileged to lead the way. As Dalmeyda proclaims, Anthia represents, in effect, Artemis.[77] In appearing as Artemis, Anthia also has a certain hairstyle. Interestingly, the term used to describe it comes from the same root as the word used in 1 Tim 2:9, *plegma*.

> Her hair was blonde, mostly loose, only little of it braided [*peplegmenē*], and moving as the breezes took it. Her eyes were vivacious, bright like a beauty's but forbidding like a chaste girl's; her clothing was a belted purple tunic, knee-length and falling loose over the arms, and over it a fawnskin with a quiver attached, arrows <...>, javelins in hand, dogs following behind.[78]

As scholars in the past have broadly viewed this term as "braided" or "plaited" hair, as used here, it is reasonable to aver that this referred to a hairstyle worn by those who served Artemis.[79] The root word, *plekō*, also appears in the bridal chamber of Anthia and Habrocomes:

> The chamber had been prepared for them: a golden bed had been spread with purple sheets, and above the bed a Babylonian canopy had been finely embroidered: there were Cupids at play, some attending to Aphrodite, who was also represented, some riding mounted on sparrows, some plaiting [*plekontes*] garlands, some bearing flowers. These were on one part of the canopy; on the other was Ares, not armed but garlanded and wearing a fine cloak, dressed for his lover Aphrodite; Eros, holding his lighted torch,

---

76. *Ephesiaca* 1.2.2.1–4; 1.2.4–5.

77. G. Dalmeyda, *Xénophon d'Éphèse. Les Épésiaques* (Paris: Les Belles Lettres, 1926) 5.

78. *Ephesiaca* 1.2.6.

79. Harland, *Associations*, 7; Contra Murphy-O'Connor, *St. Paul's Ephesus,* 179, "Anthia's dress and accoutrements in no way resemble the cult statues of Ephesian Artemis that are dated to the second century CE." The image presented by Harland and the argument of Murphy-O'Connor could be read in harmony if O'Sullivan is correct in dating *Ephesiaca* in the first century CE.

was leading him on his way. Under the canopy itself they brought Anthia and Habrocomes, put her on her bed, and closed the doors.[80]

The term *chrysion* ("gold") appears fourteen times. It describes the bedspread of Anthia and Habrocomes in their bridal chamber. In four instances it is the provision for a person taking a journey and becomes the target of pirates and brigands. Also in four instances, two of which are found in this scene, gold is the gift that Anthia and Habrocomes present in the temple of Helius.

> They were accorded public prayers, and the Rhodians offered many a sacrifice and celebrated their visit like a festival. They toured the whole city and in the temple of Helius dedicated a golden [*chrysēn*] panoply and had an inscription from its donors inscribed on a plaque: the visitors dedicated to you these weapons of beaten gold [*chrysēlata*], Anthia and Habrocomes, citizens of sacred Ephesus.[81]

Lastly, gold is part of the finery used to adorn prostitutes and rich women for burial.[82]

The next word, *sōphrosunē*, translated "chastity," is a theme in the greater literary context of 1 Tim 2:9–10 (cf. 2:9 and 2:15), and it occurs twenty-one times in *Ephesiaca*, plus there are three times when the opposite behavior is featured. In the procession that starts the story, Anthia and Habrocomes both possess this virtue,[83] but at the sight of each other, things change.

> And so when the procession was over, the whole crowd repaired to the shrine for the sacrifice, the order of the procession was dissolved, and men and women, Ephebes and girls, gathered in the same spot. There they saw each other. Anthia was captivated by Habrocomes, and Habrocomes was bested by Eros. He kept gazing at the girl and though he tried, he could not take his eyes off her: the god pressed his attack and held him fast. Anthia too was in a bad way, as with eyes wide open she took in Habrocomes' handsomeness and as it flowed into her, already putting maidenly decorum [*kataphronousa*] out of her mind: for what she said was for Habrocomes to hear, and she uncovered what parts of her body she could for Habrocomes to see. He gave himself over to the sight and fell captive to the god.[84]

---

80. *Ephesiaca* 1.8.2–3.

81. *Ephesiaca* 1.12.2.4, 1.12.2.6, 5.10.6.4 and 5.10.6.5.

82. *Ephesiaca* 5.7.1.3 for prostitutes and 3.7.4.2, 3.8.3.4 for corpses.

83. Anthia in *Ephesiaca* 1.2.6.4; and Habrocomes in *Ephesiaca* 1.4.4.5.

84. *Ephesiaca* 1.3.1–2, see also 1.4.1.3 where *kataphronōn* reflects Habrocomes's contemptuous lack of discretion.

In a moment of passion both characters abandon chastity, and this scene sets the stage for the oracle, their marriage, and the adventures that would follow. Most of the instances of *sōphrosunē* in the rest of the story are related to Anthia or Habrocomes having to defend their chastity, even to the point of being willing to die. In *Ephesiaca* to be chaste is to preserve your identity and place, and to lose this trait put characters at risk in relationship to other people and the gods.

The term *polytelēs* meaning "expensive" or "costly," appears five times. In 1 Tim 2:9–10 it is used in reference to clothing. Four times it refers to a woman's costly clothing in *Ephesiaca*, and once it refers to a lavish dinner before a wedding. In the procession to the Artemisium, Anthia is described as being "expensively" adorned (*kekosmēmenas polytelōs*).[85]

The word *prepō* ("fitting, seemly or suitable")[86] appears twice in *Ephesiaca*. It appears first as *prepontōn*, when Anthia inappropriately abandons modesty and reveals her body for Habrocomes to see. Later, she proclaims that her lovesickness is "inappropriate."[87] Her actions and the consequences were not fitting for a maiden.

The final three words, *ergōn agathōn* ("good works") and *theosebeian* ("piety toward God") will be examined together because they appear in *Ephesiaca* in relationship to each other. In *Ephesiaca ergon* appears fifteen times with a broad range of meanings, such as "work," "deed," or "action," but it also reflects "deeds of men, exhibiting a consistent moral character."[88] The last usage matches its use in 1 Tim 2:9–10 most closely and also indirectly links *ergōn agathōn* and *theosebeian* in the use of the related term *eusebeia*. When Anthia is banished by Manto to be killed by the goatherd Lampo, *Ephesiaca* reveals why he could not perform such an act.

> "But I ask you, goatherd Lampo, since you have thus far behaved respectfully [*eusebēsas*], if you kill me, give me at least a shallow grave in the ground nearby, put your hands on my eyes, and invoke Habrocomes repeatedly as you bury me: for me this would make me a happy funeral, in the presence of Habrocomes." At this the goatherd was moved to pity, aware that he was about to do an unholy deed [*anosion ergon ergasetai*] by killing a girl who had done no wrong and was beautiful. Indeed when he seized the girl, the goatherd could not abide a murder, but said this to her: "Anthia, you know that my mistress Manto ordered me to seize and mur-

---

85. *Ephesiaca* 1.2.2.4.
86. BAGD, 699.
87. *Ephesiaca* 1.3.2.3; 1.4.6.4.
88. BAGD, 307–8.

der you. But I fear heaven [*theous*] and feel pity at your beauty, so I would rather sell you somewhere far from this country, in case Manto finds out that you are not dead and becomes ill disposed toward me." She clung to his feet in tears, and said, "Please, you gods, and Artemis of my fatherland reward the goatherd for these good deeds [*theoi kai Artemi patrōa, ton aipolon uper toutōn tōn agathōn ameiepsasthe*]," and begged to be sold.[89]

Lampo could not perform an unholy deed before the gods because he feared them and showed that by exhibiting *eusebeia*. In response, Anthia prays to the gods and Artemis to reward him for his good deeds, that is, works witnessed by the gods deserving of honor.

Summary of Intertexture

Nearly every word in 1 Tim 2:9–10 appears in *Ephesiaca*. While most of the findings reinforce our understanding of the ancient cultural realities, some new ones have emerged. Most significantly, the decorum to be avoided in 1 Timothy appears in *Ephesiaca* to point to Artemis.

Ideological Texture[90]

Of the findings from intertexture analysis of 1 Tim 2:9–10 alongside *Ephesiaca*, there are three points that correlate ideologically to issues that emerged in the inner texture phase.

First, *plegma* may represent more than a prohibition of ostentatious hairstyles. It may be referring to abstaining from wearing one's hair to look like the goddess, Artemis. As Anthia led the procession to Artemis, *peplegmenē* is used to describe the appearance of her hair. It is plausible the author of 1 Tim 2:9–10 may have had this phenomenon in mind.

Second, while it is understood that "new" women may be in view, avoiding costly clothing may also be pointing to the social norm that women were to dress to imitate and serve Artemis.[91] As Anthia processed in sumptuous adornment,

---

89. *Ephesiaca* 2.11.5–8.

90. Robbins, *Exploring the Texture of Texts*, 95: "The primary subject of ideological analysis and interpretation is people. Texts are the secondary subject of ideological analysis, simply the object of people's writing and reading. The issue is the social, cultural, and individual location and perspective of writers and readers."

91. In the Roman setting women were expected to exhibit *sōphrosunē* tied to codes for deportment and decorum. Based on a closer look at terms that accompany *sōphrosunē* in the Ephesian context,

kekosmēmenas polytelōs, along with *all* the other young women of Ephesus, she was celebrated and worshipped as Artemis. To be urged to avoid such adornment could be read as a call to cease participation in cultic activities.

Third, the decorum called for in 1 Tim 2:9–10 is good deeds fitting women who profess piety to God, *theosebeia*. In *Ephesiaca eusebeia* represents behavior that showed fear and respect for Artemis and the gods. Based on the language in 1 Tim 2:9–10, women with wealth in the community of faith appear to be urged to shift their service and spending from Artemis to serving and spending money on good deeds in service to the one true God.

To place these findings from *Ephesiaca* in their ideological context, Athenaeus helps shape our understanding of the expectations of women in relationship to Artemis.

> Leto once in Delos, as they say, did two great children bear,
> Apollo with the golden hair, Bright Phoebus, god of day.
> And Artemis mighty huntress, virgin chaste,
> On whom all women's trust is placed.[92]

Notice that "all" women placed their trust in Artemis. Of course, this is a broad statement, but it reflects the ancient thinking. Women served the goddess with piety, and she watched over them.

Another example of the strong sense of pressure to conform to the cultural rules tied to Artemis is the test of virginity presented by Achilles Tatius. Any young woman who did not honor Artemis by remaining chaste would put herself in danger of the vengeance of the goddess.

> After inventing his pipes, Pan hung up the instrument, shutting it up in a cave. Some time after he made a gift of the whole spot to Artemis, making a compact with her that it should be entered by no woman who was no longer a virgin. If therefore any girl is accused of being of doubtful virginity, she is sent by public decree to the door of the grotto, and the pan-pipes (*syrinx*) decides the ordeal for her. She goes in, clad in the proper dress, and the door is closed behind her. If she is in reality a virgin, a clear and divine note is heard, either because there is some breeze in the place which enters the pipes and makes a musical sound or possibly because it is Pan

---

modesty was also tied to following cultic norms. Now in 1 Tim 2:9–10, *sōphrosunē* appears to call people away from the goddess as well as heresies and practices associated with her. See n. 94 for a more lengthy explanation of how those related themes emerge in 1 Tim 2:11–15.

92. *The Deipnosophists* 15.694D.

himself who is piping. And after a short time, the door of the grotto opens of its own accord, and out comes the virgin with a pine wreath on her head. But if she has lied about her virginity, the pan-pipes are silent, and a groan comes forth from the cave instead of a musical sound. On the third day after, a virgin priestess of the temple comes and finds the pan-pipes lying on the ground, but there is no trace of the woman.[93]

For Ephesian woman, the ancient voices seem to proclaim: "Don't mess with Artemis!"

Summary of Ideological Texture

Ideologically the language of 1 Tim 2:9–10 appears to be calling Christian women to make a radical shift. They are no longer to plait their hair and adorn their bodies with costly clothing to imitate Artemis, and they are to cease supporting her cult. Instead their modest decorum and good deeds should show their piety to God. Despite the cultural pressures of losing their place in society and their standing with others and Artemis in converting to Christianity, their decorum and deeds will show they are at home in the household of God.[94]

Sacred Texture

Sacred texture analysis compares this reading of 1 Tim 2:9–10 in light of *Ephesiaca* to other passages of Scripture.[95] The text calls the women with some measure of

---

93. *Leucippe and Clitophon* 8.6.11–14; cf. Murphy-O'Connor, *St. Paul's Ephesus*, 150–51.

94. In the larger literary context of 1 Tim 2:9–15, this reading of 2:9–10 is consistent with other scholars such as Richard Clark Kroeger and Catherine Clark Kroeger, *I Suffer Not a Woman: Rethinking 1 Timothy 2:11–15 in Light of Ancient Evidence* (Grand Rapids: Baker, 2003). In looking at some of the same ancient evidence Kroeger and Kroeger posit that women are to learn in "attentiveness and receptivity" (v. 11, p. 76); that a woman should not "teach or proclaim herself to be author of man" (as Artemis or other false teachings may have promoted; v. 12, p. 192); but that the Genesis account rather than other false accounts of the origin of man should be taught (vv. 13–14, p. 117); and lastly, a woman's understanding of her sexuality should be understood not in light of pagan sexual practices tied to cultic activities, but rather God's design from the beginning for woman to bear children. In their words, "Woman are acceptable to God within their childbearing function and need not change their sexual identity to find salvation" (v. 15, p. 177). Not only can women find a home in the household of God; it is safe there. Their actions should follow God's practices and teachings instead of the practices and teachings of Artemis (and other heretical teachings in Ephesus).

95. Robbins, *Exploring the Texture of Texts*, 120: "People who read the New Testament regularly are interested in finding insights into the nature of the relation between human life and the divine. In other words, these readers are interested in locating the ways the texts speaks about God or gods, or

wealth in Ephesus to modest *decorum* and good *deeds* fitting women who profess *theosebeia*. These two areas will be explored below.

Decorum

Regarding modest decorum for women, the most common passage viewed alongside 1 Tim 2:9–10 is 1 Pet 3:3–4 which reads:

> Your beauty should not come from outward adornment, such as elaborate hairstyles and the wearing of gold jewelry or fine clothes. Rather, it should be that of your inner self, the unfading beauty of a gentle and quiet spirit, which is of great worth in God's sight.[96]

Reading this text reveals that adornment for women should be internal rather than external. Elaborate hairstyles, expensive jewelry, and costly clothes may have been the measure of worth for "new" women *and* followers of Artemis, but before God inner beauty is what counts.

In comparing this text to 1 Tim 2:9–10, there are two key differences: the prohibitions use different terms and the calls to action, though consistent, vary. First, the prohibited hairstyle in 1 Tim 2:9–10 uses the term *plegma*, which in *Ephesiaca* appears tied to women who served Artemis in the Ephesian context. The prohibition of elaborate hairstyles (*emplokēs trichōn*) and external adornment uses language that leads the reader to avoid the dress of the worldly "new" women, prostitutes, or courtesans, rather than the imitators of Artemis, *per se*.

Second, the call to action in 1 Pet 3:3–4 is to cultivate the beauty of the inner self, whereas 1 Tim 2:9–10 call the woman to adorn herself with good deeds. Here is how they vary. The former is a general call for women to cultivate inner beauty, while the latter teaches women who would have been previously lauded for their *eusebeia* in spending money imitating and supporting Artemis to direct their money toward good deeds that show their *theosebeia*.

---

talks about realms of religious life." Sacred texture reveals the insights that have emerged and examines them alongside other texts.

96. NIV; 1 Pet 3:3–4 is in view because it most closely mirrors 1 Tim 2:9–10. Other passages consistent with this reading are explored further by Winter in *Roman Wives, Roman Widows*: 1 Corinthians 11:2–16; 1 Timothy 5:11–15; and Titus 2:3–5.

Deeds

Good deeds in the NT are a necessary complement to genuine faith as attested in James 2:14–17.

> What good is it, my brothers and sisters, if someone claims to have faith but has no deeds [*erga*]? Can such faith save them? Suppose a brother or a sister is without clothes and daily food. If one of you says to them, "Go in peace; keep warm and well fed," but does nothing about their physical needs, what good is it? In the same way, faith by itself, if it is not accompanied by action [*erga*], is dead.

In Acts 26:20 the Gentiles are called to repent and "demonstrate their repentance by their deeds." In Eph 2:8–10 *erga agatha* ("good works") are not the source of one's salvation but evidence of that salvation and what Christians were created to do. These three passages, which reflect the NT teaching that good deeds must accompany faith, appear to match the message of 1 Tim 2:9–10. Women should show their piety to God through good deeds.

While no names of rich women are mentioned in 1 Tim 2:9–10, there are three women in Acts who could represent them: Dorcas, Lydia, and Priscilla. The accounts of these women sound consistent with this reading of 1 Timothy, especially in relationship to their deeds.

Dorcas of Joppa appears in Acts 9:36. "She was full of good works [*ergōn agathōn*] and acts of charity." Here Luke uses the same term used to describes the deeds expected of women in 1 Tim 2:10. Undoubtedly her good works came at a financial cost. As saint and seamstress Dorcas is presented blessing widows in the community of faith with fine garments. Bassler argues that such good deeds would be viewed as countercultural, for according to the rules of benefaction, the rich simply did not give to people like widows: "they do *not* give to just anyone" but to those who can make a return.[97] The giving of Dorcas seems to show her piety toward God.

Lydia of Thyatira appears in Acts 16:14. She was a "a seller of purple goods" and a "worshipper of God." In the ancient world sellers of purple were clothiers with some measure of wealth. Purple cloth was expensive and could only be possessed by people with resources and worn by those with status. Lydia would have been accustomed to traveling since she appears in the text in Philippi, far from her hometown in Asia Minor. Though the term *theosebeia* is not used, she is described using a related term: *sebomenē ton theon*, "one revering God" or a "God-fearer." After hearing

---

97. Bassler, *God and Mammon*, p. 19.

Paul, Silas, and Timothy, Luke records, "When she and the members of her household were baptized, she invited us to her home. 'If you consider me a believer in the Lord,' she said, 'come and stay at my house.' And she persuaded us."[98] She extended hospitality not once but twice (cf. Acts 16:40). Though few details are given in Acts, Lydia is presented as a wealthy woman who fears God and performs deeds such as hospitality. Her faith seems to have filled her with enthusiasm to extend support to those advancing the gospel. I find it interesting that Timothy is present along with Paul. One can only wonder if the lifestyle and example of Lydia is envisioned in the teaching of 1 Tim 2:9–10.

Priscilla appears in Acts 18. She had been expelled from Rome along with her husband, Aquila (vv. 1–3). As tentmakers and travelers with Paul, they possessed some wealth and used it to support Pauline mission. After being instructed by Paul to remain in Ephesus, Acts 18 records that they heard Apollos speak in the synagogue (v. 26). Though little is known of Priscilla, her presence in the synagogue in Ephesus appears opposite the cultural norm. In a setting where women would have been expected to serve in the precincts of the Artemisium, her presence in the synagogue may reveal her allegiance to God rather than Artemis. Though she may have lost her place in the ancient world, Priscilla appears at home in the household of God.

Summary of Sacred Texture

As compared to other NT passages, the findings from reading 1 Tim 2:9–10 in light of *Ephesiaca* appear to be consistent: calling women to a countercultural lifestyle of modest adornment and good deeds that honor God. The teachings on decorum and deeds also seem to be illustrated in the examples of three Christian women in Acts: Dorcas, Lydia, and Priscilla.

Conclusion

This socio-rhetorical reading of 1 Tim 2:9–10 in light of *Ephesiaca* for biblical interpretation appears radically countercultural in relationship to the *Sitz im Leben* of the rich in Ephesus. In the first century CE, Artemis *owned* the rich women, and the rich women *owned* Artemis. The evidence presents this through their decorum and deeds: they plaited their hair and wore costly clothes to imitate the goddess while piously serving and supporting Artemis and her cult.

---

98. Acts 16:15.

In 1 Tim 2:9–10, as part of the household of God, everything changes for women regarding decorum and deeds. God now *owns* the rich Ephesian Christian women, and despite social pressures and cultural expectations, they *own* God.[99] They show their piety toward God by adorning themselves modestly and with good deeds fitting women who profess faith in God like Dorcas, Lydia, and Priscilla, three excellent role models for modern application.

---

99. Nixon in her response stated, "Hoag's conclusion that the rich Ephesian Christian women '*own* God' seems out of step with the remainder of his paper and with the concept of *theosebeia*." I offer this statement to clarify my conclusion: Those who broke away from the Artemis cult to join the Jesus-movement, which we call Christians, now belong to or are "owned" by God; no longer are they "owned" by Artemis. Likewise, even as they used to exhibit through their deeds that they "owned" or embraced Artemis before, now they demonstrate through their deeds that their faith is in God. They "own" or embrace God by demonstrating their respect and reverence, *theosebeia*, through decorum and deeds that are very different from other rich Ephesian women.

RESPONSE TO HOAG

Lyn Nixon

Gary Hoag has set himself several interesting tasks. Among them he adapts Vernon Robbins's socio-rhetorical model in order to present a fresh reading of 1 Tim 2:9–10. Also, he uses a roughly contemporary and little-referenced secular text, *Ephesiaca*, to shed light on these two verses. I want first to comment on Hoag's use of Robbins's model and then to share some thoughts about the connection between 1 Tim 2:9–10, *Ephesiaca*, and our topic of wealth and possessions.

Hoag has substantially adapted Robbins's model, which was no doubt necessary to apply such an intricate model to a text of only two verses. Hoag does not explore Robbins's five types of inner texture (repetitive-progressive, opening-middle-closing, narrational, argumentative, and aesthetic). Instead, the information he presents under the heading of inner texture concerning adornment in the ancient Mediterranean world is mostly what Robbins would call social, or perhaps cultural, *inter*texture. Especially for readers familiar with or interested in Robbins's model, it would be helpful for Hoag to clarify how he has redefined Robbins's categories of texture.[1]

A related issue is that Hoag does not explore the literary co-text of 1 Tim 2:9–10. Given both the controversies which surround 1 Tim 2:11–15 and the fact that those verses are connected to vv. 9–10 by the appearance of the most important female virtue (*sōphrosunē*) appears in both v. 9 and v. 15, it would be valuable to understand how the results of Hoag's analysis might speak into those later verses. Although I am mindful of Wayne Booth's lament, "Since everything is in one way or another related to everything else . . . to write a book at all—any book—[or a paper!] one must rule out *almost* everything that is potentially interesting,"[2] I believe a coherent reading must be demonstrably consistent with at least the entire passage under consideration.[3]

---

1. Hoag does note in a footnote that he has changed the order of Robbins's steps, but he does not describe how he has redefined Robbins's steps/categories of texture.

2. Wayne C. Booth, *The Rhetoric of Fiction* (2nd ed.; Chicago: University of Chicago Press, 1983) 404.

3. Many scholars consider 1 Tim 2:9–15 to be a complete passage. Some include v. 8 and some v. 7.

However it is categorized, the socio-cultural information on Ephesus which Hoag provides in parts two and three is very valuable. It enriches our understanding not only of 1 and 2 Timothy but also of Ephesians and Acts. I would have appreciated more information about the lifestyle expectations of Ephesian *women*—both wealthy and not wealthy. It would be interesting, for example, to know how the two sumptuary laws which regulated banquets shaped the lives of Ephesian women. In the same vein, an assessment of the impact of the *lex Iulia* and its impact on behavioral norms and actual practices would be helpful.[4]

In part three Hoag examines more closely the issue of women's adornment. He cites several ancient Jewish and Roman sources, two from the first century CE, which convincingly demonstrate that wearing costly garments and jewels was culturally connected to the enticement or deception of men.[5] Since enticement and deceit were not characteristics of the virtuous or honorable woman, following Bruce Winter, Hoag says these "new women" were breaking the social and cultural rules.

In Hoag's "prohibitions" section the distinction between the honorable and not-so-honorable Roman woman shifts to a focus on the "rich" Roman and Ephesian woman. Although Hoag does not explicitly make this point, it seems logical that the women who could afford costly garments, personal hairdressers, gold jewelry and pearls—especially if the latter were part of a woman's coiffure, as some have suggested[6]—would be women of substantial means or who were married to

---

4. Cf. Bruce W. Winter, *Roman Wives, Roman Widows: The Appearance of New Women and the Pauline Communities* (Grand Rapids: Eerdmans, 2003) ch. 3.

5. Hoag might make more of his point that "adornment . . . would become an avenue for women to gain power in the patriarchal ancient world." For example, Gordon D. Fee relates the notion of the acquisition of power back to the question of false teaching, a co-textual topic Hoag addresses only obliquely. Fee says that "both their less-than-satisfying social position in Greco-Roman society and their religious hunger, typical of the era, made women easy prey" for false teachers (*1 and 2 Timothy, Titus*, [Peabody, MA: Hendrickson, 1988] 71). Similarly, William D. Mounce notes that "according to one interpretation of 1 Tim 2:8–15, it is possible that the opponents were teaching the women to rebel openly against their husbands, and perhaps all male authority, and to dress seductively as an expression of that rebellion . . ." (*Pastoral Epistles* [Nashville: Thomas Nelson, 2000]: lxxiv [CD-Rom]). Cf. David M. Scholer, "1 Timothy 2:9–15 and the Place of Women in the Church's Ministry," in *Women, Authority & the Bible* (ed. Alvera Mickelsen; Downers Grove, IL: InterVarsity, 1986) 202; and Klyne Snodgrass, "A Case for the Unrestricted Ministry of Women," *The Covenant Quarterly* (May 2009) 37.

6. Hoag notes that a reading suggested by Mounce supports this view (cf. Mounce, *Pastoral Epistles*, 114). According to James B. Hurley, "The sculpture and literature of the period make it clear that women often wore their hair in enormously elaborate arrangements with braids and curls interwoven, or piled high like towers and decorated with gems and/or gold and/or pearls. The courtesans wore their hair in numerous small pendant braids with gold droplets or pearls or gems every inch or so, making a shimmering screen of their locks" (*Man and Woman in Biblical Perspective: A Study in Role*

or for some reason received gifts from wealthy men. Sharon Hodgin Gritz believes that "such ostentation might have made the poorer members [of the church] feel inconsequential,"[7] and there is some evidence that women of more modest resources did spend time and money trying to copy these fashions.[8]

Concerning adornment, Hoag finds that "the consensus reads 1 Tim 2:9 as consistent with Jewish moralists and respecting Roman codes for female decorum." Paul was concerned that Ephesian Christian women were in danger of becoming focused on externals—possessions and the trappings of wealth. This gave the appearance of extravagance and/or immorality and neglected those internal virtues of a godly woman whose life was adorned with her good works.[9] Certainly this mes-

---

Relationships and Authority [Leicester: InterVarsity, 1981] 199) as quoted by John R. W. Stott, *The Message of 1 Timothy and Titus: God's Good News for the World* (Leicester: InterVarsity, 1996) 84.

Whether braided hair by itself constituted an elaborate hairstyle is not clear. On one hand, there are those who believe that braided hair "would not raise the issue of impropriety" (cf. Mounce, *Pastoral Epistles*, 114). For example, Donald Guthrie considers braids to be common but fastening the plaits "with ribbons and bows" to be an elaborate hairstyle (*The Pastoral Epistles: An Introduction and Commentary* [2nd ed.; Leicester: InterVarsity; Grand Rapids: Eerdmans, 1990] 85). On the other hand, S. M. Baugh believes braiding itself was elaborate: "During this period, Greek hairstyles for women were for the most part simple affairs: hair was parted in the middle, pinned simply in the back or held in place with a scarf or headband" ("A Foreign World: Ephesus in the First Century," in *Women in the Church: An Analysis and Application of 1 Timothy 2:9–15* [2nd ed.; ed. Andreas J. Köstenberger and Thomas R. Schreiner; Grand Rapids: Baker, 2005] 35). However, Baugh recognizes that hairstyles became increasingly more elaborate during the Roman principate: "The women of the imperial household originated new styles; by the Trajanic period they had developed into elaborate curls, braids, high wigs, pins, and hair ornaments that were quickly copied by the well-to-do throughout the empire: 'See the tall edifice rise up on her head in serried tiers and storeys!' (Juvenal, *Satire* 6)."

7. Sharon Hodgin Gritz, *Paul, Women Teachers, and the Mother Goddess at Ephesus: A Study of 1 Timothy 2:9–15 in Light of the Religious and Cultural Milieu of the First Century* (Lanham, MD: University Press of America, 1991) 127.

8. J. M. Holmes points out that "gold chains were worn by Roman barmaids, and some poor women in antiquity wore large pearl earrings" (*Text in a Whirlwind: A Critique of Four Exegetical Devices at 1 Timothy 2.9–15* [Sheffield: Sheffield Academic, 2000] 64).

9. Cf. Winter, *Roman Wives, Roman Widows*, 108; and Scholer, "1 Timothy 2:9–15 and the Place of Women in the Church's Ministry," 201–2. Scholer believes "Paul encourages dress and adornment for women that . . . presents the church as of good reputation and without offense." More practically, Gritz points out that "the arranging of hair could occupy a large part of women's time and thought" (*Paul, Women Teachers, and the Mother Goddess at Ephesus*, 127) leaving them little time for the true priorities. Philip H. Towner adds that "Paul would not want Christian women to be typed as 'new' women since that would bring the church's witness and mission into jeopardy" (*The Letters to Timothy and Titus* [Grand Rapids, Eerdmans, 2006] 197).

sage concerning wealth and possessions relates to the church today—and not just to its women.[10]

To explore whether something additional might be in view in this passage, Hoag turns to *Ephesiaca*. He bases his analysis on the ten words the two texts have in common—words that cover two-thirds of the nouns, adjectives, and verbal forms contained in 1 Timothy. From the ten common words Hoag makes several suggestions for reading the letter. First, Paul's mandate to avoid braiding may be more than a prohibition of elaborate hairstyles. It may refer to refraining from "wearing one's hair to look like the goddess, Artemis." Additionally, since in *Ephesiaca* women dressed to imitate Artemis, Paul's desire that women avoid costly clothing and sumptuous adornment may be a call to cease participating in cultic activities. Finally, since *eusebeia* in *Ephesiaca* represents behavior that shows fear and respect for Artemis and the gods, by referring to *theosebeia* (piety to God) in 1 Tim 2:9–10, Paul may be urging wealthy Christian women "to shift their service and spending from Artemis to serving and spending money on good deeds in service to the one true God."

Although I think all of Hoag's conclusions are correct—Christian women are not to imitate, serve, or spend money on Artemis or, in our day, on any other "idol," I am not fully convinced that those conclusions derive from the examples offered from *Ephesiaca*. To see this, we need to take a closer look at some of these words in their contexts.

One word is *gynē*, the word generally translated "women" in 1 Tim 2:9–10.[11] It is a common word in *Ephesiaca*, and Xenophon uses it with its meaning "wife" when he comments that at this festival it was customary "to find husbands for the girls and wives for the ephebes [young men]" (1.2.3).[12] However, it is not the word used to describe the heroine of the story, Anthia, age 14, as she first appears leading the girls in festival procession to the shrine of Artemis. Anthia and the other girls are described not as *gynai* but as *parthenoi*, a word for an unmarried female of marriageable age (1.2.2, 1.2.3, 1.2.5, etc.)[13]

---

10. Modern practices that come to mind as examples are "body art" such as tattooing and piercing.

11. Some scholars believe 1 Tim 2:9–10 refers specifically to wives. See Towner, *The Letters to Timothy and Titus*, 205; Thomas R. Schreiner, "An Interpretation of 1 Timothy 2:9–15: A Dialogue with Scholarship," in *Women in the Church*, 92–94; and Gritz, *Paul, Women Teachers, and the Mother Goddess at Ephesus*, 125, for a range of opinions on this question.

12. All references to *Ephesiaca* are to *Anthia and Habrocomes by Xenophon of Ephesus*, ed. and trans. Jeffrey Henderson (Cambridge: Harvard University Press, 2009).

13. There is a reference to Anthia as a good potential wife in 1.7.3. Note that Anthia and Habrocomes

Another group of the common words *is* used to describe Anthia during the procession and afterwards: "adorn" (*kosmeō*), "costly" (*polytelēs*), "braided/plaited" (*plegma*), "fitting/seemly/suitable" (*prepō*), and "chastity" (*sōphrōn/sōphrosynē*). This last word deserves more attention than Hoag gives it, especially since Abraham Malherbe indicates it was "the primary virtue of women in antiquity."[14] It is notoriously difficult to translate with one English word.[15] In its second entry BDAG offers "practice of prudence, *good judgment, moderation, self-control* . . . Esp. as a woman's virtue *decency, chastity*."[16] *Sōphrosynē* appears in 1 Tim 2:9 and 15.[17] By Hoag's count it also appears twenty-two times in *Ephesiaca*, although the example he gives in part four is actually of a form of *prepō*, as he notes a few paragraphs later. Although Hoag does not mention it, this is the word used to describe Anthia's "vivacious eyes" as she marches in the procession; they are "bright like a beauty's but forbidding like a chaste girl's [*sōphronos*]" (1.2.6).[18] "Chaste" seems to imply more than physical chastity; there is also a sense of "purity" or "modesty." In this, it is similar to the way the word is used in 1 Tim 2.

Anthia is from an aristocratic and presumably wealthy family.[19] She and all the girls in the procession march "sumptuously adorned," and "each of the girls was

---

are both under the control of their parents, who are the ones who determine to "join the children in marriage" (1.7.2) and all the resources the children enjoy are those of their parents. Anthia does not appear yet to be a woman in the sense to which Paul is referring in 1 Tim 2.

14. Abraham J. Malherbe, "The *Virtus Feminarium* in 1 Timothy 2:9–15," in *Renewing Tradition: Studies in Texts and Contexts in Honor of James W. Thompson* (ed. Mark Hamilton, Thomas H. Olbricht, and Jeffrey Peterson; Eugene, OR: Pickwick, 2007) 59.

15. Malherbe ("The *Virtus Feminarium* in 1 Timothy 2:9–15," 53) notes that "modern New Testament scholars have . . . recognized the virtual impossibility of translating the word group; they have had to be content to render the Greek word according to the contexts in which it occurs, as meaning moderation, restraint, modesty, prudence, and self-control or to write summary accounts of its meaning." On p. 58 he adds that *sōphrosynē* is related to *to prepon*, what is fitting. Forms of this word occur in both 1 Tim and *Ephesiaca*.

16. BDAG, 987.

17. Malherbe ("The *Virtus Feminarium* in 1 Timothy 2:9–15," 48) suggests that "this *inclusio* invites us to view the entire section as practical demonstrations of a woman's moderation or prudence."

18. Although Gritz (*Paul, Women Teachers, and the Mother Goddess at Ephesus*, 41) believes the cultus of Artemis "included wild orgies in which her votaries castrated themselves in dedication to her service," Baugh ("A Foreign World," 25–26) notes "there is simply no evidence from Artemis Ephesia's cult practices to substantiate her as a fertility or mother goddess. Instead, what we do know of her worship shows it to have been a typical hellenic state cult . . . . Fertility and orgiastic rituals in the Greco-Roman world were much different." The latter coheres with Hoag's understanding of the importance of chastity and virginity for the Artemis cult.

19. Cf. 2.9.4, in which Anthia tells Lampo of her "erstwhile high estate." See below n. 28 for a

adorned as for a lover."[20] Anthia is wearing a purple tunic, which would be costly attire, but there is no mention that she is wearing any jewelry. She is carrying a quiver and arrows in honor of Artemis. Additionally, her hair was "mostly loose, with only little of it braided, and moving as the breezes took it." This does not sound like an elaborate hairstyle.

As Anthia processes Xenophon implies that she is seemly and her behavior is fitting/suitable/decorous.[21] There is no hint that her attire, her accessories, or her hairstyle in any way violate the code of proper moral behavior. She appears to be dressed more like a potential bride than a courtesan or "new woman," and Xenophon says it was customary for the young people to find spouses at this festival.[22] Although Paul would not approve of this method of advertising for a spouse, this is not the situation he addresses in 1 Tim 2:9–10.

Admittedly Anthia does immediately put "maidenly decorum out of her mind" (1.3.2) when she sets eyes on Habrocomes. But as Hoag notes in part five, this behavior would not have been acceptable for a young woman who worshipped *Artemis*.[23] Anthia and Habrocomes do not meet clandestinely or behave in a way that would sully their honor or tarnish their virtue; rather, both young people fall into a decline. An oracle suggests to their parents that the two lovesick young people should marry,[24] and after the wedding the couple is sent on a trip which leads to adventures that rival any modern soap opera. At one point Anthia is given to Lampo the goatherd, who is told to make Anthia his wife, by force if necessary. Anthia begs Lampo to take pity on her and preserve her chastity, and Lampo swears he will not defile her.

Hoag's discussion of the Greek words "good works" (*ergōn agathōn*) and "piety to God" (*theosebeia*), both of which appear in 1 Tim 2:10, considers a later dialogue

---

description of some uses of the wealth of the parents of Anthia and Habrocomes.

20. There are words missing from the only extant manuscript of this story right before "each of the girls," which could affect the meaning of that phrase.

21. Anthia puts "maidenly decorum [*prepontōn*] out of her mind" only at the end of the procession when she lays eyes on Habrocomes, an arrogant young man who has earned the wrath of the god Eros by claiming to be superior to Eros in both physical beauty and power. Eros has decided to vanquish and punish Habrocomes. When the two young people see each other, Habrocomes is bested not by Anthia's deceit and enticement but by Eros.

22. More elaborate clothing and jewelry is deemed suitable in Scripture for a bride. See below for examples.

23. Hoag says, "Any young woman who did not honor Artemis by remaining chaste would put herself in danger of the vengeance of the goddess."

24. Interestingly, the oracle consulted was at the temple of Apollo at Colophon, and the goddess mentioned by the oracle is not the virgin huntress Artemis but the Egyptian Isis.

between Anthia and Lampo (2.11.4–8). In this dialogue Anthia uses the related term *eusebeia* (2.11.5). However, in this instance *eusebeia* carries its meaning of giving respect to another human and refers to the respect Lampo has shown Anthia by not defiling her.[25] This is not the meaning *eusebeia* has in 1 Timothy where it invariably involves reverence of God (cf. 1 Tim 2:2, 6:11, etc.).[26]

However, although the word *eusebeia* does not appear in the sense of "piety" in *Ephesiaca*, it is true that the expected behavior is that which shows fear and respect for Artemis and other gods. Some scholars have argued that "εὐσέβεια had special significance in Ephesus in connection with Artemis and that its frequent use in the PE [Pastoral Epistles] may be an answer to the pagan claims."[27] In that case an argument can be made that by the use of the related and more specific word *theosebeia* in 1 Tim 2:10, Paul is opposing the respect, worship, and service of Artemis and other pagan gods, as these are demonstrated in *Ephesiaca*.[28]

---

25. In 2.11.5 *eusebēsas* is translated "behaved respectfully" not "piously." This is confirmed in 2.12.3 where Lampo explains to Habrocomes his previous "respectful behavior toward her," i.e. Anthia.

26. Hoag's conclusion that the rich Ephesian Christian women "*own* God" seems out of step with the remainder of his paper and with the concept of *theosebeia/eusebeia*.

27. Mounce, *Pastoral Epistles*, 84. *Ephesiaca* does not provide direct support for this argument.

28. There are other concepts in the two texts concerning the identity of the deity and the service due the deity that can be used to make this point without attempting to find parallel uses of the common words and, in particular, to find parallels that equate Anthia with the women to whom Paul refers in 1 Tim 2. One of the concepts is worship. People seeing Anthia at the shrine have worshipped her as Artemis, and in the procession some spectators declare she is the goddess, and all of them pray (1.2.7). Throughout the novel the characters worship and pray to a variety of local gods and goddesses. Paul clearly would not countenance worship of any human or of any god or gods other than the one true God—a point he makes with the word *theosebeia*. Secondly, there is the issue of "good works" or "deeds" in 1 Tim 2:10. According to Hoag, "good" and "works" do not appear side-by-side in *Ephesiaca*. Although not exactly of the same character as the "good works" described in 2 Cor 9 or in the story of Dorcas (Acts 9:36, to which Hoag refers) as Hoag notes, the goatherd Lampo refrains from doing an "unholy deed" [*anosion ergon*] i.e., killing Anthia, "a girl who had done no wrong and was so beautiful" (2.11.6). Anthia begs the gods to "reward the goatherd for these good deeds" [*agathōn*] (2.11.8). This act of mercy, performed by a lowly goatherd, is surely closer to Paul's idea of "good deeds as fitting women who profess piety to God" than the pagan acts Xenophon attributes to women (and also men) of prayer, worship, and sacrifice (including human sacrifice by a bandit gang [2.13.2]) to both humans and many and various local gods and goddesses, service in the temple of Artemis, the dedication to Helius of a golden panoply with an inscribed plaque (1.12.2) as well as locks of hair (5.11.5-6) seeking oracles, and the like. Related to this, one of the ten common words may actually deserve more attention in Hoag's work. This word, which ties to the symposium topic of wealth and possessions, is "gold" (*chrysion*). The bridal bed of Anthia and Habrocomes is described as "golden," and the bedding and canopy are extravagantly decorated (1.8.2–3). The rich cargo on board their honeymoon ship, including "lots of . . . gold" (1.10.4), makes the young couple a target for pirates. As mentioned above, Anthia and Habrocomes dedicate a golden panoply to Helius. Anthia is adorned in gold first by a would-be

Concerning sacred texture, there are two additional passages Hoag might consider. One is Prov 31:10–31, which speaks of the woman of noble character, who "opens her arms to the poor" (v. 20), is "clothed in fine linen and purple" (v. 22) and also "with strength and dignity" (v. 25), and who "fears the Lord" (v. 30). The other is the contrast in Revelation between the great harlot, "dressed in purple and scarlet, and . . . glittering with gold, precious stones, and pearls" (17:4), who represents the depths of blasphemy and idolatry, and the "Holy City, the new Jerusalem, coming down out of heaven from God, prepared as a bride beautifully dressed for her husband" (21:2).[29]

In these passages the total absence of external beauty and adornment is not mandated. Rather, like 1 Tim 2:9–10 and 1 Pet 3:3–4, what is highlighted is that a Christian's priority in spending time and financial resources is to be the development of internal beauty which reflects love for and service of the one true God—and no other. Again, this is a topic of great relevance in the church today.

I thank Hoag for his thoughtful paper and for the wealth of socio-cultural information he offers. He has broken new ground in using the novel *Ephesiaca* to illuminate the social and religious situation faced by the first-century Christian community in Ephesus. I look forward to reading his dissertation.

---

replacement for Habrocomes when she is believed dead (3.7.4) and later by a pimp who attempts to offer her in prostitution (5.7.1). Clearly, none of these uses of gold or other material resources is the "good works" Paul encourages in 1 Tim 2.

29. Some OT passages which speak to the adornment of a bride are Isa 61:10; Jer 2:32; and Ps 45:9, and 13–14.

WEALTH, LORDLESS POWERS, AND THE RULE OF CHRIST

Mark Husbands

In a frank and informative essay David Held, a professor at the London School of Economics and Political Science, asks:

> Would anyone freely choose a distributional pattern of scarce goods and services which causes hundreds of millions of people to suffer serious harm and disadvantage independent of their will and consent (and 50,000 dying every day of malnutrition and poverty-related causes), unless they had a privileged stake in the existing social hierarchy? Would anyone freely endorse a situation in which the annual cost of supplying basic education to all children is $6 billion, water and sanitation $9 billion, and basic health to all $13 billion, while annually $8 billion is spent in the U.S. on cosmetics, nearly $20 billion on jewelry and $17 billion (in the U.S. and Europe) on pet food?[1]

In the face of the harrowing scale of global poverty and human needs with forty-six percent of the world's population living on less than two dollars per day, little to no effort is required to establish the claim that we live in a profoundly disordered world. A visit to globalrichlist.com all too quickly and easily identifies one's place in the world economy. Based on figures from the World Development Bank Research Group, an annual income of $47,500 places one in the company of the top one percent of the richest people in the world.[2] Far from engendering guilt, knowledge of the alarming scale and reality of global poverty might help us to enter more deeply into a meaningful theological interpretation of Scripture and faithfully enact ways in which genuine love and care for each other constitutes a profound social and economic witness. Early in *Sources of the Self: The Making of the Modern Identity,* Charles Taylor insists that "to know who you are is to be oriented in moral space, a space in which questions arise about what is good or bad, what is worth do-

---

1. David Held, "Becoming Cosmopolitan: The Dimensions and Challenges of Globalization," in *Globalization and the Good* (ed. Peter Heslam; Grand Rapids: Eerdmans, 2004) 11–12.

2. "How do we calculate it?" at http://globalrichlist.com/how.html, accessed on September 19, 2011.

ing and what not."[3] The modern loss of confidence in the reality of the self is entirely consonant with the modern tragedy of a loss of moral order. Without a clear and compelling account of the moral space or order within which we are called to obedience and fellowship (cf. 1 Cor 11:17–34), we are unable to grasp and best determine our proper relation to a reality as powerful as "mammon" or wealth.

Jewish and Christian traditions effectively maintain that creaturely life is best oriented around a moral vision that guides the lives and being of God's people. The covenantal promises of God establish a moral space within which God's people have been drawn into a living fellowship with God. This confidence in the divine promise, order, and care of God is, as we shall see, patently on display in the plaintive and beautiful song of Mary, who like Hannah years before (cf. 1 Sam 1:11, 2:1–10) displays a remarkable confidence in the goodness and moral order of God (Luke 1:46–55).

Although early Christians did not possess a working knowledge of the instruments and methodologies of economic analysis, they certainly possessed a profound and hard-worn knowledge of economic inequality. In spite of the harrowing experiences of poverty and injustice they knew themselves to be a people constituted by the moral order and renewal of the covenant revealed in the teaching of a *new* Moses on the mount (Matt 5–7).[4] It is highly instructive that when Jesus turns to provide his disciples with vital moral teaching about mission, the law and the prophets, reconciliation, fidelity, love for one's enemies, and the giving of alms to the poor, he does so by teaching them how to pray. The Lord's Prayer is itself an invocation or petition for the coming of God's kingdom, with all that this holds for a shared life of justice and mercy.

In an effort to recover a number of the most fruitful ways of thinking about wealth and possessions, we shall offer a brief account of Karl Barth's exposition of the Lord's Prayer. As it turns out, Barth offers a moving account of prayer as human revolt against the disorder and lordless powers that twist, distort, corrupt, and ruin the lives of those who seek to live outside of the moral order revealed in Christ. Prior

---

3. Charles Taylor, *Sources of the Self: The Making of Modern Identity* (Cambridge: Harvard University Press, 1989) 8.

4. When we speak of a "*moral order,*" we have in view the sense that the kingdom of God orders human life and community such that God can be seen to have established, according to Karl Barth, an "order of life, right, freedom, peace and joy which is good for man as his creature, covenant partner, and child, which saves and keeps him." This very action, as the grace and mercy of God, is to be understood as a judgment that in the sacrifice and death of Jesus Christ has already been executed upon all disorder and unrighteousness. Cf. Karl Barth, *The Christian Life* (Grand Rapids: Eerdmans, 1981) 263.

to taking up Barth's discussion of prayer, however, we will draw the connection between Christology and political authority by looking at the example of Athanasius. His theology provides a clear vantage point from which we might better see how a high Christology offers essential resources with which to resist earthly powers. The powers in question are, for Athanasius, political and ecclesial. Following his argument may help us to recover constructive ways in which we too might be able better to resist authorities and powers that seek to compromise Christian witness and moral life. Our treatment of wealth, lordless powers, and the rule of Christ begins with a brief exposition of the Magnificat.

The key issue that this argument seeks to address is this: What constitutes the moral space within which the church can offer wholly free and faithful praise to God? Consequently, we argue that no properly Christian understanding of wealth and possessions can be had apart from an understanding of the rule of Christ. In short, the moral space within which Christians must come to understand wealth and possessions is one in which the triune God opposes all that refuses the good order and praise of the Lord in whom the reconciliation and redemption of all things is accomplished. The following argument seeks to retrieve a more adequate understanding of wealth by setting it within the larger context of a biblical and theological account of righteousness. Recognizing that Christians often find themselves in a disordered relationship to creaturely life, including wealth and possessions, we submit that a positive retrieval of the authority and rule of Christ may well serve to encourage the renewal and restoration of the church's witness and moral life. With this in view, we turn to a treatment of the Magnificat.

Poverty, Power, and the Promised Messiah

The Magnificat of Mary (Luke 1:46–55) offers one of the most important biblical treatments of justice, judgment, and the mission of Christ. As such, it sets the context for subsequent theological reflection on wealth, lordless powers, and the rule of Christ. When examined from the perspective of seeking to determine the concrete economic and political dimensions of God's promises to Israel, a number of fascinating dimensions come to light:

> [46]My soul magnifies the Lord,
>
> [47]and my spirit rejoices in God my Savior,
>
> [48]for he has looked with favor on the lowliness of his servant. Surely, from now on all generations will call me blessed;

> 49for the Mighty One has done great things for me, and holy is his name.
>
> 50His mercy is for those who fear him from generation to generation.
>
> 51He has shown strength with his arm; he has scattered the proud in the thoughts of their hearts.
>
> 52He has brought down the powerful from their thrones, and lifted up the lowly;
>
> 53he has filled the hungry with good things, and sent the rich away empty.
>
> 54He has helped his servant Israel in remembrance of his mercy,
>
> 55according to the promise he made to our ancestors, to Abraham and to his descendants forever. Luke 1:46–55 (NRSV)

The early verses of this song (vv. 46–49) are understandably focused upon Mary's immediate sense of God's blessing, for she is the chosen one through whom Yahweh has answered Israel's yearning for the promised Messiah. In the course of Mary's praise and thanksgiving we are given an unmistakable picture of the moral space within which the needs and identity of God's people will be met. As the song proceeds (vv. 50–55), we realize that the birth of Jesus of Nazareth is set within a cosmic, political, economic, and moral frame distinguished by the categories of divine covenant, judgment, and mercy along with proclamation of God's love for the vulnerable, poor, and hungry children of Abraham. In effect, the Magnificat offers us one of the most poignant declarations of God's solidarity with Israel, a people yearning for deliverance from under the oppressive rule of the Roman Empire. Made plain in all of this is the fact that Jesus' life and ministry are incomprehensible *apart* from the context of opposing powers, be they political, economic, social, or religious.

While we would be foolhardy to reduce Jesus' ministry and identity merely to that of conflict with opposing powers, any account of his teaching concerning the kingdom of God that fails to consider concrete economic and political powers will invariably offer no more than a partial and therefore insufficient portrayal of the saving work of Christ. Too often our thoroughly modern practice seeks to quarantine religious belief and commitments in the hope that political and economic life may flourish apart from the putatively irrational judgments of religious believers. When this is combined with the all too widely held and mistaken assumption that Jesus' teaching is no more than religious instruction for individuals, it becomes readily apparent that modern readers of the biblical text are ill-prepared to encounter a Jesus and a faith that integrates a serious commitment to the rule and promise of God with the everyday affairs of commerce, care for neighbor, active opposition to political and economic oppression, and the pursuit of justice and mercy for the broken. Arguably, only when Jesus' declarations "the kingdom of God is at hand" (Mark

1:14) and "blessed are you who are poor, for yours is the kingdom of God" (Luke 6:20) are heard against the backdrop of military violence, conquest, and economic oppression does the full force of Jesus' opposition to the oppressive imperial rule of the Roman empire clearly come into focus.

St. Athanasius on the Solidarity of Christ

Persuaded by Paul's teaching in Col 2:9 that in Christ "the whole fullness of God dwells *bodily*," we maintain that the ontological ground and basis for a Christian understanding of power and authority rests upon the Pauline affirmation that Christ is "the head of every ruler and authority" (2:10). This principle renders it all the more difficult—and so it should be—to offer one's fealty to the dominant claims of either the State or liberal economic theory. Not only does this passage suggest a profoundly countercultural notion of the moral shape of the Christian life, but it demands a corresponding break with dominant secular forms of political authority. Stated more positively, it maintains that all earthly powers and authorities have their proper identity and purpose within the order or rule of God. Of course, this raises the issue of what happens with creaturely thrones, authorities, rulers, or powers that resist or ignore the rule and authority of Christ. Here Oliver O'Donovan rightly claims that when these powers turn against the objective order of Christ's rule, they become "tumultuous and tyrannous adversaries in this condition of darkness, against whom we wrestle (Eph 6:12)."[5] A worthy perspective on the relationship between Christ and opposing powers can be gained by looking at the development of Athanasius's theology and ministry in the years following the first ecumenical council in 325. An illuminating correspondence can be drawn here between the way in which Arius and his followers relate to earthly powers and the way many contemporaries seek to accumulate and use wealth. In both cases, when Christ is not acknowledged as Savior and Lord, it is all the more likely that people will place inordinate confidence in creaturely powers and resources. Furthermore, the dramatic condemnations of Athanasius illustrate the fact that a high Christology poses numerous threats to those in authority who misuse political and ecclesial powers.

On the face of it, the great ecumenical council of 325 was a promising sign of mutuality, respect, and cooperation between the powers of the church and empire. The unprecedented occurrence of a Christian emperor sponsoring an ecclesiastical gathering of a significant number of the most prominent bishops of the church is it-

---

5. Oliver O'Donovan, *Resurrection and Moral Order: An Outline for Evangelical Ethics* (Grand Rapids: Eerdmans, 1986) 123.

self significant. That many of these bishops had undergone persecution in the course of seeking to defend the orthodox teaching of the church makes the significance of this gathering truly extraordinary. The sight of "over three hundred bishops, several of them confessors marked with the scars and mutilations of the recent fury of the Roman emperors, riding in imperial coaches to the first ecumenical council"[6] appeared to prefigure a messianic banquet signaling the sudden end of the reign of the antichrist.

It is crucial to realize that the critical difference between the catholic and Arian parties represents a critical distinction in how each party viewed the appropriate relation of the church to the Empire. This difference has much to teach us about the way in which Christianity *should* relate to powers in general. The relationship between one's Christology and understanding of political authority has much to teach us about the Christian life and witness. Much can be gained from seeing the way ancient Christians and Arians employed the lord/satrap model of authority.

Arians and catholic Christians alike believed that Christ was the head of the Church, that God had ordained the emperor to rule over earthly affairs, and that kingship (either divine or earthly) should be understood in terms of the analogy of a traditional lord/satrap relationship. One of the key points of disagreement had to do with the precise way in which their competing Christologies led them to employ the lord/satrap model in a given direction. Believing that the Son of God (satrap) was ontologically subordinate to the Father (lord), Arians applied the lord/satrap model in a way that subordinated the church to the empire (their earthly lord and sovereign). Catholic believers strongly resisted this move, believing that the incarnate Word is consubstantial with the Father. Accordingly, they maintained that the Son (satrap) shares in the authority of the Father (as lord). While the full implications of Arian Caesaropapism could not be as easily discerned at the beginning of the fourth century as it could toward its end, controversies surrounding the Arianizing Constantius (337–361) and Julian the Apostate (361–363) served to underscore the crucial significance of the catholic refusal to equate the authority of the emperor with that of the Supreme God. Arian support for imperial authority failed to secure the critical distance required of the church when, as it turned out, emperors such as Constantius enacted oppressive and vicious reprisals against catholic Christians. It is at this critical juncture that the ministry and writing of Athanasius sheds substantial light upon the vital difference that obtains between Arians who seek to uphold a

---

6. George Huntston Williams, "Christology and Church-State Relations in the Fourth Century," *Church History*, 20/3 (Sept, 1951) 5.

vision of the utter transcendence of God, while refusing to acknowledge the rule of Christ over earthly powers, and Christians who, like Athanasius and Paul before him, insisted that Christ is all in all.

By refusing to countenance an ontological subordination of the Son to the Father, Athanasius gave to the church a profound account of God's solidarity with the broken. This, as we shall see, stands in direct correspondence to Mary's depiction of the mission and identity of the incarnate Word. Far from imagining that God is shrouded in divine transcendence and majesty, as did the Arians, Athanasius proclaimed a divine Lord who willingly chooses to enter into full union with humanity. If Athanasius's tract *Contra Gentes* constitutes an argument for the necessity of the restoration of humanity, *De Incarnatione* demonstrates how all of this takes place by showing the purpose, truth, and outcome of the incarnation of the Son of God.

In the opening of *De Incarnatione* we learn that the divine Word became flesh in such a way that the "loving-kindness and goodness of His own Father" is decisively revealed to us "in a human body for our salvation." Developing this claim Athanasius continues:

> It is, then, proper for us to begin the treatment of this subject by speaking of the creation of the universe, and of God its Artificer, that so it may be duly perceived that the renewal of creation has been the work of the self-same Word that made it at the beginning. For it will appear not inconsonant for the Father to have wrought its salvation in Him by whose means He made it.[7]

Evidently Athanasius is seeking to secure the belief that the Son and the Father were involved in the creation of the world and therefore share in its renewal. The very center of this renewal is the saving appearance of the Son whose incarnation is an expression of God's grace and mercy. Showing mercy upon our plight, the Son condescended to take upon himself our corruption. According to Athanasius his arrival honors humanity in the same manner as when a king takes up residence in a city.

Seen against the backdrop of the use of the lord/satrap model, Athanasius's reference to Christ as King is seen to have considerable significance. More to the point, a high Christology critically undermines the basis upon which Arians and emperors alike understood the identity and rule of Christ. Look at the way in which Athanasius speaks of the cosmic significance of Christ as the Monarch of all: "So,

---

7. Athanasius, *De Incarnatione (On the Incarnation of the Word)* NPNF2 IV:36.

too, has it been with the Monarch of all. For now that He has come to our realm, and taken up his abode in one body among His peers, henceforth the whole conspiracy of the enemy against mankind is checked, and the corruption of death which before was prevailing against them is done away."[8]

Far from remaining aloof, hidden in divine transcendence, *this* Monarch (Christ) has drawn near to us. So near, in fact, that he has not only blessed or, in the words of the Eastern tradition, deified humanity, but has made our common cause *his*. Surely this is what is meant by Mary in her beautiful song: "He has shown strength with his arm; he has scattered the proud in the thoughts of their hearts. He has brought down the powerful from their thrones and lifted up the lowly" (Luke 1:51–52).

According to Athanasius, the purpose and truth of the incarnation is revealed in the condescension of the consubstantial Son of God for us and for our salvation. Over against the Arians who refused to concede that God truly joined himself to flesh, Athanasius insists that the incarnate Word is the self-same Lord who was both crucified at Golgotha and raised from the dead, standing bodily before Thomas with the mark of nails in his hands. Bringing the full magnitude of the incarnate Word's bodily solidarity into focus, Athanasius writes concerning 2 Pet 1:4, "For what the human Body of the Word suffered, this the Word, dwelling in the body, ascribed to Himself, in order that we might be enabled to be partakers of the Godhead of the Word."[9] In this we learn that the purpose of the divine incarnation of the Word is the full redemption and reconciliation of humanity with God in Christ.

Of considerable importance is the claim that Jesus "suffered and yet suffered not," by which Athanasius means that because the Word is by nature divine and human these two natures come together without canceling out their respective properties. According to Athanasius Jesus suffers inasmuch as he is truly human. Similarly, the Word does not suffer, for the divine nature is impassible. More than this is at work, for it was the impassible Word "which was destroying the infirmities in the Body."[10] What Athanasius means by saying that the incarnate Lord "suffered and yet suffered not" is that Christ suffered impassibly. None of this mitigates against the fact that it is the incarnate and divine Word who has taken upon himself our nature and offered himself as our sacrifice, thereby showing the full extent of his humility and identification with humanity. Once again, it is Athanasius's high Christology

---

8. Ibid., IV:41.

9. Athanasius, "Letter 59, to Epictetus," *NPNF*2 IV:572.

10. Ibid.

that leads him properly to understand the way in which Christ's suffering effectively communicates the full extent of the Word's solidarity with humanity:

> And if we wish to know the object: attained by this, we shall find it to be as follows: that the Word was made flesh in order to offer up this body for all, and that we partaking of His Spirit, might be deified a gift which we could not otherwise have gained than by His clothing Himself in our created body, for hence we derive our name of "men of God" and "men in Christ." But as we, by receiving the Spirit, do not lose our own proper substance, so the Lord, when made man for us, and bearing a body, was no less God; for He was not lessened by the envelopment of the body, but rather deified it and rendered it immortal.[11]

Reflecting an Eastern understanding of the scope of Jesus' redemptive activity, Athanasius firmly grasps how the incarnation of the Word—in his condescension and full participation in our suffering and death—is indeed the *constitutive* ground of the restoration of humanity. Far from resting upon juridical categories of debt, ransom, or penalty, Athanasius shares with Origen, Cyril, Gregory of Nyssa, John of Damascus, and Gregory of Nazianzus the conviction that the Word assumes our flesh in order that we may partake of his Spirit and be deified. Athanasius maintains that the Word was not diminished by taking on flesh, but rather healed or deified that which was otherwise subject to death. Towards the close of *De Incarnatione* Athanasius reflects yet again upon the inexhaustible mystery of the Incarnate, offering us the consummate phrase: "For He was made man that we might be made God," adding that he endured the "insolence of men" so that those who were suffering may be preserved by his own impassibility.[12]

One could well be excused for wondering how this apparent excursus on patristic Christology bears upon our discussion of wealth and possessions. As it turns out, the Arian controversy discloses a number of rather painful lessons about the nature of power and wealth.

At the Council of Milan (355) it came to the attention of the Arianizing emperor Constantius that a number of bishops were refusing to hold communion with Arians. Perhaps not surprisingly, he immediately summoned these bishops in the hope of determining why such evidently obdurate individuals were siding with Athanasius. Well aware that their manifest support for Athanasius could lead to certain banishment, if not death, bishops Paulinus, Lucifer, Eusebius, and Dionysius

---

11. Athanasius, *De Decretis (Defence of the Nicene Definition)* NPNF2 IV:159.
12. Athanasius, *De Incarnatione,* (NPNF2 IV:65).

of Milan took pains to remind the Emperor that no ecclesiastical canon permitted them to have communion with those deemed to be heretics. In reply Constantius boldly declared: "Whatever I will, be that esteemed a Canon."[13] By subordinating the Son to the Father and the church to the emperor, Arians mistakenly believed that security lay in offering tribute to earthly powers. The emperor was all too ready to dispense with established doctrine or tradition if they proved to be impediments to his own judgment. In the end Arians and Constantius alike cut themselves off from the full recognition of God's solidarity with humanity by privileging earthly power over against the teaching and authority of the church.

The connection between this period of Christian history and our broader concern with a Christian understanding of wealth and power is more clearly seen in light of a fragment of Athanasius's *History of the Arians* (355–57). In the midst of a long narrative of imperial incursions upon catholic churches by Constantius, Athanasius recounts numerous ways in which the Arian churches were complicit in the widespread imperial persecution of catholic Christians. Towards the end of this fragment we learn that the Arians "again devised another yet more cruel and unholy deed; cruel in the eyes of all men, but well suited to their antichristian heresy."[14] Athanasius has in view Jesus' command to care for the poor in Luke 12:33; Matt 25:35 and 40. In light of this teaching Athanasius boldly condemns the mistreatment of the destitute and widows at the hands of Arians. Not only did these followers of Arius fail to care for the vulnerable, but apparently they defended the use of a law that punished those who showed mercy and cared for poor.[15] Athanasius reports that "persons were brought to trial for acts of kindness which they had performed; he who shewed mercy was accused, and he who had received a benefit was beaten; and they wished rather that a poor man should suffer hunger, than that he who was

---

13. Athanasius, *Historia Arianorum* (History of the Arians) *NPNF2* IV:281.

14. Ibid., IV:292.

15. We ought not confuse the actions of Arians at this point with Arius himself. Many thanks are due to Jeff Tyler who helped me to discern a much more balanced picture of Arius's social concern than I would have otherwise seen. There is indeed evidence to show that Arius had a well-earned reputation for offering spiritual care to women (many of whom would have been widows). See Peter Brown, *The Body and Society: Men, Women, and Sexual Renunciation in Early Christianity* (New York: Columbia University Press, 1988) 266. Arius, it must be remembered, refused to countenance the belief that Jesus was of the same nature as God the Father. By way of contrast, he depicted a "savior" who shared in the human struggle towards virtue. Cf. Diarmaid MacCulloch, *Christianity: The First Three Thousand Years* (New York: Viking, 2010) 213. The despicable actions of Arians noted above, however, may well reveal a willingness to side with secular power rather than offer support for the poor and destitute in their midst.

willing to shew mercy should give to him."[16] By way of contrast, throughout his ministry Athanasius gave specific instruction for Christians to love their neighbor and extend kindness to the poor. Athanasius concludes his first Festal letter with the following:

> Let us remember the poor, and not forget kindness to strangers; above all, let us love God with all our soul, and might, and strength, and our neighbour as ourselves. So may we receive those things which the eye hath not seen, nor the ear heard, and which have not entered into the heart of man, which, God hath prepared for those that love Him, through His only Son, our Lord and Saviour, Jesus Christ.[17]

What then does the Arian controversy teach us about wealth, power, and the rule of Christ? Here was a community whose people regarded themselves as Christians, but they failed to understand, confess, and worship Christ rightly as the incarnate, eternal, and consubstantial Word. Failing to see the full participation of God in the world by failing to honor the kingly rule of Christ, Arians misunderstood the proper subordination of imperial authority to Christ. Placing confidence in a center of power outside of the gospel, Arians mistakenly choose power and privilege over solidarity with the poor and vulnerable.

By way of contrast, Christians like Athanasius read the kenotic hymn of Phil 2 and were unashamed of God's condescension and solidarity with the lowly and poor. Athanasius rightly teaches that we would be entirely lost if not for the condescension of the incarnate Word. This is readily on display in his statement: "Lord Jesus Christ, Who is the Very Life; and that none other could teach men of the Father, and destroy the worship of idols, save the Word, that orders all things and is alone the true Only-begotten Son of the Father."[18] Only God has the authority and power to do away with sin and to satisfy the just requirements of the law. Indeed, in Christ we find the most poignant and revealing display of a loving, powerful Lord who "lifts up the lowly" (Luke 1:52) by taking upon himself broken, alienated, and sinful humanity. As Mary faithfully proclaimed, Jesus of Nazareth has come to "fill the hungry with good things" to send "the rich away empty."

Our examination of Athanasius's Christology has revealed a number of pivotal ways in which a high Christology constitutes the fundamental ground of genuine

---

16. Athanasius, *Historia Arianorum*, IV:293.
17. Athanasius, *Letters of Athanasius*, "Festal Letter 1" *NPNF2* IV:510.
18. Athanasius, *De Incarnatione*, *NPNF2* IV:47.

revolt against heretical and/or imperial authorities. More than this however, by refusing to bind the identity, witness, teaching, and ministry of the church to imperial authority, Athanasius was free to call Christians to care for the poor and vulnerable. The lesson to be learned here is this: belief in the consubstantiality of the Father and the Son demands a corresponding commitment to the objects of God's love. Here, the incarnation is rightly seen as the revelation of God's decisive solidarity with the brokenness, alienation, and sin of the world. Athanasius expresses this by saying: "He, the incorruptible Son of God, being conjoined with all by a like nature, naturally clothed all with incorruption, by the promise of the resurrection" adding that all of this took place with the result that "the actual corruption in death has no longer holding-ground against men, by reason of the Word, which by His one body has come to dwell among them."[19] Far from remaining aloof in transcendent glory, the incorruptible Son of God became incarnate so that the poverty of brokenness, sin, and death no longer has its hold upon us, with the result that we are reconciled to God.

So far we have shown the depths of the Father's love for us in Christ and the ways in which a high Christology required catholic Christians to resist the Arian subordination of the church to the emperor. Now we need a clearer sense of the moral space within which Christians must come to understand wealth and possessions. A positive retrieval of the authority and rule of Christ may help us see the redemptive work of the triune God, opposing all that refuses the good order and praise of the Lord in whom the reconciliation and redemption of all things is accomplished. We will offer a brief theological exposition of a few biblical passages, keeping in mind the central question: What is the right order within which the church can offer wholly free and faithful praise to God? Then we shall develop our account of justice, wealth, and possessions by turning to the moral theology of one of the twentieth centuries most important theologians, Karl Barth.

Moral Order and the Biblical Witness

In Second Corinthians generosity is a decisive criterion of whether or not the churches of Macedonia had in fact received the grace of God. Paul wrote, "We want you to know, brothers and sisters, about the grace of God that has been granted to the churches of Macedonia; for during a severe ordeal of affliction, their abundant joy and their extreme poverty have overflowed in a wealth of generosity on their

---

19. Athanasius, *De Incarnatione*, NPNF2 IV:41.

part" (2 Cor 8:1-2). Their example of faithfulness in the midst of economic hardship stands as a model for Paul, who added: "For, as I can testify, they voluntarily gave according to their means, and even beyond their means, begging us earnestly for the privilege of sharing in this ministry to the saints" (2 Cor 8:3-4). As compelling as the example of Macedonian Christians is, Paul further illustrated the need for the Corinthian Christians to share their wealth by reminding them of the sacrifice of Jesus Christ: "For you know the generous act of our Lord Jesus Christ, that though he was rich, yet for your sakes he became poor, so that by his poverty you might become rich" (2 Cor 8:9). A few verses later Paul added, "I do not mean that there should be relief for others and pressure on you, but it is a question of a fair balance between your present abundance and their need, so that their abundance may be for your need, in order that there may be equality" (2 Cor 8:13-14).[20] Evidently, Paul knew that Christians do not have an absolute claim upon their wealth or possessions. It is this fact that allowed him to submit a financial appeal to fellow Christians to share their wealth with others so that there may be equity between the rich and the poor.

While it is true that the biblical canon fails to offer us a comprehensive economic program, there is no gainsaying the fact that holy Scripture provides a compelling moral vision in which we hear the call for God's people to alleviate poverty, to care for the hungry, homeless, naked, orphans, and resident aliens. At various points Israel was called to collect tithes for the poor (Deut 14:28-29), to leave fallen produce on the ground (Deut 24:19-21), and in the words of Isaiah, to "loose the bonds of injustice, to undo the thongs of the yoke, to let the oppressed go free" and "to share your bread with the hungry, and bring the homeless poor into your house" (Isa 58:6-7). It is not insignificant that the command to care for the alien, orphan, and widow in Deut 24:19-21 is accompanied by the exhortation "Remember that you were a slave in the land of Egypt" (Deut 24:22). Once again, issues of poverty and political power are drawn closely together. God knows that the human condition is so distorted by sin that even those who have been freed from bondage in Egypt might, left to themselves, refuse to share the abundance of their harvest with those who are most vulnerable. How much harder is it for those who have only known affluence and prosperity to care for the poor and hungry?

Paul had to remind the Corinthians of the incalculable generosity of the sacrifice of Christ as the basis of his moral exhortation to share their abundance with

---

20. The NRSV translates *isotēs* as "fair balance," but the terms "equity" or "equality" constitute a more powerful and accurate translation.

the poor. David Held in the quotation at the beginning of this essay suggests that our failure to care for the poor stems from our vested interest in the inequitable distribution of income which allows us to consume a disproportionate measure of the world's global resources. No doubt, Held is right, as far as he goes. Due to its limited scope, however, his argument is insufficient. For reasons that shall become patently clear, Christians living in Western Europe and North America must be open to the charge that forces even greater than self-interest may be at work in our disordered relationship to wealth, possessions, and the consumption of global resources. It turns out that one of the most constructive ways of gaining perspective on wealth and possessions lies in considering what stands in the way of developing a more just and equitable use of wealth and resources. It is here where the moral theology of Karl Barth is most helpful.

Barth on Prayer and the Righteousness of God

Karl Barth saw that our inability to discern the genuine powers and forces at work in the modern world follows directly from a number of critical decisions tied to a dominant rational and scientific worldview. So clearly did Barth see the spiritual threat of what he terms "lordless powers" that without embarrassment he claimed that we live in a world that is "largely demon-possessed, possessed, that is, by the existence and lordship of similar or, at times, obviously the same lordless forces"[21] of which the people of the NT speak with familiarity.

Well aware that others might too quickly accuse him of offering a naive or perhaps mythical picture of reality, Barth—and much to his credit—casts his lot with global South and Eastern Christians. He writes: "A magical picture of the world? Might it be that our fellow Christians from the younger churches of Asia and Africa, who come with a fresher outlook in this regard, can help us here? We hope at least that they will not be too impressed by our view of the world and thus be afflicted by the eye disease from which we ourselves suffer in this matter."[22] There is now considerable evidence pointing to the fact that Christians in Africa, China, and India—to name just a few of the places around the world where Christian growth is exponential in scale—have a more compelling and accurate grasp of the reality of spiritual forces or powers so central to Jesus' ministry and the promise of delivery. What is

---

21. Karl Barth, *The Christian Life*, Translation of Lecture Fragments, *Church Dogmatics* IV.4 (trans. Geoffrey W. Bromiley; Grand Rapids: Eerdmans, 1981) 218.

22. Ibid. 219.

more, without this kind of knowledge and perspective, we can make no real sense of Jesus' use and application of Isa 61 in the synagogue (Luke 4:16–22) or on the street with Bartimaeus (Mark 10:46–52).

In *The Christian Life* (*Church Dogmatics* IV/4, sec. 78) we find a lucid exposition of the second petition of the Lord's Prayer, "Your kingdom come. Your will be done, on earth as it is in heaven" (Matt 6:10). As is customary for Barth, each new section of the *Church Dogmatics* begins with a thesis, and here he says:

> Christians pray to God that he will cause his righteousness to appear and dwell on a new earth under a new heaven. Meanwhile they act in accordance with their prayer as people who are responsible for the rule of human righteousness, that is, for the preservation and renewal, the deepening and extending, of the divinely ordained human safeguards of human rights, human freedom, and human peace on earth.[23]

Here we see the connection between prayer for the coming of God's righteousness and creaturely moral action directed toward securing human rights, freedom, and peace. Put differently, the struggle for justice in the face of the sinful disorder of the world takes the form of prayer.

Barth is acutely aware of the ways in which persons seek to emancipate themselves from the lordship of God. In their attempt to do so, they fall victim to the harrowing force of lordless powers. Barth traces this move all the way back to the beginning of time. In Gen 3:5 we hear the serpent declare: "For God knows that when you eat of it your eyes will be opened, and you will be like God, knowing good and evil." Here, Barth argues, we find a decisive and critical first step towards the myth and illusion of human freedom and autonomy. Put differently, self-assertion does not issue in freedom or autonomy, but brokenness and bondage. Barth adds, "In the foolish and hopeless attempt to escape from the sphere of God's lordship, it is not so simple for man to become and be even a little God and Lord with the implied approximation to God's supremacy and controlling power in the fashioning of human existence."[24] The argument concerning the futility of seeking to become a lord unto oneself is strengthened by reference to Goethe's *The Sorcerer's Apprentice*. Drawing our attention to the forbidding consequences of efforts to free ourselves from the lordship of God, Barth writes:

---

23. Ibid., 205.
24. Ibid., 214.

His capacities when he uses them, as Goethe describes so vividly and with such frightening profundity in his poem *The Sorcerer's Apprentice,* become spirits with a life and activity of their own, lordless indwelling forces. To be sure, he thinks he can take them in hand; control them, and direct them as he pleases, for they are undoubtedly the forces of his own possibilities and capacities, of his own ability. In reality, however, they escape from him, they have already escaped from him. They are entities with their own right and dignity. They are long since alienated from him. They act at their own pleasure, as absolutes, without him, behind him, over him, and against him, according to the law by which they arose, in exact correspondence to the law by which man himself thought that he should flee from God.[25]

Given the central thesis of this paper, that no proper Christian understanding of wealth and possessions can be had apart from an understanding of the rule or kingdom of God, Barth's exposition of the second petition of the Lord's prayer demands that we take seriously the "reality" of all that stands in the way of the good order of God revealed in the righteousness and rule of Christ.

When power breaks free from its proper order and purpose, as has happened in the development of the modern nation-states, we find conditions ripe for the political absolutism spoken of by Thomas Hobbes in his 1651 work, *Leviathan*. Here Michael Gillespie's informative treatment of the theological significance of Hobbes is instructive. Hobbes offers us a powerful image of a god "less to be loved than feared." *This* god offers no more than arbitrary standards of good and evil, which, in turn, has led to the development of a science that perhaps only hesitatingly grants the existence of a distant god, all the while seeking to "emulate his power and artifice through the mastery of the causal order of the world."[26] It is not difficult to see why Barth commends Hobbes for providing a negative example of the risks of political absolutism. Barth thought Hobbes deserves praise for his vision and knowledge about this topic and added, "It should be part of Christian vigilance to see and know what he saw and knew."[27] Christian vigilance is what led Barth to permit the question of mammon or wealth to occupy such an important place in his exposition of the Lord's Prayer.

Barth's discussion of mammon as one of a number of lordless powers, under whose control and force all too many have fallen victim, conforms to his general

---

25. Ibid.

26. Michael A. Gillespie, *The Theological Origins of Modernity* (Chicago: University of Chicago Press, 2008) 254.

27. Barth, *The Christian Life,* 222.

claim that a rational or scientific world view consistent with Hobbes' *Leviathan* betrays the false belief that it is *we* who control things like wealth and possessions and not they us. Listen to how Barth expresses the point:

> He thinks he can take them in hand, control them, and direct them as he pleases, for they are undoubtedly the forces of his own possibilities and capacities, of his own ability. In reality, however, they escape from him, they have already escaped from him. They are entities with their own right and dignity. They are long since alienated from him.[28]

Along similar lines he claims that lordless powers, such as mammon, have a profound hold upon us, even though they are products of our own making. Barth identifies them as "the secret guarantee of man's great and small conventions, customs, habits, traditions, and institutions. They are the hidden wirepullers in man's great and small enterprises, movements, achievements, and revolutions."[29] Barth appeals to Jesus' teaching in Matt 6:24 and Luke 16:13 in which we encounter the warning: "No one can serve two masters; for a slave will either hate the one and love the other, or be devoted to the one and despise the other. You cannot serve God and wealth." Barth rightly sees that money or wealth is presented as a second, competing lord.[30]

Having grown accustomed to thinking of wealth instrumentally, we are often at a loss in finding satisfying explanations for global and domestic financial inequality. Barth's depiction of mammon challenges us to think more deeply about the insidious influence of money upon public opinion, social policy, personal consumption, and political debate. Money, Barth writes, "is a flexible but powerful instrument which, supposedly handled by man, in reality follows its own law." This lordless power can "in a thousand ways establish some opinions and even convictions and suppress others. It can also create brutal facts. It can cause the market to rise and then to fall again. It can arrest this crisis and cause another. It can serve peace yet pursue cold war even in the midst of peace. It can make ready for a bloody war and finally bring it about."[31] Mammon is able to execute such influence in the context of a vacuum created by individuals and cultures that falsely imagine that wealth is intrinsically harmless, something that we possess. This may be true, Barth suggests,

---

28. Ibid., 214.
29. Ibid., 216
30. Ibid., 223.
31. Ibid., 224.

until such time as we decide that we can have and use money *apart from* God. As a lordless power, mammon fills this vacuum and becomes an "absolutist demon" such that individuals become "its football and slave."[32]

Taken as a whole, the terrifying reality of these lordless powers and the ensuing alienation and disorder that follow in their wake need not constitute a bitter end for humanity. This is where Barth's ethics of prayer constitute a powerful and constructive response to the brokenness of a world in which lordless powers like mammon have their putative reign.

According to Barth, the human struggle for righteousness begins with the invocation: "Thy kingdom come." Not only is invocation for the coming of God's kingdom exceedingly important as an act of creaturely revolt; at the same time it correctly identifies the kingdom and rule of God with Christ:

> The kingdom of God is God himself, who in the act and revelation of his own divine righteousness certainly frees man and calls him to a being in human righteousness but who still remains free over against all the inner and outer works of human righteousness, who does not merge into any of them so that people might say, "Lo, it is here or there" (Lk. 17:21), who can thus free all people for such works, and call them to them, precisely in his indestructible sovereignty.[33]

It is vital to note that Barth is running at least two lines of argument in tandem. First, the kingdom of God is spoken of in terms of God's own identity and action—with the result that the knowledge of God follows from divine freedom and *prome-ity*. For this reason, the kingdom of God is not to be confused with human action, for the moral life properly *follows from* rather than *inaugurates* the free movement of God toward us. The Lord's Prayer is, as Barth reminds us, an act that "carries with it the unreserved certainty of being heard."[34] In similar ways, Barth shows that this petition "looks toward an act of God as the goal and end of all human history and of all the history of faith and the church within it."[35] Christian prayer, in other words, has an undeniably eschatological character and content; its antecedent is the unique history of the incarnate Lord as the truly new and concrete reality.

---

32. Ibid.
33. Ibid., 244.
34. Ibid., 245.
35. Ibid., 247.

Second, the underlying premise of Barth's reading of the NT and his understanding of the kingdom of God leads him to view the history of Jesus Christ as *the* eschatological reality and decisive event. Early in the *Church Dogmatics* we encounter this key lesson about the centrality of Christ to the order and redemption of the world: "Dogmatics has no more exalted or profound word—essentially, indeed, it has no other word—than this: that God was in Christ reconciling the world unto Himself (2 Cor 5:19)."[36] Almost twenty years later he said: "'The kingdom of God is at hand' means 'the Word was made flesh and dwelt among us' (Jn. 1:14). In him the divine righteousness and order contest, defeat, overcome, and set aside human unrighteousness and disorder."[37]

Accordingly, one of the most significant features of Barth's exposition of the Lord's prayer is the claim that the kingdom of God *is* Jesus Christ. The extraordinary importance of this lies in the way Barth anchors the moral life (imperative) within the constitutive reality of the person and work of God (indicative). As he rightly claims, only here are signifying and being (*significare* and *esse*) one thing, not two.[38] The force of all this is more clearly on display in the following passage where we see the benefit of locating the meaning of the locution "the kingdom of God" in Christ:

> Jesus Christ is the new thing . . . *He* is the total and definitive limitation of human unrighteousness and disorder, of the interim demonic world of unchained powers: the conqueror of this world, the victorious enemy of all the enmity of man against God, one another, and themselves. *He* at that time was in his history, on the path that he trod to the end in his time, the imminent kingdom of God.[39]

Because Christ is the kingdom of God, the resurrection appearances constitute an important key to understanding the rule of Christ. Expressed somewhat differently, as realized eschatology, the risen Lord lays bare the nature of human obedience to the present rule of God.

> The One revealed and knowable to them as this Son and Lord was Jesus raised again from the dead—the same in a totally different way—who appeared to them in the Easter days . . . he in the future of his history now revealed to them and not concealed, the kingdom of God in what was now

---

36. Karl Barth, *Church Dogmatics*, II/2 (ed. G. W. Bromiley and T. F. Torrance; Edinburgh: T. & T. Clark, 1957) 88.

37. Barth, *Christian Life*, 249.

38. Ibid., 250.

39. Ibid., 52.

revealed to them as the universal future of its hitherto particular and to that extent concealed coming.[40]

To his credit, Barth addresses the obvious problem straightway. On what basis is it possible for those who did not witness the Easter event to be moved from pure recollection of this narrative to real expectation and hope for the final consummation of God's rule and dominion?[41] How, in other words, can this startling revelation of a past event, so central to the witness and life of the church, constitute the ground upon which in our day we faithfully enter into the struggle for human righteousness? Barth's response is one that focuses upon the ongoing work and power of the Holy Spirit. He writes: "The Holy Spirit is the *forward* which majestically awakens, enlightens, leads, pushes, and impels, which God has spoken in the resurrection of Jesus from the dead, which he has spoken and still speaks to the world of humanity: *forward* to the new coming of Jesus and the kingdom."[42]

As we have seen, Barth's grasp of the eschatological force of the NT leads him to speak of the life, death, and resurrection of Jesus as an utterly new and definitive reality on our horizon. This divine interruption of human existence arises by virtue of the presence and power of the Holy Spirit. Unlike lordless powers that enslave and distort human existence, the Spirit liberates and empowers Christians to call upon God, praying, "Thy kingdom come."[43]

In the final section of *The Christian Life,* entitled *"Fiat Iustitia"* Barth offers a lucid, unadorned, and concrete exposition of the moral life. Invocation here is depicted as "the most authentic, powerful, and effective thing that can be done on the human side."[44] When Christians bravely invoke God, Barth declares, they are "caught up by what they pray, their whole life and thought and word and deed are set in motion, oriented to the point to which they look with the petition."[45] To invoke God, therefore, is to engage in a fundamentally *moral* act in which the intrinsic meaning of the petition "Thy kingdom come" subsists in a prior moral field in which the gospel and the renewal of the Spirit makes possible the very invocation of God.

---

40. Ibid., 255.
41. Ibid., 255–56.
42. Ibid., 256.
43. Ibid.
44. Ibid., 261.
45. Ibid., 262.

For this reason, Barth represents the moral agent as one who has been claimed, freed, and empowered for a life of moral action and faithfulness.

In characterizing invocation as an activity *for* human righteousness, Barth has in view not only the question of the shape of the moral life but its goal and purpose. Christians have been empowered to *act* in the domain of the relative possibilities presented to them. While human righteousness is always imperfect, the provisional and tenuous character of creaturely moral action for Barth does not mitigate the responsibility we carry for concrete moral action. At every turn Christians are to resist the temptation of passivity: "What is required, with a full sense of one's limitations, is to become active."[46] It is no small matter that God has summoned the human agent to invoke God in prayer and then to carry out corresponding human works of righteousness.

The final point concerns the degree to which Barth understands moral action as being essentially humanist in scope. As we shall see, moral acts, for Barth, properly reflect God's own mercy and genuine interest in human subjects. In their public witness to the gospel Christians are called and empowered to make their fellow human subjects the focus of their obedient moral action. Not setting aside their own share in the disorder and unrighteousness of the world, they nonetheless act as "righteous sinners." Far from making fellow subjects little projects or a means to some further good, Barth's account of moral action is focused rightly upon the task of seeking to restore the dignity and well-being of people caught in the disorder of the world. Fitting moral action is characterized by Barth as a "wrestling and fighting and suffering for a provisional bit of human right."[47]

Drawing his discussion of the kingdom of God and the corresponding struggle for human righteousness to a close, Barth reminds us of the fundamental obligation that has come upon Christians to act as "shining lights of hope, to all men" and to pray, "Come, Lord Jesus." When Christians pray these words, Barth writes:

> . . . they may not and cannot abandon man himself in spite of all his disguises. They will always see in him a fellow man and not just a future brother, and they must treat him as such. They must assist him in full commitment in this time between times and thus bring him the promise and be for him credible witnesses that God, like themselves, has not abandoned him and will not do so, that his kingdom, the kingdom of the

---

46. Barth, *The Christian Life*, 265.
47. Ibid., 270.

Father, Son and Holy Spirit, has come and will come even for him, that Jesus Christ is his hope too.[48]

Conclusion

Der rote Faden, or central theme, of the biblical witness with respect to wealth and possessions is this: God's people are called to care for the poor and vulnerable. In the words of Isaiah, God's people are called to "loose the bonds of injustice, to undo the thongs of the yoke, to let the oppressed go free" and "to share your bread with the hungry, and bring the homeless poor into your house" (Isa 58:6–7). It is not insignificant that the biblical command to care for the alien, orphan, and widow (Deut 24:19–21) is followed by the telling exhortation: "Remember that you were a slave in the land of Egypt" (Deut 24:22). At the very least this shows that wealth, possessions, and poverty cannot be understood apart from socio-economic conditions and political power.

In view of the Magnificat with its highly charged polemic against earthly powers and authorities that seek power and their own advantage at the expense of the poor, hungry, and vulnerable, we have argued that Jesus' teaching about the kingdom of God (Mark 1:14) and God's blessing upon the poor cannot be rightly understood unless it is heard in the context of the military violence, conquest, economic disparity, and oppressive imperial rule of the Roman empire. This contextual observation forms the backdrop against which we have sought to show ways in which one's grasp of earthly power and authority can twist or distort one's understanding of the identity and work of Christ.

Athanasius's courageous and longstanding defense of a high Christology provided him with the basis upon which to offer a profound exposition of God's solidarity with humanity. It also allowed him to develop the conceptual and theological basis to resist competing claims for lordship and power. Against an Arian misuse of the lord/satrap model, Athanasius correctly maintains that no earthly lord or emperor can properly govern apart from the authority and unique mission of the consubstantial and incarnate Word. One of the most important contributions of Athanasius's theology is the way in which he decisively maintains that the Son of God humbled himself to the point of death so that we might be delivered from our poverty and be restored to saving fellowship with the true Lord and Father of all.

---

48. Ibid., 271.

No fully Christian discussion of wealth and possessions can take place without serious examination of the harrowing scale of global economic inequality. Instruction is found in Paul's exhortation to the churches in Corinth and in his appeal to both the generosity of Macedonian Christians and the self-offering of Christ himself. Christians do not have an absolute claim upon their wealth or possessions. This fact allowed Paul to submit a financial appeal to fellow Christians to share their wealth so that there may be equity between the rich and the poor. Barth's ethics of prayer provided further means to see the intersection of power, solidarity, care for the broken, and the rule of Christ. Barth's ethics accurately assesses the hidden yet forceful "lordless powers" that function as "the hidden wirepullers in man's great and small enterprises, movements, achievements, and revolutions."[49]

In the face of the devastating effect of the lordless powers upon the lives of those who have sought to live in rebellion against God, Barth admonishes us to enter more fully into genuine moral action and solidarity with others. The key to our analysis has been the realization that the issue of wealth and possessions cannot be understood apart from the broader context of a moral order in which economic relationships are deeply rooted in the questions of the kingdom of God. Moreover, the theological and moral thrust of our argument has cast light upon the economic and political significance of the love and mercy of God on display in the incarnation, suffering, death, and resurrection of Christ. May we, in turn, seek to bear faithful witness to the one who, in fundamental solidarity with the broken, is the desire and hope of the nations (Hag 2:7).

---

49. Barth, *The Christian Life*, 216.

RESPONSE TO HUSBANDS

William Myatt

The primary problem addressed by Professor Husbands is expressed in this sentence taken from his opening paragraph: "Without a clear and compelling account of the moral space or order within which we can act, discern, and worship, we have little hope of being able to make sense of a reality as powerful as wealth." By turning primarily to St. Athanasius of Alexandria and (some would say) St. Barth of Basel, Husbands attempts to locate this space without remaining "subject to the reigning values" of the surrounding culture. Such values may be grounded in deficient theologies, such as Arius's theory of the atonement[1] and its notions on authority, or in deficient understandings of human intellect, as in the "rational and scientific worldview" challenged by Barth.

Of significance for Husbands's retrieval of the Athanasian and Barthian projects is a concern with the manner in which any theological system affects the "least of these," those on the underside of theological construction. In retrieving an Athanasian theology of atonement, for example, we find that the incarnation of the embodiment of the impassible God enables the "preservation" of the suffering. Or, in retrieving a Barthian theology of prayer, we find that Christian piety is "essentially humanist" reflecting "God's own mercy and genuine interest in human subjects." With these concerns I am very much in agreement. Any theology constructed on the other side of such abuses of power as those of Christendom, the religious wars, and colonialism—not to mention such singularly evil events as the violence of the Crusades, the abuses of the Peasant Wars, or the atrocities of the Holocaust—must be attentive to the radical ambiguity of Christian theology and of any theology attempting to retrieve historical-theological expressions. It should make the potential dangers of its project a constitutive and not merely teleological aspect of its method. Husbands has retrieved from the Christian tradition resources which enable the pursuit of human dignity and, where necessary, the "revolt against the dehuman-

---

1. During the conversation which followed my response, Professor Husbands kindly corrected my terminology. His concern was not with Athanasius's and Arius's theologies of atonement but with their theologies of incarnation.

izing disorder of creaturely life." In so doing he has addressed the precarious relationship between social structures and theological method, a maneuver that enables Christian theology to challenge such unhealthy structures. For this I enthusiastically applaud him.

However, I am hesitant to adopt his critique fully. For in his challenge toward reigning cultural paradigms, indeed in his challenge of secularism, one may observe the perpetuation of what we could call a secularist methodology. In brief, I wonder whether the evaluative method Husbands uses is robust enough to redirect the dysfunctional relationship between theology and power into a newly formed, Christian moral space attentive to the dignity of every human being.

Let me begin with Husbands's correction of Arius by way of Athanasius. My primary question here could be stated using Husbands's own phraseology: Is it adequate to correct the "Arian error" according to a Christology which is more "correctly maintained" by Athanasius? Husbands is appropriately concerned with the assumed secularity of so many political and economic arguments, constructed as if the bracketing of religious belief were possible. In my estimation his challenge to this assumption is spot on, but his running comparison between the two historical theologians finally rests on what could conceivably be called a "secular" foundation.

Arius's and Athanasius's respective theologies of atonement are evaluated over against one another as better or worse interpretations of the revelation of God, quintessentially located in the Bible. In this regard the governing evaluative matrix emerges finally as a controlled set of data to be analyzed, dissected, and evaluated on the way to the most provable theory. In order for two interpretations to be judged more or less accurate, there is the assumption of a third, empty space wherein the evaluation may occur "objectively," "scientifically," and we could risk, "secularly." Is not the assumed point of entry into this evaluative space merely a perpetuation of the dangers of technocracy that Husbands wishes to challenge? If so, one may question whether Husbands has fully shifted away from a secular order for moral evaluation into "the proper [post-secular but, one hopes, no less Christian] order within which wealth and possession have their use and significance."

In consideration of Husbands's use of Barth, I begin again with a point of agreement. Borrowing from the French philosopher Paul Ricoeur, I label this point of agreement a "hermeneutic of suspicion." One need not read far into the second half of the paper to locate an example of this hermeneutic. According to the opening quote of David Held, the present perdurance of radical economic inequality is attributed to the "privileged stake in the existing social hierarchy" that is maintained by those whose interpretation determines the economic policies in which the inequality exists.

In continuity with Held's suspicion is that of Karl Barth. There has scarcely been a theologian in Christian history whose posture of suspicion could rival that of Barth. Husbands notes Barth's suspicious comportment in a variety of ways. Situating his treatment of Barth in the biblical notion of a human condition "distorted by sin," Husbands highlights Barth's skepticism of the "dominant rational and scientific worldview," Barth's encouragement for Christians to "see how and what [Thomas Hobbes] saw and knew,"[2] and Barth's prophetic proclamation that those "powers" we humans naively think we control—mammon being the most saturated example—are actually beyond our control. Mammon has escaped our powers and exists as something like the Godfather of history, pulling the wires, as it were, of our social evolutionary trajectory. Barth's concern with these surreptitious powers motivates him to suggest not merely that Christians should protect themselves by preserving the lordship of God but should also understand prayer as a dynamic activity, moving them toward that great "meanwhile" during which they act "for the preservation and renewal, the deepening and extending" of human rights.[3] This teleological aspect of prayer is instituted by the Holy Spirit, who is the "forward" trajectory of prayer's motion, and it may result ultimately in revolt. With all of these concerns, I am in thorough agreement with Husbands.

Yet, not unlike my critique of his use of Athanasius, I wonder if the methodological world Barth inhabits—and thus the theological application constructed by Husbands—is also inadequately sensitive to the tendencies toward technocracy and power which linger within the very infrastructure of so many theological projects. Barth regularly mentions the ungraspable nature of God, that mysterious aspect of God which protects against the temptation to declare, "Lo, it is here or there!"[4] However, in my reading, Barth's theology as preaching and his insistence on the objectivity of God rests on the assumption that revelation is, well, "there." God's revelation is observable enough to elicit evaluative appraisals, appraisals that issue forth into experimentally defensible positions. How else could Barth hold to his classic paradoxes, if not according to the belief that they are simply "there" and should be presented as such, with as little personal engagement from the theologian as pos-

---

2. Karl Barth, *The Christian Life*, translation of lecture fragments, *Church Dogmatics* IV.4 (trans. Geoffrey W. Bromiley; Grand Rapids: Eerdmans, 1981) 222.

3. Ibid., 205.

4. Ibid., 224, invoking Luke 17:21.

sible? Barth's theological method is thus likewise disclosed as ironically modern, more "secular" than may be assumed.

Has Husbands located that "moral space" in search of which his paper initially set out? I believe he has. My questions challenge the assumed adequacy of this space. As I have suggested, I am afraid it is not exactly where one may expect it to be, especially if it is located by way of theological method as opposed to theological claims. Given the methodology operative in Husbands's comparison of Athanasius and Arius and his treatment of Barth's dependence on the object of revelation, one may appropriately ask whether there is not a lurking secularity in Husbands's method. Although the overall direction of his project is most welcome, I hesitatingly submit that the infrastructure which undergirds it is finally inadequate for accomplishing the Christian goals he hopes to obtain.

MONEY AND POSSESSIONS

Will Willimon

The most honest sentence in the most truthful book that I know—Flaubert's *Madame Bovary*—is, "Of all the winds that blow upon love, the coldest is the request for money." In this gathering we have been talking about God and money. We have agreed that money is powerful, and one of the most powerful aspects of money is its power to unmask us, to tell the truth about us. I know that the church tends toward triviality—until you ask Christians for their money. Then the discussion gets interesting.

I remember as a young pastor my first church. I was pouring out my frustrated heart to an older, experienced pastor about my failed efforts to get the church in gear, trying to get things moving. What could I do?

He said, "Here's a suggestion that I find works. And it's easy to do: next Sunday demand that they give you $50,000 for mission work in Zimbabwe. And I believe Jesus will show you just how good a church you've got in the subsequent discussion." Money is powerful. Money brings out some of the best things we do and some of the worst.

The night before I came here I was at dinner with a group of pastors. One of the pastors at the table was a distinguished scholar/pastor, pastor of a large, predominately African American congregation. He confirmed my observations about money. He said, "You know, I go around the world talking about race and racial injustice, but I tell you that things don't usually get testy in nice, liberal mainline Christian gatherings until I put the other 'R' word on the table."

I asked, "The 'R' word?"

He replied, "Reparations. Then suddenly all this innocuous liberalism wilts." (By the way, I noticed that the pastor who made that comment to me was wearing a nice pair of gold cufflinks, as well as monogram initials on his shirt, and he was consuming a meal that I estimate cost about $160.)

Money matters are ambiguous, not only in life but also in Scripture. Here's a question for you: when is a conference about the evils of money a participation in the evils of money? It is hard to know. Thus, I bring you to our Scripture for today: Luke 16.

> Jesus said to his disciples, "There was a rich man who heard that one of his managers was squandering his property. So he summoned him and said, 'Hey you! What is this I hear about you stealing from me? Give me an accounting of your management.'
>
> The manager said to himself, 'What am I to do now that my master is taking away my position? I am not strong enough to dig and I too ashamed to beg. I've decided what I will do so that when I am dismissed as manager people will welcome me into their homes.'
>
> Summoning his master's debtors one by one, he asked the first, 'How much do you owe my master?'
>
> He answered, 'One hundred jugs of olive oil.'
>
> 'Take your bill, sit down quickly, and make it fifty.' Then he asked another, 'How much do you owe the master?'
>
> He replied, 'One hundred containers of wheat.'
>
> 'Here, take your bill and make it eighty.'
>
> And his master commended this dishonest manager because he had acted shrewdly. But the children of this age are more shrewd in dealing with their own generation than are the children of light. I tell you, make friends for yourselves by means of dishonest wealth, so when it is gone they can welcome you into their eternal homes."

A significant moment in my religious development came when I was 16. I had seen her across the classroom from me in typing class and was impressed by her . . . development. So I invited her out. After pizza, we were sitting there in the park and I told her, "I don't know you really well but I really like you."

She said, "I really like you."

I said, "More than like, I think I love you."

She said, "Really?"

One thing led to another and I said, "Yes I have always admired you across the typing class, and if I could just adjust this button for you . . ." At the end of that evening having—once again—failed in my intentions, I was sitting there thinking to myself, "I thought I was a good person. I can't believe that I would tell that many lies!"

It was a moment of revelation for me. I thought I was fairly nice until then. And I think I am making an appropriate analogy here between sex and money. Others have made it before. There is an interesting connection between my self-deceit and my use of money.

One of my favorite passages is from the Acts of the Apostles where they are having a church meeting and they are talking about the annual Fall Stewardship

Emphasis, and Ananias and Sapphira (two members of the Administrative Board) have come forward to offer their gifts. Peter said, "Hey you two, how come you've lied to the Holy Spirit and kept back some of the proceeds of the sale of your land?" I love that story because, well, who among us pastors hasn't wanted to kill a church trustee at some time or another? It is so good to see them get what they deserve! And at an otherwise boring church meeting!

But an interesting thing about that story (in light of this conference) is you would think Peter would say, "How dare you be so greedy and materialistic?" But he did not say that. He said, "How dare you to lie to the Holy Spirit?" There is just something about money and deceit that go hand in hand, and there is something about money that reveals the perplexity and the depth of my self-deceit.

It is not just money itself that is a problem; it is when you take money and set it next to Jesus. That is when money has a way of becoming a medium of revelation. Thus, I bring you back to our Scripture for today.

Jesus said to his disciples, just to us, the in crowd, the children of light: "A rich man had this little manager whom he heard was stealing from him." (Now, whose side are you on in the story? I know you class-hating democrats. You are on the side of the little manager against the rich man. You are thinking to yourself that the little manager is probably taking only what he really deserves for all the work he has done. He is probably underpaid.)

So the little manager said to himself, "What am I to do? I am too lazy to go out and do honest manual labor. I am too proud to beg. Oh, I know what I will do; I will cheat my master out of the money that other people owe him. He called the debtors in and the swindle began: "Hey, how much do you owe my master? Take $100 off. Remember me next week when I get sacked." Huge sums are being written off here. It bothers me that you took the side of this little wretch!

Of course you say, "I liked him before I got to know him that well. I thought he was a member of the *deserving* poor. I didn't know he was one of the illegal poor."

So the swindling manager went back to the master to show him the cooked books, and the master looked down. (He could see numbers scratched out and messed with). The master said, "You business genius you. I wish other people in my company would show this much entrepreneurial spirit! I tell you I wish I had a little more children of this age in this company rather that these priggish little, tight children of light that don't know how to make a dollar."

Now, I have no idea why Jesus would tell an outrageous story like this to people like us. I have lived forty years with this story, and I do not know what it means. But it is interesting to watch you listening to this story. You know at first we are on the side of the little manager against the rich guy because we are always against the rich. When we find out what a seedy character this little manager is, we are back up in the front office with the boss saying, "I see what you have been putting up with all these years. This guy is stealing you blind."

Then at the end of the story when the boss praises the little crook for his crimes, we have had it with all of them. They are stealing out on the assembly line but also stealing up in the front office, commending thievery, and there is no good guy in this story. In a way, listening to your wonderful academic papers at the end this week, you have made me ask myself, "Where do I stand. Is there a good guy in the story in our dealings with money? Where is there a high, righteous place to stand?"

"Can we be honest for just five minutes, even though this is Chicago?" That is not from me; it is from one of Carl Sandberg's poems. But as a preacher, I am thinking money is helpful in promoting honesty in the way that God gives us money, placing money against us in order to be for us.

In my last congregation, if you were to ask me the greatest pastoral care challenge in that congregation, I would have immediately responded that the biggest burden for our families is *affluence.* That would have seemed odd because it was an inner-city congregation full of shop keepers, school teachers, and blue collar people.

My analysis was that they were the first generation in their family to have a surplus of funds. I learned, in my interaction with families in my own church, that it does not take a lot of money to ruin a teenager. You can do it for about $225. My people did not think of themselves as affluent. They had no moral skills of discernment or resistance for dealing with a surplus of money. The wreckage around them showed both the power of money and the impotence of many church people to know what to do with it.

In that congregation I preached a stirring sermon on money and stewardship and the evils of money. At the end of the sermon this grand dame of the congregation emerged under full sail and said to me, "Thank you for your sermon. Well said."

"Thank you," I graciously responded, "it is good to get a compliment from you for a change."

Then she asked, "Are we to take this to mean that you probably will not be expecting a raise this year? I am sure the finance committee will be glad to hear that."

If you can't fool laity, who can you fool? Where would we be as a church, if when I confronted you about your sin with money, you confronted me? We might be emerging as a church that values the truth more than simply getting along. We might be on our way of being visibly the Body of Christ. My wife and I, after prayerful consideration in taking my present job, decided that we would give back to the church about 40% of my salary. We do it as a witness; it just seems right. (How many of you give that much of your salary?) Well, I hope you are impressed by our stewardship, but when I tell you that my salary is about $121,000 a year plus housing, well, I bet you are a bit less impressed by my giving.

It is complicated. In fact, I would say from what I have heard in your papers in the last couple of days, "People, don't try this at home! Don't do this by yourself. If you want to try to live a righteous life in regard to money, you had better believe in a God who forgives sin and you had better know how to ask for it."

I am in a church that appears to have too few theological resources for dealing with the complexity of the blessings and curses of wealth. My church, in its beginnings, had an ecclesiology that was high enough and functional enough to help early Methodists look at the lures of the world and say, "No thanks, I've had enough."

There is not much wrong with our financial ethics that could not be solved by a more vibrant ecclesiology. I was in a new church last weekend, a new kind of hip congregation with contemporary music, etc. The preacher said, "We now come to what we call 'the offering.' The offering is when we give our money to help fund the work of the church. If you are a visitor, we are just glad to have you here today. Just relax, enjoy the service, and should you decide to affiliate with us, as we hope you will, then you can help us support the church too."

I sat there thinking, "Hey, it's Hoover, Alabama. Why wait a week to get started on their greed? Let's get going now. Put it in the plate!" I wanted to say, "Hey, this is an offering! It's not a metaphor. It's not a symbol. Put it in the plate!"

One of the promises of salvation in Jesus Christ offers that maybe *even* I could be, through the miraculous grace of God, delivered from some of my natural inclinations. I had to wait until I reached sixty-five before I could be delivered from the inclination that I had at sixteen. But maybe there is hope for me even sooner in regard to money. Jesus Christ enables us to tell the truth about ourselves, not so that we can simply be honest, repentant, and guilt ridden, but so that we can live the truth about ourselves.

It is not enough in this faith just to stand up and be honest about my sins. (This is the Methodist moment in my sermon.) I also have to take up the disciplines that enable me to live a more sanctified, holy life.

I was discussing with an imminent professor and preacher the challenge of being a prophetic preacher. How do you teach students to stand up and deliver and preach the gospel, regardless of whether the people hear or refuse to hear? He said to me, "Something that I found helpful, just as a personal discipline in cultivating more courageous preaching, is to refuse to participate in my university's health insurance plan."

I asked, "What does that have to do with anything?"

He replied, "Do you know how many Americans don't have health insurance? I realized that health insurance was insulating me from things that people whom Jesus loves must deal with all the time. So, I refused to participate in health insurance, and I just told the university that I was not going to fill out the forms and to use the money for someone else. It is just wonderful. I go in for treatment, and they say, 'I need to take that cyst off.' 'How much are you going to charge?' I ask. And the doctor says, 'I don't know. Your insurance will cover it. How the heck did you get in here?' And I reply, 'You mean you don't know how much it will cost? Twenty-five hundred dollars to have this little thing taken off? How many hours would you spend to take this little thing off? Will you take $250?' You can really have some good conversations. Like, 'Did you really come into the practice of medicine for this? I bet you didn't even know how much you would make as a doctor when you started out. Let me help you recover some better reasons to be a doctor.' So if you just junked your health insurance, it will help you to do some great gospel preaching."

Money reveals the truth about us. That is true, but let us also remember that we are in the hands of Jesus Christ who can use even money as an encouragement to live the truth in adventurous ways.

Oh, is this sermon you have just heard, not only an experience in telling the truth, but also avoiding the truth? Probably.

ANNOTATED BIBLIOGRAPHY

Atkins, Margaret, and Robin Osborne, editors. *Poverty in the Roman World*. Cambridge: Cambridge University Press, 2006. This book explains the meaning of poverty in antiquity and why the poor were an important group in the Roman world. In essays which range widely with regard to place and time across the Roman Empire, the contributors address both the reality and the representation of poverty and examine the impact which Christianity had upon attitudes towards and treatment of the poor.

Bader-Saye, Scott. "Fear in the Garden: The State of Emergency and the Politics of Blessing." *Ex Auditu* 24 (2008) 1–13. Bader-Saye explores fear in Eden and in Gethsemane and urges Christians to be courageous in the face of political maneuvers that offer a false security. He points to Eden as the place where humans first know fear. The theme of this *Ex Auditu* volume is the idolatry of security.

Baker, David L. *Tight Fists or Open Hands? Wealth and Poverty in Old Testament Law*. Grand Rapids: Eerdmans, 2009. Baker provides a detailed survey of every OT law relating to possessions and gives attention to parallel laws elsewhere in the ancient Near East. This is a fundamental work for biblical exegesis relevant to the subject.

Bassler, J. *God & Mammon: Asking for Money in the New Testament*. Nashville: Abingdon, 1991. Bassler examines early church writings dealing with requests for money and connects this to the practical economic concerns of the church: salaries for ministers, funding ministry programs, and paying bills. Drawing from the documents of the early church, Bassler leads today's church in thinking about the theological, social, and ethical dimensions of requests for money.

Blomberg, Craig L. *Neither Poverty Nor Riches: A Biblical Theology of Possessions*. Downers Grove, IL: InterVarsity, 1999. Blomberg provides a Christian response to problems of poverty and wealth. He treats OT and NT texts and themes, as well as intertestamental literature, to construct a biblical understanding of the issues. Blomberg provides a serious scriptural challenge to the church's response to poverty and wealth.

Brand, Chad, and Tom Pratt. *Seeking the City: Wealth, Poverty, and Political Economy in Christian Perspective*. Grand Rapids: Kregel, forthcoming. The authors approach social justice, equating it with economic justice, with some fear and trembling. The aim of this work is to present the immense task of reimagining current economic systems, calling teachers, political and social leaders, and prophets to approach the task humbly. Though it seems Brand and Pratt see just economic reform as an impossible task, they seek to infuse hope for those engaged in the effort.

Brown, Peter. *Poverty and Leadership in the Later Roman Empire*. Menahem Stern Jerusalem Lectures. Hanover, NH: University Press of New England, 2002. Brown explains the situation of the poor in the Roman Empire, the actual nature of the relations between the

Christian church and the poor, and the true motivations behind the Christian rhetoric of love for the poor. He draws not only on the standard Greek and Latin sources for the later Roman Empire, but also on Jewish sources to document the interactions between Middle Eastern provincial societies and classical Roman traditions.

Carter, Christopher L. *The Great Sermon Tradition as a Fiscal Framework in 1 Corinthians: Towards a Pauline Theology of Material Possessions.* London: T. & T. Clark, 2010. Carter traces Paul's thought on possessions to Jesus and treats the following topics: the authenticity of the great sermon tradition, Paul's general interest in the historical Jesus and his specific knowledge of the great sermon tradition, the fiscal worldview of the great sermon, 1 Corinthians in relation to the great sermon tradition, and Paul and Jesus in relation to Jewish and Greco-Roman fiscal thought.

Claar, Victor V., and Robin J. Klay. *Economics in Christian Perspective: Theory, Policy and Life Choices.* Downers Grove, IL: InterVarsity, 2007. Claar and Klay use case studies to explain economic and biblical ways of thinking about important public policy issues. They address critical topics such as evaluating market economies, engaging poverty relief, growing energy needs, managing global economic development, assessing government fiscal macroeconomic policies, and pollution control.

Coles, Romand. *Rethinking Generosity: Critical Theory and the Politics of Caritas.* Ithaca, NY: Cornell University Press, 1997. Coles analyzes generosity in Kant, Adorno, and Habermas, and argues for a "receptive generosity" that can recognize and welcome the other as a subject. Using the theoretical framework of a world where no one group claims absolute privilege, he explores how we might understand and motivate generosity.

Collier, Paul. *The Bottom Billion: Why the Poorest Countries Are Failing and What Can Be Done About It.* Oxford: Oxford University Press, 2007. Collier reveals that fifty nations, home to the poorest one billion people, pose the central challenge of the developing world. These small nations drop further behind due to problems like corrupt governance, civil war, and unfair trade practices. Collier proposes a plan for the G8 industrialized nations to help through trade policies, new laws against corruption, new international charters, and carefully calibrated military interventions.

Collins, Chuck, and Mary Wright. *The Moral Measure of the Economy.* Maryknoll, NY: Orbis, 2007. This work is a guide written especially for Catholics in answer to the growing need for economic justice and a strong moral foundation in today's society. The chapters focus on moral and ethical responses to economic problems and urge readers to uphold a countercultural higher moral standard in the use of wealth, government, and business power.

Corbett, Steve, and Brian Fikkert. *When Helping Hurts: How to Alleviate Poverty Without Hurting the Poor.* Chicago: Moody, 2009. This book is arranged as a teaching manual for churches or organizations interested in mission work. Using case studies, economic growth strategy, and practical learning exercises, Corbett and Fikkert show how care with economic strategy helps in extending a holistic gospel and ministry to the poor.

The book helps to direct mission-minded efforts in engaging poverty by understanding the systems that propel it.

Countryman, L. William. *The Rich Christian in the Church of the Early Empire: Contradiction and Accommodations.* New York: Edwin Mellen, 1980. Countryman discusses early Christian attitudes towards wealth, including the writings of Clement of Alexandria and Cyprian of Carthage. The book covers topics such as redemptive almsgiving, stewardship of time and treasures, and the danger of riches for both possessor and church.

Day, Dorothy. *Selected Writings: By Little and By Little.* Edited by Robert Ellsberg. Maryknoll, NY: Orbis, 1983. Dorothy Day was a social activist and cofounder of the Catholic Worker movement, and this volume collects her rich and humane theological reflections on being Christian in the United States in the twentieth century. She gives particular attention to wealth and economy. Day's firsthand accounts reveal the social and economic dynamics of her work with the poor.

DeBode, Eric, and Ched Myers. "Towering Trees and 'Talented' Slaves." *The Other Side* 35:3 (May–June, 1999) 11–17. The parable of the talents is presented as predicting the rejection of Jesus. DeBode and Myers contend that Jesus uses the economic language of talents and investment to reveal the third slave as the hero of the story, one who does not conform to the expectations of the rich master.

Delgado, Sharon. *Shaking the Gates of Hell: Faith-Based Resistance to Corporate Globalization.* Minneapolis: Augsburg Fortress, 2007. Delgado provides a faith-led response to global corporations whose expansion damages the cultures and economies of people around the world. The focus of much of her work is on damage done to creation and to the political and economic structures of less developed nations.

De Neui, Paul H., editor. *Complexities of Money and Missions in Asia.* Pasadena: William Carey Library, 2012. This collection of essays explores the dynamics of missionary work in an Eastern economic context. Much of the book deals with Buddhist culture and the varying expectations of the missionary role as it relates to finances, possessions, and lifestyle. This book also provides important insight regarding the use of funds in missionary work in Asia.

DeSoto, Hernando. *The Mystery of Capital: Why Capitalism Triumphs in the West and Fails Everywhere Else.* New York: Basic, 2003. DeSoto points to the Western legal structure of property and property rights as the central reason for capitalism's success in some countries as opposed to others. The assets and talent of a nation are central, DeSoto, suggests, to success in a capitalist system.

Dinsmore, Julia K. *My Name is Child of God . . . Not "Those People": A First-Person Look at Poverty.* Minneapolis: Augsburg Fortress, 2007. Dinsmore shares her story of growing up in a large Irish Catholic working class family in Minneapolis and draws together the experiences of living in poverty, the role of the church and music in her life, and the many remarkable people who populated her life and the lives of her family. Through her stories and reflections Dinsmore puts a face on poverty and challenges readers to answer God's call to respond to poverty and its effects.

Easterly, William. *The White Man's Burden: Why the West's Efforts to Aid the Rest Have Done So Much Ill and So Little Good*. New York: Penguin, 2006. Easterly points out the flaws in Western humanitarian aid systems and argues that these organizations, often government run, do not seek valuable feedback from the populations they attempt to help. These organizations often ignore the deeper systemic problems in the economies of recipient countries. After an initial section of statistical analysis that presents the problem, Easterly suggests methods of ground-level, indigenous planning that will help to fix the broken system.

Finn, Richard. *Almsgiving in the Later Roman Empire: Christian Promotion and Practice 313-450*. Oxford: Oxford University Press, 2006. Finn describes the increasingly complex views of Christian almsgiving as they related to the bishop's position and power relative to other benefactors. He highlights the use of alms as a source of honor and leadership in the benefactor system and connects alms with the virtues of justice and generosity.

Franks, Christopher A. *He Became Poor: The Poverty of Christ and Aquinas's Economic Teachings*. Grand Rapids: Eerdmans, 2009. Franks contrasts Aquinas with Aristotle, John Locke, and Alasdair MacIntyre in constructing Thomian economic thought. The author reclaims a clear reading of Aquinas's teaching and contends that he drew heavily from the example of the mendicant life of Jesus and his disciples. Franks deals specifically with Aquinas's work on usury and poverty.

Gaiser, Frederick J., editor. *Word & World: Theology for Christian Ministry* 30:2 (Spring 2010). The theme of this issue of *Word & World* is "Faith and Economics." The articles included treat OT and NT voices on economics, Jesus and money, the relation of Holy Communion and economy, and Martin Luther's view of usury. The articles emphasize the practice and application of the scriptural accounts of justice, money, and community.

González, Justo L. *Faith and Wealth: A History of Early Christian Ideas on the Origin, Significance, and Use of Money*. San Francisco: Harper & Row, 1990. Starting with the fifth century, this book systematically treats major documents of early Christianity concerning wealth and poverty. González includes Greek and Roman thought as well as scriptural foundation for the progression of economic thinking. He shows especially the significance of Acts 2 and 4 as influences on the content of these early Christian documents.

Grant, R. M. *Early Christianity and Society*. San Francisco: Harper & Row, 1977. Grant treats the economic dimensions of Christian life in the Roman Empire. Some of the specific subjects covered are taxation, occupations, almsgiving, and private property. He also devotes attention to endowments, temples, and churches.

Hands, A. R. *Charities and Social Aid in Greece and Rome*. Ithaca, NY: Cornell University Press, 1968. Hands gives a comprehensive historical account of philanthropy in Greek and Roman society. This study provides a backdrop for understanding the context in which Christian economic structures were formed.

Hengel, Martin. *Property and Riches in the Early Church: Aspects of a Social History of Early Christianity*. Philadelphia: Fortress, 1974. In this brief study Hengel examines the views of property and riches from the teachings of Jesus, early Christian communities, and early church leaders. He compares Christian views of wealth with Judaism and ancient philosophy and applies his conclusions to Christian life today.

Holman, Susan R. *God Knows There's Need: Christian Responses to Poverty*. Oxford: Oxford University Press, 2009. Holman argues that patristic writers like Gregory of Nyssa, Gregory of Nazianzus, John Chrysostom, and Basil of Caesarea sensed the needs of the poor and led Christians to respond through almsgiving and welcoming all into the body of Christ. Working from their example, she compels the reader to respond to the sick, the hungry, and the homeless today.

———, editor. *Wealth and Poverty in Early Church and Society*. Grand Rapids: Baker, 2008. This collection of essays deals with patristic thought on issues of wealth and poverty. The essays examine poverty in the NT period, in early Christian groups from Egypt, Asia Minor, and early Byzantium and then engage patristic theology with today's discussion of public policy and religion.

Hoppe, Leslie J. *There Shall Be No Poor Among You: Poverty in the Bible*. Nashville: Abingdon, 2004. Hoppe portrays the socioeconomic structures of ancient Israel and Roman Palestine and then examines the evidence of the OT, NT, Apocrypha, and rabbinic literature regarding poverty. Hoppe concludes that poverty is never idealized in Scripture and that God clearly values social justice between rich and poor.

Houston, Walter J. *Justice—The Biblical Challenge*. London: Equinox, 2010. This is a well-informed and accessible survey of issues relating to social justice. Those looking for a fuller and more technical study of the same subject by a leading and committed expert might care to consult his book *Contending for Justice: Ideologies and Theologies of Social Justice in the Old Testament* (Library of Hebrew Bible/Old Testament Studies 428; London: T. & T. Clark, 2006).

Interpretation 65.2 (April, 2011). This whole issue of *Interpretation* is focused on usury. The essays deal with views on usury in Scripture and the denunciation of oppressive lending practices in church tradition, but also the increasing embrace of usury by Christians by the end of the seventeenth century. Essays also treat usury in the context of economic crisis and the relation between usury and capitalism.

Johnson, C. Neal. *Business As Mission: A Comprehensive Guide to Theory and Practice*. Downers Grove, IL: InterVarsity, 2009. Johnson offers a practical guide for "kingdom-strategic business ventures," recognizing the potential of global economic activity as a channel for mission work. The book merges mission and business models with special concern for issues such as management, sustainability, and accountability. Johnson provides planning strategies and step-by-step guidance for Christian entrepreneurs who seek to bring faith and work together.

Johnson, Kelly. *The Fear of Beggars: Stewardship and Poverty in Christian Ethics*. Grand Rapids: Eerdmans, 2007. This study of Christian economic practice shows how dependence and voluntary poverty had a constructive and social significance in Christian history and how anxieties about begging shape stewardship rhetoric and classical economic thought. Johnson challenges the reader to examine the root of fear, including the desire for individual security. At the same time, beggars fear many things in their life on the street. In examining the relationship between the wealthy and beggars, Johnson calls for a renewal of humble stewardship practices.

Johnson, Luke Timothy. *Sharing Possessions: What Faith Demands*. Rev. ed. Philadelphia: Fortress, 2011. This work approaches Christian possessions from a scriptural perspective. Johnson begins with biblical passages that support the mandate for Christian ownership of property. He offers a theological approach to possessions and to sharing possessions in Christian community. He also focuses on Christian almsgiving.

Jung, L. Shannon. *Food for Life: The Spirituality and Ethics of Eating*. Minneapolis: Augsburg Fortress, 2004. As theologian, ethicist, and food enthusiast, Jung underscores the religious dimensions of eating on an individual and global scale. He confronts various eating disorders that affect global cultures and offers Christian practices as a remedy. Jung details the spiritual practice of eating and drinking through activities like church ministries, gardening, cooking, and engaging cultural food norms.

———. *Hunger and Happiness: Feeding the Hungry, Nourishing Our Souls*. Minneapolis: Augsburg Fortress, 2009. Jung reveals a global-scale tension between food consumption and spiritual "fullness," pointing out that the countries that are the best fed often eat at the expense of others in the world who go hungry. Ethical food practices, Jung contends, lead not only to more people getting enough food but also to a healthier spiritual self. Cheap food for some is not always a good thing for everyone else.

Knapp, John C. *How the Church Fails Businesspeople (and What Can Be Done About It)*. Grand Rapids: Eerdmans, 2011. Knapp draws from his expertise as a business ethicist to argue that the church's ambiguity in teaching about vocation, money, and business have led to uncertainty among Christians about discipleship in the workplace. After an overview of the work and church "worlds," Knapp seeks to merge them through a responsible approach to biblical teaching about money and work.

Landes, D. S. *The Wealth and Poverty of Nations: Why Some Are So Rich and Some So Poor*. New York: W. W. Norton, 1999. This historical exploration of global wealth and poverty tries to pinpoint the causes of growth in some countries and decline in others. Landes contends that the use or exploitation of geography, science, technology, and economic opportunity have led some countries to huge amounts of growth. Landes elevates the cultural values of work, thrift, honesty, patience, and tenacity in industrialized nations as a key characteristic of growth.

Lim, David S. *Transforming Communities: Biblical Concepts of Poverty and Social Justice*. Mandaluyong City, Philippines: OMF, 1992. Drawing largely from Genesis, Acts, and the Epistles, Lim depicts healthy communities that exercise stewardship, good dominion, and justice as guided by Christ and Scripture. These communities should seek to alleviate the poverty of others (in and outside of the community), live a simple lifestyle that rejects overconsumption, and construct viable economic systems that are ecologically sound and politically just. The result is a new economic order that focuses on reducing wants rather than increasing wealth.

Lindberg, Carter. *Beyond Charity: Reformation Initiatives for the Poor*. Minneapolis: Augsburg Fortress, 1993. This historical analysis portrays the scope of medieval European thought about poverty, charity, and social welfare. Lindberg depicts the changes in this thought that began with the European reformers. The second half of the book includes some primary material from Luther, Erasmus, Huss, and others. The collected work gives a good image of the changes in the Christian understanding of poverty around the time of the Reformation.

Lohfink, Gerhard. *Jesus and Community: The Social Dimension of the Christian Faith*. Philadelphia: Fortress, 1984. Lohfink responds to the claim that Jesus did not found a church by studying the call to community in Israel and Jesus' attempt to gather Israel. The church, like Israel, is called to be a contrast society and a light to the nations. Lohfink states that the church already existed as the people of Israel; Jesus continued this church by gathering those who followed him and sanctifying them through his death. Some of the economic and social implications are detailed in Lohfink's exploration of Jesus' community.

Longenecker, Bruce W. *Remember the Poor: Paul, Poverty, and the Greco-Roman World*. Grand Rapids: Eerdmans, 2010. In a challenge to the common view that Paul had no concern for the poor, Longenecker highlights Paul's concern in this historical, exegetical, and theological study. After an overview of first century Greco-Roman approaches to poverty, this book constructs a reading of Paul's letters that reveals great concern for the poor in his instruction to early Christian communities. The second half of the book deals with texts specific to the debate.

Longenecker, Bruce, and Kelly D. Liebengood, editors. *Engaging Economics: New Testament Scenarios and Early Christian Reception*. Grand Rapids: Eerdmans, 2009. This collection of essays treats the role of economics in the formation of early Christian communities. Some subjects include patronage in Paul's writing, community-shared possessions, economic ethics as a mark of transformation in Luke-Acts, and economic humility in James. The latter section of the book deals with the expression of Christian economic thought in the first four centuries of the church.

Malherbe, Abraham J. "Godliness, Self-Sufficiency, Greed, and the Enjoyment of Wealth: 1 Timothy 6:3–19, Part 1." *Novum Testamentum* 52 (2010) 376–405. This exegetical study of 1 Timothy interprets the background and intent of the text. Malherbe suggests that the teaching in 1 Tim 6 is most striking in its insistence on the enjoyment of wealth. This is the first article in a two-part examination of the text.

———. "Godliness, Self-Sufficiency, Greed, and the Enjoyment of Wealth: 1 Timothy 6:3–19, Part 2." *Novum Testamentum* 53 (2011) 73–96. In this second part Malherbe discusses how the latter part of 1 Tim 6 engages with socioeconomic thought of its time. He focuses on the warnings made to the wealthy and the exhortation to use and enjoy wealth and compares it to the thought of the Epicureans, Stoics, and Cynics.

McDaniel, Charles. *God & Money: The Moral Challenge of Capitalism*. New York: Rowman & Littlefield, 2007. McDaniel addresses the myth that market-driven capitalism and the values of Christian faith fit well together. He does not see these as complementary systems but urges that capitalism must be tempered and even challenged by Christian morals and beliefs. He draws on individuals such as Reinhold Niebuhr, G. K. Chesterton, Peter Berger, and John Paul II to promote a "redemptive economy" where core Christian beliefs undergird the inevitable capitalism of our day.

Meilaender, G. "To Throw Oneself into the Wave: The Problem of Possessions." In *Preferential Option for the Poor,* edited by R. J. Neuhaus, 72–86. Grand Rapids: Eerdmans, 1988. Meilaender uses the lens of possessions to address God's preference for the poor. He argues God is more concerned about the condition of the heart and about being poor in spirit. He treats the role of possessions in people's spiritual posture and the positive and negative impacts possessions can have. He concludes that it is impossible to make generalizations about possessions and that they must be held in tension between enjoyment and renunciation.

Miller, Vincent. *Consuming Religion: Christian Faith and Practice in a Consumer Culture.* New York: Continuum, 2003. Miller explores the way fragmentation, which is characteristic of a consumer culture, affects religious practice so that religious symbols and convictions, like commodities, float free of history and reason. The book confronts the damage consumer culture has done to the formation of identity and to Christian faith and discipleship.

Mitchell, Christopher Wright. *The Meaning of* brk *"to bless" in the Old Testament.* Society of Biblical Literature Dissertation Series 95. Atlanta: Scholars, 1987. This volume from the SBL Dissertation Series analyzes all 402 occurrences of *brk* in the OT. Part of Mitchell's work addresses the contexts of blessing: God blessing humans, humans blessing humans, and humans blessing/praising God. This emphasizes the relational tone of blessing in the Hebrew Scriptures.

Mullin, R. *The Wealth of Christians.* Maryknoll, NY: Orbis, 1984. Mullin confronts the contemporary attitudes toward charity by revisiting early Christian history and thought regarding philanthropy. Individualistic views of property and wealth are challenged with early Greco-Roman, Jewish, and Christian thought. Mullin calls the Western church to put aside culturally ingrained selfishness and revive an early Christian ethic of giving.

Nardoni, Enrique. *Rise Up, O Judge: A Study of Justice in the Biblical World.* Peabody, MA: Hendrickson, 2004. This book surveys the evolution of social and liberating justice from the OT through the NT. Nardoni takes a historical-critical approach and applies the biblical material to the contemporary world. He examines the exodus as an event of liberating justice and the norms of justice seen in the laws of the covenant.

Newhauser, R. G. *The Early History of Greed: The Sin of Avarice in Early Medieval Thought and Literature.* Cambridge: Cambridge University Press, 2006. Newhauser addresses the early onset of avarice within the church, even back to the first century CE. He claims that the desire to amass wealth beyond that which is necessary occurred much before the rise of money economies.

Novak, Michael. *The Spirit of Democratic Capitalism*. Rev. ed. New York: Rowman & Littlefield, 1990. Novak presents the benefits and congruences of capitalism in relationship to Christian values. He recognizes that Christian values should not be subordinate to capitalist ideology but argues rather that capitalism is humanity's best resource thus far for stewarding God's resources.

———. *Will It Liberate? Questions about Liberation Theology*. Long Island, NY: Madison, 1991. Novak answers basic questions concerning liberation theology and the role of the Christian church. Novak comes from a perspective that Latin American poverty is largely due to systemic economic issues. He argues that questions about liberation theology do not arise from its spirituality but rather from the interpretations of the economic and social realities.

Owensby, Walter L. *Economics for Prophets: A Primer on Concepts, Realities, and Values in Our Economic System*. Grand Rapids: Eerdmans, 1988. Owensby argues that much of the biblical prophetic voice addressed historic economic realities rather than predicted the future. From this perspective Owensby takes a three step approach of teaching the basics of economic systems, applying these basics to real world situations, and critically examining these frameworks through a theological lens to encourage readers to be a prophetic voice in the realities of current economic issues.

Pattison, Bonnie L. *Poverty in the Theology of John Calvin*. Eugene, OR: Pickwick, 2006. Pattison divides her work into two sections. The first highlights the history of theological thought on poverty from the patristics through the Reformation. The second focuses on John Calvin's belief that affliction and poverty are the primary marks and manifestations of God's Kingdom. She focuses on the intersection of spiritual and physical poverty in Calvin's thought on Christology, Christian life, and ecclesiology.

Peters, Rebecca Todd, and Elizabeth Hinson-Hasty, editors. *To Do Justice: A Guide for Progressive Christians*. London: Westminster John Knox, 2008. This collection of essays provides practical resources for Christians dealing with the social problems of our day. Each article addresses a contemporary issue from biblical, social, and theological perspectives and then provides practical application by outlining basic policy for each topic.

Phan, Peter C. *Social Thought: Message of the Fathers of the Church*. Wilmington, DE: Michael Glazier, 1984. Phan compiles the social and political ideologies of a wide range of church fathers. He presents their primary texts and his own brief commentary. He deals with Clement of Rome and Ignatius of Antioch, moves to third-century fathers, Greek patristic literature, John Chrysostom, Augustine, and a range of Latin patristic authors.

Putnam, Robert D., and David E. Campbell. *American Grace: How Religion Divides and Unites Us*. New York: Simon and Schuster, 2010. This sociological study examines the ways religious differences are negotiated in the United States. Of particular interest is their attention to fast-growing "nones," those who say they have no religious commitment.

Ramsey, B. "Christian Attitude to Poverty and Wealth." In *Early Christianity: Origins and Evolution to AD 600,* edited by I. Hazlett, 256–65. Nashville: Abingdon, 1991. Ramsey argues the church grew out of a poor community and that poverty was central to the ideologies of the early church. He presents five basic facts from the NT concerning poverty and wealth: 1) the early church had both poor and rich members, 2) there was a concern for aiding the poor, 3) the occasional observation of a preference for the poor, 4) the proposal of voluntary poverty for the sake of Christ, and 5) the shared resources of early Christian communities. Ramsey emphasizes the importance of the poor and oppressed in the NT texts and the applicability these texts have for today.

Rhee, Helen. *Loving the Poor, Saving the Rich: Wealth, Poverty, and Early Christian Formation.* Grand Rapids: Baker, forthcoming. Helen Rhee shows how the early Christian church appropriated and made Jewish and Greco-Roman practices of benevolence their own. Specifically she highlights the central role wealth and poverty played in the identity formation of early Christians and the application this identity has for the church today.

———. "Wealth, Poverty, and Eschatology: Pre-Constantine Jewish and Christian Social Thoughts and the Hope for the World to Come." In *Patristic Social Ethics: Issues and Challenges*, edited by J. Leemans, B. Matz, and J. Verstraeten, 64–84. Washington, DC: Catholic University of America Press, 2011. This article examines how eschatology, following Jewish tradition, influenced the ethics of wealth and charity for the poor in early Christianity.

Richards, Jay W. *Money, Greed, and God: Why Capitalism is the Solution Not the Problem.* San Francisco: HarperOne, 2009. In his eight chapters Richards addresses eight myths concerning capitalism. He shows the congruences between the Christian life and capitalism and that an individual can both be a "good Christian" and a "good capitalist."

Rindge, Matthew S. *Jesus' Parable of the Rich Fool: Luke 12:13–34 Among Ancient Conversation on Death and Possessions.* Early Christianity and Its Literature 6. Atlanta: Society of Biblical Literature, 2011. Rindge examines the relationship between death and possessions in Luke's parable of the Rich Fool (Luke 12:16–21) and takes into account the intertextual dialogue of the Second Temple period. Rindge examines key texts from Jewish and Greco-Roman sources and the divergent views on stewarding possessions revealed therein. From this complex web of perspectives he shows the poignancy of Luke's parable in the context of the Second Temple period.

Roth, C. P., translator. *St. John Chrysostom on Wealth and Poverty.* Crestwood, NY: St. Vladimir's Seminary, 1984. This collection of six sermons focuses on issues of wealth and poverty from the narrative of Lazarus and the rich man (Luke 16:19–31). These sermons are as applicable today as when first delivered.

Sachs, Jeffrey. *The End of Poverty: Economic Possibilities for Our Time.* New York: Penguin, 2005. Through the use of first-person narrative and critical analysis Sachs explains the contour of the world economy and the reasoning behind the divergence of wealth across the globe over the past two hundred years. He then examines specific countries and evaluates the options that lie ahead. He integrates his own experience with his analysis to suggest the possibility of ending world poverty and the moral obligation each individual has in taking part in the solution.

Schmidt, Thomas E. *Hostility to Wealth in the Synoptic Gospels.* Journal for the Study of the New Testament Supplement Series 15. Sheffield: Sheffield Academic, 1987. Schmidt deals first with socio-economic circumstances in first-century Palestine and method. He surveys hostility to wealth in Ancient Near Eastern and in Jewish material, and then treats the theme in each of the Synoptic Gospels. He argues that hostility to wealth does not depend on socio-economic circumstances but is a fundamental religious and ethical tenet in the teaching of Jesus.

Schneider, John R. *The Good of Affluence: Seeking God in a Culture of Wealth.* Grand Rapids: Eerdmans, 2002. Schneider argues against the commonly held notion that wealth is inherently bad and that God's hope for all of creation comes from a perspective of abundance. He addresses modern perspectives on the negative view of capitalism while relying heavily on a biblical examination of wealth and abundance in which he encourages the proper stewardship and responsibility of that wealth.

Schwartz, Glenn. *When Charity Destroys Dignity: Overcoming Unhealthy Dependency in the Christian Movement.* Lancaster, PA: World Mission Associates, 2007. Schwartz first defines the dependency syndrome and provides a history regarding its development. He examines various institutions and their dependency and places specific emphasis on missions. In part two of his book he offers solutions for dependency and provides practical illustrations for moving toward a healthy self-reliance.

Sider, Ronald J. *Rich Christians in an Age of Hunger: Moving from Affluence to Generosity.* 4th ed. Dallas: Word, 2005. Sider confronts issues of world hunger and poverty head on. He challenges readers with the basic truths of global poverty and the relative wealth that many Christians possess. He deals with poverty from a biblical perspective and also treats the causes of poverty. He also presents his own suggestions for policy and implementation to combat world hunger.

———. *Just Generosity: A New Vision for Overcoming Poverty in America.* 2nd ed. Grand Rapids: Baker, 2007. Sider deals with specific social programs in America and discusses the benefits and necessities of policy in promoting positive change. He has a clear biblical approach but encourages the involvement of government programs as a necessity for tackling issues of poverty in the United States.

Smith, Christian, and Michael O. Emerson, with Patricia Snell. *Passing the Plate: Why American Christians Don't Give Away More Money.* Oxford: Oxford University Press, 2008. This work examines attitudes and practices surrounding stewardship and tithing in the United States and argues that the problem is not greed but a set of social, ecclesial, and theological issues.

Sobrino, Jon. *No Salvation outside the Poor: Prophetic-Utopian Essays.* Maryknoll, NY: Orbis, 2007. Inspired by the witness of Oscar Romero and Ignacio Ellacuria, Jon Sobrino presents five essays dealing with issues of poverty and equality. He applies the promises of the Christian faith, specifically the kingdom of God and the hope for the resurrection, to the poor and oppressed communities of our time and encourages his readers to reflect on the meaning of discipleship within this context.

Soulen, R. Kendall. *The God of Israel and Christian Theology*. Minneapolis: Augsburg Fortress, 1996. Soulen argues for an understanding of Scripture as a narrative of consummation rather than only of redemption. He hopes to overcome the supersessionism and gnosticism common in Christian readings of Scripture.

Stackhouse, Max L., editor. *On Moral Business: Classical and Contemporary Resources for Ethics in Economic Life*. Grand Rapids: Eerdmans, 1995. This comprehensive work synthesizes both theological and philosophical viewpoints on business and economic issues. It draws from sources ranging from Aristotle, Karl Marx, Adam Smith, Max Weber, Reinhold Niebuhr, and Walter Rauschenbusch to excerpts from Catholic and Protestant documents concerning social thought and business morality. This compilation does not provide commentary but simply presents a wide range of thought and ideology.

Torvend, Samuel. *Luther and the Hungry Poor: Gathered Fragments*. Minneapolis: Augsburg Fortress, 2008. Torvend shows Luther's concern for the poor and oppressed as he reconstructs fragments of Luther's earliest writings. He argues that Luther was not only committed to theological reform but social reform as well as his own community faced issues of hunger and homelessness. Torvend bookends his discussion with introductory remarks concerning Jesus' words on hunger and with a conclusion that calls his readers to implement "structured generosity" within their own context.

United States Conference of Catholic Bishops. "Stewardship: A Disciple's Response, Tenth Anniversary Edition." Washington, D.C.: United States Conference of Catholic Bishops, 2002. In this pastoral letter the United States bishops offer a broad understanding of stewardship in relation to Scripture, spirituality, social responsibility, and church membership.

Van Til, Kent A. *Less Than Two Dollars a Day: A Christian View of World Poverty and the Free Market*. Grand Rapids: Eerdmans, 2007. Van Til argues that the combination of a capitalist economy with a free market does not allow for proper provision of human sustenance. His work in Latin America has led him to examine critically the inadequacies of the system and its lack of equitable distribution across the globe. Focusing on these issues as the foundation for his text, Van Til then provides a biblical perspective on poverty and the application of these values in today's society. He draws heavily on the ideas of political theorist Michael Walzer and nineteenth-century theologian-statesman Abraham Kuyper.

Vogt, Virgil. *Treasure in Heaven: The Biblical Teaching about Money, Finances, and Possessions*. Ann Arbor: Servant, 1982. Vogt argues that God has been showing his people how to deal with their possessions from the very beginning and that the revolutionary teachings of Jesus are crucial to surviving the tumultuous state of economics today. He concludes with a rallying cry for full mobilization of the resources of Christians throughout the world for the kingdom of God.

Vrolijk, Paul D. *Jacob's Wealth: An Examination into the Nature and Role of Material Possessions in the Jacob Cycle (Gen 25:19–35:29)*. Leiden: Brill, 2011. In this in-depth study of Gen 25:19–35:29 Vrolijk highlights the importance of studying the wealth of the patriarchs and specifically the narrative of Jacob. He shows that proper attitudes toward material possessions are essential for understanding the relationship dynamics in the narrative.

Wagner, W. H. "Lubricating the Camel: Clement of Alexandria on Wealth and the Wealthy." In *Festschrift: A Tribute to Dr. William Hordern*, edited by W. Freitag, 64–77. Saskatoon: University of Saskatchewan Press, 1985. Wagner's article looks at the way Clement of Alexandria in *Who Is a Rich Man That Is Saved?* "lubricated" the camel by his figurative interpretation of Mark 10:17–31 (about the rich young ruler) and thereby made the salvation of the rich possible with almsgiving.

Weaver, Rebecca H. "Wealth and Poverty in the Early Church." *Interpretation* 41 (1987) 368–81. Weaver shows that an examination of the literature from the early church reveals two main themes: the importance of almsgiving and a negative attitude toward the rich. Weaver supports her thesis by examining the work and thought of Clement of Alexandria, Cyprian of Carthage, John Chrysostom, and Augustine and shows the consistency in their addressing these two main issues.

Wheeler, S. E. *Wealth as Peril and Obligation: The New Testament on Possessions*. Grand Rapids: Eerdmans, 1995. Wheeler argues many people attempt to find definitive answers to moral questions from biblical texts and that this method is prone to difficulty and misinterpretation. She describes several approaches and then frames her proposal for how best to interpret the Scriptures. She focuses on four key texts: Mark 10:17–31; Luke 12:22–34; 2 Cor 8:1–15; and James 5:1–6.

Williamson, H. G. M. *He Has Shown You What is Good: Old Testament Justice Then and Now*. Cambridge: James Clarke, 2012. This little book is based on a series of lectures for a church audience and gives fuller details of the thinking that lies behind Williamson's paper in this volume.

Winslow, D. F. "Poverty and Riches: An Embarrassment for the Early Church." *Studia Patristica* 18:2 (1989) 317–28. This article provides a critique of the social gap between early Christian rich and poor and the way the church dealt with wealth and poverty, often seeming to focus more on the salvation of the rich than the alleviation of poverty.

Witherington, Ben, III. *Jesus and Money: A Guide for Financial Crisis*. Grand Rapids: Baker, 2010. Witherington provides a biblical framework for a proper stewardship of resources in difficult times. From the perspective that "all things belong to God," he analyzes OT and NT texts and encourages readers to move beyond tithing to sacrificial giving.

Wright, Christopher J. H. *Living as the People of God: The Relevance of Old Testament Ethics*. Leicester: InterVarsity, 1983. Wright has written several books that helpfully deal with the application of the ethical teaching of the OT to the vastly different Christian community in the modern world. This one is perhaps the best.

Yamamori, Tetsunao, and Kenneth A. Eldred, editors. *On Kingdom Business: Transforming Missions Through Entrepreneurial Strategies*. Wheaton: Crossway, 2003. This work presents a new model for missions and encourages individuals to begin for-profit businesses to support and sustain ministries. Case studies and essays describe the successful implementation of this model.

NORTH PARK THEOLOGICAL SEMINARY SYMPOSIUM ON THE THEOLOGICAL INTERPRETATION OF SCRIPTURE

SEPTEMBER 29–OCTOBER 1, 2011

MONEY AND POSSESSIONS

PRESENTERS

JONATHAN BONK
International Association for Mission Studies, President

GARY HOAG
Trinity College, University of Bristol, Ph.D. Candidate

MARK HUSBANDS
Hope College, Leonard and Marjorie Maas Associate Professor of Reformed Theology

KELLY JOHNSON
University of Dayton, Associate Professor

BRUCE LONGENECKER
Baylor University, Professor of Religion and W. W. Melton Chair

HELEN RHEE
Westmont College, Associate Professor of Church History

HUGH WILLIAMSON
University of Oxford/The Oriental Institute, Regius Professor of Hebrew

WILLIAM WILLIMON
Bishop of North Alabama United Methodist Conference

RESPONDENTS

JAMES K. BRUCKNER
   North Park Theological Seminary, Professor of Old Testament

GREG CLARK
   North Park University, Professor of Philosophy

AARON KUECKER
   Trinity Christian College, Associate Professor of Theology

WILLIAM MYATT
   Loyola University, Ph.D. Candidate

BRADLEY NASSIF
   North Park University, Professor of Biblical and Theological Studies

LYN NIXON
   University of Wales, Ph.D. Candidate

LIZ MOSBO VERHAGE
   North Park University, Adjunct Professor

EX AUDITU

Volumes Available

Vol. 1 (1985) consists of selected articles presenting the issues inherent in the theological interpretation of Scripture.

Vol. 2 (1986) discusses the theme: "Church and State Relationship." In addition, there are two lead articles: one by Peter Stuhlmacher on "EX AUDITU and the Theological Interpretation of Holy Scripture," and the second by Ben F. Meyer on "The Primacy of Consent and the Uses of Suspicion."

Vol. 3 (1987) "Creation."
Vol. 4 (1988) "The Church and Israel (Romans 9–11)."
Vol. 5 (1989) "What is Salvation?"
Vol. 6 (1990) "Prophetic and/or Apocalyptic Eschatology."
Vol. 7 (1991) "Christology and Incarnation"
Vol. 8 (1992) "Worship."
Vol. 9 (1993) "Resurrection."
Vol. 10 (1994) "The Church."
Vol. 11 (1995) "Biblical Law and Liberty."
Vol. 12 (1996) "Holy Spirit."
Vol. 13 (1997) "What is a Human?"
Vol. 14 (1998) "The Theological Significance of the Earthly Jesus."
Vol. 15 (1999) "Idolatry and the Understanding of God."
Vol. 16 (2000) "The Task of Interpreting Scripture Theologically."
Vol. 17 (2001) "Biblical Ethics."
Vol. 18 (2002) "Spiritual Formation."
Vol. 19 (2003) "The Authority and Function of Scripture."
Vol. 20 (2004) "Judgment."
Vol. 21 (2005) "Health and Healing."
Vol. 22 (2006) "Justice."
Vol. 23 (2007) "Christianity's Engagement with Culture."
Vol. 24 (2008) "The Idolatry of Security."
Vol. 25 (2009) "Conversion."
Vol. 26 (2010) "Atonement."
Vol. 27 (2011) "Wealth and Possessions."

Pickwick Publications
An Imprint of Wipf & Stock Publishers
199 West 8th Avenue, Ste. 3
Eugene OR 97401
www.wipfandstock.com
twitter.com/wipfandstock
www.facebook.com/wipfandstock
www.facebook.com/pages/Pickwick-Publications/103143236431970

www.ingramcontent.com/pod-product-compliance
Lightning Source LLC
Chambersburg PA
CBHW081350230426
43667CB00017B/2788